Aperture® 3

PORTABLE GENIUS

Aperture® 3

PORTABLE GENIUS

by Josh Anon and Ellen Anon

Wiley Publishing, Inc.

Aperture® 3 Portable Genius

Published by
Wiley Publishing, Inc.
10475 Crosspoint Blvd.
Indianapolis, IN 46256
www.wiley.com

For general information on our other products and services or to obtain technical support, please contact our Customer Care Department within the U.S. at (877) 762-2974, outside the U.S. at (317) 572-3993 or fax (317) 572-4002.

WILEY

About the Authors

Josh Anon has been a nature photographer for most of his life, with his interest in photography starting when he received his first Kodak 110 camera at the ripe old age of 4. Camera in hand, he received a B.S. in computer science from Northwestern University in Evanston, Illinois.

After graduating, Josh started working at Pixar Animation Studios in Emeryville, California. There he has worked on *The Incredibles, Ratatouille, Toy Story 3,* and more. Currently he is a camera and staging artist.

He has traveled the globe searching for the next great picture, be it 100 feet deep on the Great Barrier Reef, on a cold and windy beach in the South Atlantic, or inside the Arctic Circle. His award-winning images, represented by the prestigious Jaynes Gallery and available on www.joshanon.com, have appeared in a variety of galleries, calendars, and other publications, including the San Diego Natural History museum, Nature's Best, Photo Media, The Kiteboarder, and more. Josh teaches photography, both privately and for the Panasonic Digital Photo Academy, and he and his mother, Ellen, have also coauthored *Aperture Exposed* (Sybex, 2006) *Photoshop CS5 for Nature Photographers* (Sybex 2010), and more. He is also a cofounder of DSLRU (www.dslru.com).

Josh continues to develop software in his free time, currently focusing on FlipBook, which is movie-making software for iPad, iPhone, and iPod Touch.

When not shooting, making cartoons, or coding, Josh can be found kiteboarding.

Ellen Anon got her start with photography at age 5, but for years it remained a hobby as she took a very long fork in the road, eventually earning a Ph.D. in clinical psychology. Finally, a broken foot in 1997 forced her to take a break from work as a psychologist and she used the time to study photography. She debated briefly between building a traditional darkroom in her home and creating a digital darkroom. Because she's not fond of being closed up in small dark spaces with strong smells of funky chemicals, she opted for the latter. Ever since, photography has been a two-part process for her. Making the image in the field is step one, and optimizing it in the digital darkroom is step two. Being creative with it is the icing on the cake!

Ellen is now a freelance photographer, speaker, and writer. Her goal with her photographs is to go beyond the ordinary in ways that she hopes stimulate others to pause and appreciate some of the beauty and wonder of our earth. Ellen's images are included in collections in several countries. She is represented by several stock agencies, and her photos have been showcased in galleries, used in numerous publications (including Sierra Club's *Mother Earth* and Inner Reflections 2010 calendar). In addition, she has been Highly Honored in Nature's Best Photography Windland Smith Rice

International Awards and Highly Commended in the 2008 BBC/Shell Wildlife Photographer of the Year competition. She is honored to be a member of the Aperture Advisory Board and is an Apple Certified Trainer for Aperture.

In addition to *Aperture 3 Portable Genius*, Ellen is the coauthor, along with Josh, of the series *Photoshop CS5 for Nature Photographers: A Workshop in a Book* (Sybex, 2010), and *Aperture Exposed* (2006). She has contributed chapters to several other books and she creates video training materials on digital software for several companies including www.maccreate.com. Ellen leads both photographic- and digital darkroom–oriented workshops and is a featured speaker at various events. She is an active member of the North American Nature Photography Association (NANPA) and is an instructor for its high school scholarship program. She is honored to be a member of Nik software's Team Nik.

Credits

Senior Acquisitions Editor
Stephanie McComb

Project Editor
Jama Carter

Technical Editor
Paul Sihvonen-Binder

Senior Copy Editor
Kim Heusel

Editorial Director
Robyn Siesky

Editorial Manager
Rosemarie Graham

Vice President and Executive Group
Publisher
Richard Swadley

Vice President and Executive Publisher
Barry Pruett

Business Manager
Amy Knies

Senior Marketing Manager
Sandy Smith

Project Coordinator
Katie Crocker

Graphics and Production Specialist
Andrea Hornberger

Quality Control Technician
Jessica Kramer

Proofreading
Penny Stuart

Indexing
BIM Indexing & Proofreading Services

To my family, for having a second refrigerator just for film. –Josh Anon

To Jack, Josh, and Seth for always being there for me. – Ellen Anon

Acknowledgments

First and foremost, we both owe our family a big thank you for their continued support and encouragement. Neither of us would have made it where we are today without the support of Jack, Seth, and each other.

Someone once said it takes a village to raise a child. We don't know whether that's true or not, but it sure feels like it takes a village to create a book like what you hold in your hands. Specifically, we owe special thanks to Stephanie McComb, our Acquisitions Editor, and Jama Carter, our Project Editor. They somehow always managed to stay calm even when we were being stubborn.

We also owe our gratitude to our technical editor, Paul Sihvonen-Binder, for making sure that we really are leading you in the right direction.

We both want to thank our friends at Apple involved with Aperture, especially Kirk Paulsen, Martin Gisborne, and Joe Schorr for working hard to create such an amazing program that's completely optimized our workflows.

Josh wants to thank his friends and co-workers at Pixar, including Trish Carney, Jeremy Lasky, Patrick Lin, Eben Ostby, and Matt Silas. You guys always provide great inspiration and are just awesome people. To his friend Michelle Safer: thank you for always being there to provide moral support. Last but certainly not least, he owes his continued gratitude to his high school English teacher Claudia Skerlong, for teaching him to write well; although he thinks he heard she once started a betting pool about whether his authoring a book (to say nothing of four) or Armageddon would happen first.

Ellen wants to extend a special thanks to her son Josh for being the lead author on this book and smoothing the way. It is a special pleasure to coauthor books with you! She also wants to thank all the people who have requested that she and Josh do another Aperture book. She also wants to thank Dr. Gary Brotherson and Dr. J.P. Dailey for their flexibility and perseverance in safeguarding her eyesight while enabling her to travel to remote places in search of the next photographic adventure.

Contents
at a Glance

Contents

chapter 4

How Can I Use Metadata to Organize
and Find My Images?   90

chapter 5

How Do I Use Faces and Places
to Categorize My Images?   120

chapter 6

What Tools Can I Use to Make My Images Better?   144

What Options Do I Have to Create a Physical Copy of My Photos?   198

chapter 8

How Can I Share My Images Digitally?   232

Introduction

In many ways, Aperture needs no introduction. It's professional photo management done by Apple, the same folks who brought you iPhoto, iPhone, and more. We could lavish it with praise for the next few hundred pages and describe to you how happy we are with the photographic workflows we've developed with Aperture, but while that praise would be completely true (perhaps garnished with a touch of hyperbole to add some humor), that wouldn't leave much room to explain how Aperture can help your workflow. Instead, we'll simply say that Aperture has helped us optimize our digital workflows more than any other piece of software (and between the two of us, we've tried them all) so that we can quickly process thousands of images and spend more time shooting and less time at our computers.

When you first look at it, though, it's tough to understand how this neutral-gray window can do so much, and more importantly, what all these weird words like *stacks* and *projects* mean. Don't worry: we're here to help.

The next few hundred pages will take you through Aperture, from understanding the basic terms in Chapter 1 to advanced topics in Chapter 10. As you read, we encourage you to import some images and videos into your Aperture library and to try clicking the buttons we describe for yourself.

Don't feel obligated to read this book from start to finish, however. While we've tried to build the text so that the chapters follow roughly a digital workflow order and build on each other, feel free to skip around, especially if you've used Aperture before.

Lastly, while it's easy to sometimes feel overwhelmed by all the features in a program like Aperture, don't be. There's no test at the end of this book, and you don't have to use every possible feature to its fullest to integrate Aperture into your workflow. That's part of what's so great about Aperture — it's flexible enough to fit into your workflow instead of forcing you to fit into its workflow.

How Do I Get Started with Aperture?

©Josh Anon

Aperture in some ways is like iPhoto on steroids, but in other ways it's a completely different beast. Unlike iPhoto, it's designed to be an incredibly flexible image, video, and audio file asset management tool so that it can integrate into your existing workflow. However, this flexibility means that Aperture has more jargon, settings, and buttons than iPhoto. This chapter helps demystify Aperture's jargon and shows you key fundamentals you need to know when using Aperture.

Understanding Why Aperture Is a Key Part of Your Workflow

Most photographers agree that the time you spend behind the lens shooting is the best part of being a photographer, and all the other stuff (processing an image, categorizing it, trying to sell it or use it to promote business) is really just annoying. While digital photography enables you to be more creative as a photographer, from being able to see right away whether you got the shot or not to being able to experiment as much as you want with the only cost being disk space, the "other stuff" arguably gets more frustrating because now you have to manage digital files instead of physical film and learn to use multiple programs to develop and output your images. That's where Aperture comes into play. Aperture is a central point for all of your image management, from the moment you download an image from camera to computer until you search for an image and click Print to make a physical copy for a client. Aperture makes it relatively easy and fast to organize and manage your digital files, and that lets you spend more time having fun shooting. However, Aperture isn't the only digital asset management tool out there. Let's look at what Aperture gives you over iPhoto, Bridge, and Lightroom.

Seeing the difference between Aperture and iPhoto

If you've been using iPhoto to manage your images, then you know that our explanation of why Aperture is a key part of our workflow could apply to iPhoto, too. While iPhoto is great for managing images of your family and friends taken with your point and shoot, it's really limited when you put it under a microscope. For example, while you can make basic retouching adjustments in iPhoto like a levels adjustment, Aperture lets you fine-tune those adjustments to develop your image exactly the way you want it to look, perhaps adjusting the levels in just one color channel or using the quarter-tone controls (which we cover in Chapter 6) to adjust the levels in a specific part of your image. If you really like the effect your adjustment creates, you can save it as a preset to easily apply to other images, even on import. Aperture 3 has the ability to brush those adjustments selectively onto just part of your image, meaning you can make one levels adjustment in the sky and another on the ground, something iPhoto just can't do. Oh, and if you prefer using curves to levels, Aperture 3 has a curves adjustment, too.

However, more advanced image adjustment controls aren't the only difference between iPhoto and Aperture. Aperture provides tools to manage a far larger library than iPhoto can manage. For example, Aperture lets you make complicated searches for images, such as the search in Figure 1.1 that finds all your top-rated images taken in 2010 that were taken in San Francisco and have the keyword *water*. If you want to know specifics about Aperture's tools to help categorize and search for images, check out Chapters 5 and 6. Aperture is also a lot more flexible with managing your photos, and unlike in iPhoto, images in Aperture can easily be stored on multiple hard drives. Aperture 3 also adds great new tools to merge and split off collections of images, making it easy to share image collections between two machines.

1.1 An image search that's easy to do in Aperture but just not practical in iPhoto.

Lastly, while there are similar features in iPhoto and Aperture, like Faces, Places, books, and slide shows, they are just more powerful in Aperture. Aperture's Book tool, which we cover in Chapter 7, has advanced layout options that let you completely customize the image and text boxes on your page, or even use a photo to create a two-page background spread. Aperture's slide shows, explored in Chapter 8, let you go beyond iPhoto's click-and-play slide shows, creating custom titles, transitions, and music. You can even include HD video within an Aperture slide show.

In summary, while iPhoto is great for the casual consumer, just as you move from a point-and-shoot camera to a dSLR to upgrade your photography, moving to Aperture from iPhoto lets you upgrade your image-management tools.

Choosing Aperture over Bridge and Lightroom

For many photographers, Adobe Photoshop is the number one tool of choice for image work, and we certainly agree that it's a great image-manipulation program (although Aperture's adjustment tools combined with third-party Aperture plug-ins have made it so that we do more than 90 percent of our manipulation work in Aperture instead of Photoshop). You might be asking yourself why you shouldn't just use Adobe products, such as Adobe Bridge or Adobe Lightroom.

Bridge

Bridge, which comes free with your copy of Photoshop or Photoshop Elements, gives you basic organization features, such as letting you add keywords and captions to your images, and because it lets you open your RAW files in Adobe Camera Raw, you can adjust your images in it, too.

However, the key reason to choose Aperture over Bridge is that Bridge is really more of a File Browser that lets you do a couple of basic tasks with your files. Aperture, on the other hand, is a full asset management tool with a database behind the scenes tracking all your images. With Bridge, it's still up to you to manage where your files live, and tasks like searching for a particular image are quite clunky compared to an asset-based tool like Aperture. Furthermore, because Adobe wants to promote Lightroom over Bridge, Bridge lacks many features that are useful to photographers, like being able to spell-check keywords and captions. Adobe has explicitly chosen to omit those features.

Lightroom

While in some ways the Lightroom versus Aperture debate is a bit like a religious Mac versus PC debate, there are specific reasons that we find Aperture to be a much better choice than Lightroom for our workflows. The main reason is that Lightroom has different modules that you must switch between for different tasks, whereas Aperture does not. Practically speaking, adjustments affect editing decisions, and it's faster to make those decisions in Aperture than in Lightroom. For example, you may frequently look at an image and say, "This is good, but if I straighten it, will it be great?" In Aperture, you can press one keyboard shortcut and then drag the mouse to straighten the image. In Lightroom, you need to switch from the Organize to the Develop module, adjust the image, and then switch back to the main module to continue making editing decisions. Less time having to switch modes to make a decision means more time shooting and having fun!

We prefer Aperture for specific, technical reasons as well. One is that Aperture has a more powerful hierarchy (we dig into the specific parts of its structure shortly) that you can customize, such as moving albums wherever you want them to be, whereas Lightroom has a relatively flat hierarchy with limited customization options. In Aperture 3, like in Lightroom, you are able to brush adjustments onto an image, but Aperture provides far more control over how those adjustments are applied, such as only affecting the highlights or shadows. Furthermore, only a few adjustments in Lightroom can be brushed onto an image, whereas most adjustments in Aperture can be selectively applied. Aperture's new curves control is far more powerful than Lightroom's parametric curves, too. Then there are also features that Lightroom just doesn't have; for example being able to manage audio files and being able to make a book. Lightroom also lacks any form of Faces and Places.

We should mention that while we far prefer Aperture to Lightroom, Lightroom is not a bad program, and if you have a PC, it's a very good choice. However, if you have a Mac, we enthusiastically recommend that you use Aperture.

Working with Aperture's File Structure

If you've used a program like Bridge before, then you're accustomed to the folder hierarchy on your hard drive being exactly what you see in Bridge, and when you move images around within Bridge or make new folders, it also creates new folders and moves files around on your hard drive for you. Programs such as Aperture (and Lightroom) take a different approach. Your images live in a particular location on your hard drive (more on this in a minute) and appear within a different structure within Aperture. When you move images around within Aperture, between albums for example, they don't move around on your hard drive (although there are special commands to let you move the files around your disk), and when you create a new folder within Aperture, that folder doesn't actually exist on your hard drive. Let's take a minute to explore how Aperture stores files and the different terms for the various collections of images.

Note We frequently use the word *image* to talk about any file in Aperture, including movie and audio files, as Aperture treats them all in essentially the same way, especially as far as the file structure is concerned.

Understanding the Aperture library and where your files live

One of the fundamental concepts in Aperture is a library. A library refers to a collection of images. On your hard drive, a library, like the one in Figure 1.2, stores and tracks information about an image, ranging from the various-sized thumbnails that Aperture uses to display the image to the image's metadata, information about the faces in your images, and information about what adjustments you've made to an image. If you choose, Aperture will also store your image files themselves within a library (more on this in a minute), but your image files can also live outside the library instead. An Aperture library appears as a bundle within the Finder (a bundle is a special type of folder that appears as if it were a single file) and discourages you from digging inside your library. If you dig inside your library, you might accidentally do something, such as move a key file, which causes a problem in Aperture.

Unlike in iPhoto where you tend to just have one photo library, you will most likely have multiple libraries with Aperture. For example, you could have a library on an external drive containing every image that you've ever taken and a second library on your laptop's internal hard drive that has a library with images from the previous shoot or two.

By default, Aperture creates a library in your Pictures folder. Chapter 10 explains how to work with multiple libraries.

1.2 An Aperture library as seen in the Finder. Notice that it appears as just a single file, even though it contains other files within.

When Aperture is closed, double-click on a library in the Finder to launch Aperture with the contents of that library.

Genius

Understanding referenced and managed files

Referenced and managed files refer to where your image files are stored. Put simply, referenced files are stored in whatever folder on your hard drive you select, and Aperture stores a reference to their location within the library. If you move the files around on your disk, you have to tell Aperture to update its reference (we cover working with referenced files in depth in Chapter 3). Managed files, on the other hand, are stored within the Aperture library. You don't need to worry about where they are on your hard drive because they'll always just be inside your library, and if you want to access the image files you must do so via Aperture rather than the Finder.

Choosing to use referenced or managed files is largely a personal choice, and within Aperture they are treated exactly the same. The main benefit to managed files is that you don't have to worry about into what folder on your drive you're importing your images because they're all just going into your Aperture library. You might find it preferable to use managed files because they help prevent you from losing track of your images.

However, the main benefit to referenced files is that you can store your images wherever you want, even on a separate hard drive. Aperture stores previews of your images inside the library that you can view in Aperture, even if the full image files can't be found. This means that you can keep your full Aperture library on your MacBook Pro's hard drive so that you can always have your images with you, but you can store all the large image files on a large, external drive.

Referenced files that you see in Aperture but whose image files can't be found are called *offline images*. Aperture indicates an offline image with the badge overlay indicated in Figure 1.3.

A second benefit to referenced files is that if you want to use another program to work with your images, such as Adobe Bridge, without going through Aperture, you can because your image files are not locked away inside of the library bundle. Just be careful about reorganizing your image files outside of Aperture. If you move the file on your hard drive, you need to tell Aperture where the file's new location is so that it doesn't think the image is offline. Chapter 3 covers working with referenced files in depth.

Badge indicates an offline image

1.3 A badge overlay over a thumbnail in Aperture indicating an offline image.

Understanding how images are organized within Aperture

Aperture has special terms to explicitly describe which image you're working with: the *master* file on disk or a *version* within Aperture. Furthermore, a key concept to understand about Aperture is that files within Aperture have their own hierarchy that isn't guaranteed to be anything like the file hierarchy on your disk. When you move an image around within Aperture, it doesn't also move it between folders on your hard drive. As such, Aperture has a special vocabulary to describe how masters and versions are organized into projects, albums, folders, and stacks.

Master images

A master is the original file you imported into Aperture, whether it's a RAW, JPEG, TIFF, DNG, and so on. Aperture never modifies the master file; you can always return to your original master image no matter how many adjustments you make within Aperture.

Versions

A version is a representation of a master file that you work with within Aperture. It refers to the master file but is not the master file. No matter how many changes you make to a version, you aren't changing the master. This is called nondestructive editing.

Something special about Aperture is that you can make multiple versions of an image with different adjustments applied to each, as shown in Figure 1.4. And unlike iPhoto, which makes a full copy of the master file each time and uses a lot of hard drive space, Aperture only stores the changes you make to each image. Then, when you ask to see a particular version, Aperture loads the master behind the scenes and applies the changes you made to create this version.

1.4 All three versions of this image share the same master file, and each new version only takes a few kilobytes more hard drive space to create.

Working with versions can get a little confusing. Although all of Aperture's built-in adjustments are nondestructive and are stored as information on top of a master file, Aperture also supports third-party adjustment editors such as plug-ins to create high dynamic range (HDR) images, as well as external editors like Photoshop. In order for these third-party programs to see the adjustments you make to an image, Aperture makes a TIF or PSD file from your version for the other tool to work with. What this means is that if you make a bunch of adjustments to an image within Aperture and want to open it in Photoshop, rather than trying to describe to Photoshop how Aperture converted the RAW file and then the changes you made on top of that, Aperture just collects everything together, makes a new TIF file, and then tells Photoshop to open that TIF file.

Genius Even if you're using referenced files, this new file that Aperture makes from your version will be stored within your Aperture library. You can relocate the Aperture-created master wherever you want after it's created, as discussed in Chapter 3.

This new version has a master file on the hard drive, but it's not the master file that you imported from your camera, and this version with its new master consumes far more disk space than a normal version.

If you see the badge overlay indicated in Figure 1.5 within Aperture, it means that this version also has an Aperture-created master aside from the original master you imported.

Badge indicates an
Aperture-created master

1.5 This badge overlay on a thumbnail or image means that this version has an Aperture-created master.

Projects

Within an Aperture library, you will group your master files and versions into projects. A project might represent an entire shoot, multiple shoots of the same subject, a part of a shoot, or just a completely random collection of images. Each time you import an image, you must determine into what project to place it. If you delete a project, you are removing the master files contained within it from your library. There is no limit on how many projects you can create.

Albums

Albums are a collection of image versions that you create manually. Versions may exist in more than one album (for example, you might put an image in both a *Brooks Wedding Dinner* album and a *Show to Bride* album). Albums can either exist within a project to provide a finer-grained grouping of images or at a library level if they contain images from multiple projects. For example, we typically create a project for a shoot such as *Japan – February 2010* and then create albums within the project to represent specific parts of the shoot such as *Tsurui Day 3 AM*. Later, we create a library-level album, such as *Images to Copyright*, containing images from every project that we need to submit for copyright registration. No matter how many albums within a library you put an image into, Aperture will not create a new copy of the master file on disk. Furthermore, deleting an image from an album does not remove it from your library or hard drive.

There are special types of albums, called Smart Albums, whose contents are created dynamically. For example, Aperture has built-in Smart Albums at the library level (called Library Albums) for 5-star images (the highest rating you can give), videos, images created in the last week, and more. Each time you add or adjust an image and make it meet one of these criteria, such as rating an image with 5 stars, Aperture automatically adds it to the appropriate Smart Album. Smart Albums are covered in depth in Chapter 4.

Folders

A folder is a container for projects, albums, and other folders. As you create more and more projects, you may find it helpful to use folders to group related projects together so that you're not always scrolling through a long list of projects. For example, we have a folder in our library called Kiteboarding (shown in Figure 1.6) that contains folders for each beach we shoot at, and those subfolders contain our projects. We also have albums within the Kiteboarding folder (and not a child folder) with images of specific riders pulled from all the beaches we've shot each rider at.

Stacks

While not strictly part of Aperture's hierarchy, Aperture calls a small collection of images that are related in some way a *stack*. The difference between a stack and a project or album is that a stack of images tends to essentially be one image, but just slightly different versions of that image, whereas a project or album might contain many stacks of images.

For example, Aperture can automatically group bursts of images taken close together into a stack. If you shoot a sporting event and import the images into one album, you would have many different stacks representing each burst of action. Additionally, if you want to create multiple versions of a single image with different adjustments, you could group these different versions into a stack for organization. Each time you open your image in an external editor such as Photoshop, Aperture automatically stacks the previous version and this new externally edited version together. Stacks are covered in more detail in Chapter 3.

1.6 Here's what part of our Aperture library looks like. Notice how projects, albums, and folders all have different icons, how folders help us organize our library, and how we have albums at both the library and project levels.

A Brief Tour of Aperture's Interface

Now that you've learned some of Aperture's basic jargon, let's look at Aperture itself. The first time you launch Aperture, you see the Welcome screen in Figure 1.7. You can get back to this Welcome screen at any point by choosing Help⇨Welcome to Aperture. Here, you find video tutorials to help you learn about Aperture 3's new features and to help you get started importing your iPhoto library into Aperture, a topic we cover in Chapter 2. Close this window to begin using Aperture itself. The main parts of the interface you see right away are the Inspector, Browser, and Viewer, and this section explores these pieces in depth and explains how to work with the Library Inspector, which you use to manage Aperture's file hierarchy.

Understanding the Inspector, Browser, and Viewer

The three key parts of Aperture's interface are the Inspector, the Browser, and the Viewer. These three areas are shown in Figure 1.8.

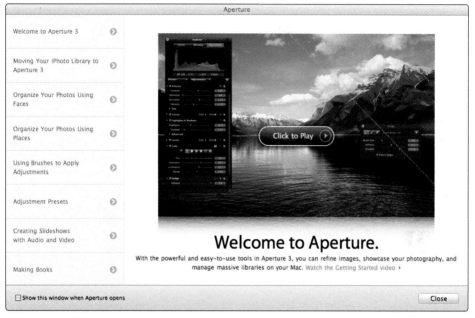

1.7 Aperture's Welcome screen.

Viewer

Inspector

Browser

1.8 Three areas of the Aperture interface that will serve you well.

Inspector

The Inspector has three tabs within it to let you inspect different items. The initial tab is the Library tab. The Library Inspector has two groups, as shown in Figure 1.9. At the top is a library-wide group that lets you see all your projects, all your images, every face in your library, and more (we discuss this section shortly). Below that is the Projects & Albums group that has both built-in Library Albums — Smart Albums that search your entire library for certain groups of images — as well as all your projects, albums, and folders.

To create an empty project, choose File⇨ New⇨Project. To create an empty album within a Project, select that project and choose File⇨New⇨Album. To create an empty, library-level album, select the Library Albums group and choose File⇨New⇨ Album, or click and drag a project-level album out of the project until Aperture displays a box around the Projects & Albums text. To create a new folder, choose File⇨New⇨Folder.

▼ LIBRARY
- Projects
- Photos
- Faces
- Places
- Flagged
- ▶ Trash

▼ PROJECTS & ALBUMS
- Badges
- Badge Book
- ▼ Library Albums
    - ★ or better
    - ★★★★★
    - In the Last Month
    - In the Last Week
    - Rejected
    - Videos
- 20 key
- ▶ Kiteboarding
- ▶ Alaska August 2009
- ▶ Alaska March 2008

1.9 The Library and Projects & Albums groups within the Library Inspector.

At the very top of the Library Inspector is a search field that filters the contents of the Library Inspector. This search field does not search inside the metadata of your images. It simply searches your project, album, and folder names for a match. Next to the search field is an Action pop-up menu. This menu contains the following four commands:

- **Add to Favorites/Remove from Favorites.** Over time, you will end up with many items in your Library Inspector. To filter the list so that you only see your favorite items, select Favorite Items from the search field's pop-up menu. To mark an item as a favorite, select it in the Library Inspector and choose Add to Favorites from the Action pop-up menu.

- **Keep Albums & Projects Arranged By.** This submenu affects how items at the same level (such as all the top-level items, all the items directly under a project, and all the items directly within the same folder) are sorted within the Library Inspector. Choose

Name from this submenu to cause all the items in the Library Inspector to be sorted alphabetically. Choose Kind to cause the items to be grouped by kind. Choose Manual so that you can drag and drop items to rearrange them however you want. Even if you choose Name or Kind, you can manually rearrange an item at any point and Aperture will automatically switch to Manual sorting.

- **Export Project/Folder/Album as New Library.** We cover this topic more in Chapter 10, but the quick explanation is that any item in Aperture can be exported as a new library to make it easy to share groups of images.

- **Maintain Previews for Project.** By default, Aperture maintains large previews of your images for use in other applications such as iWork. However, these previews can take a lot of hard drive space, and it's often useful to not maintain them for an entire project. We cover previews and this command more in Chapter 10.

At the very bottom of the Library Inspector is a bar marked Vault. Vaults are special Aperture-created backups of your library. We cover Vaults and other backup options in Chapter 10.

By clicking the Metadata tab at the top of the Inspector, you switch from the Library Inspector to the Metadata Inspector. As you might expect, this inspector allows you to edit your image's metadata. This inspector is covered in depth in Chapter 4. The last tab, Adjustments, lets you switch to the Adjustments Inspector, which contains tools to adjust your image. The Adjustment Inspector is covered in Chapter 6.

If you're working on a small screen, it's often useful to hide the Inspector and to only show it when needed. To hide the Inspector, choose Window ⇨ Hide Inspector; to reveal it, choose Window ⇨ Show Inspector. The keyboard shortcut for hiding and showing the inspector is I (with no modifiers). There are menu commands for quickly switching to the Library, Metadata, and Adjustment Inspectors under View ⇨ Inspector, but more useful are the keyboard shortcuts to switch to those views: Control+P for the Library Inspector (think P for Project), Control+D for the Metadata Inspector, and Control+A for the Adjustment Inspector. W (with no modifiers) is also a keyboard shortcut for View ⇨ Inspector ⇨ Next Tab, which lets you quickly cycle among Inspector tabs.

Note If you're working with a tablet display like a Wacom Cintiq, you might find it useful to move the Inspector to the right side of the screen. Choose View ⇨ Inspector ⇨ Swap Position.

Browser

The Library Inspector lets you switch between collections of images within your library, and the Browser lets you see the contents of those collections. The three views within Browser are Filmstrip, Grid, and List, which you can switch by clicking the buttons marked in Figure 1.10. Filmstrip (the default) and Grid are similar in that they both show primarily thumbnails of your image (we cover customizing what other data you see in Chapter 3), but Filmstrip will only have one row of images that scrolls from side to side. Grid view arranges your images into a grid that you scroll up and down. List view turns Browser into a table where each column has a different piece of metadata, such as the image's date, aperture, and shutter speed. Another way of switching views is to choose View ⇨ Browser ⇨ Filmstrip (Control+F), Grid (Control+G), or List (Control+L). In all three views, there is a thumbnail size slider that lets you make the displayed thumbnails larger or smaller.

Sorting menu   Filter button

View buttons   Search field

Thumbnail size slider

1.10 Browser with a few key buttons and controls highlighted.

Browser also has a sorting pop-up menu that lets you determine how your images are sorted, be it by date, rating, or more. Switch between Ascending and Descending in the Sorting pop-up menu to change the sort direction. When in List view, you can also click the column header to sort by that criteria, and click the header again to change the sort direction. If you prefer, it's also possible to manually arrange the images by clicking and dragging an image (or group of images) wherever you want it to be. If for some reason the sorting and filtering controls aren't visible, choose View ⇨ Browser ⇨ Show Sort and Filter Controls (⌘+Shift+F). Similarly, if you want to hide those controls, choose View ⇨ Browser ⇨ Hide Sort and Filter Controls.

Caution
If you start to work with your images in the Browser while Aperture is still importing your images, it tends to revert to Manual sorting. We highly recommend making sure you're sorting by Date when editing your photos so that it's easier to see sequences of images.

At the top right of Browser is a search field. As you might expect, if you start typing in it, Browser will filter its contents to only show images whose name or other metadata match the text you're typing. If you click on the search field's pop-up menu, you will see commands to quickly filter Browser based on image ratings and labels. By clicking the Filter button to the left of the search field, you open the Filter dialog, as shown in Figure 1.11, which lets you refine your filter even further. We cover this more in Chapter 4, but this control is where you can make advanced queries like "filter Browser so that it only shows images taken last Tuesday containing Eric's face."

1.11 The Filter dialog and button.

Sometimes, when looking for an image, you'll find it useful to make Browser larger. There are two ways to do so. If you're working in Split View, which has both Browser and Viewer on-screen at the same time, click the dark line between Browser and Viewer and drag it up and down to adjust

Browser's size. Unfortunately, Aperture only lets you drag Browser so that it takes up about 60 percent of the screen. To hide Viewer and make Browser take the entire screen, click the Browser button in the toolbar indicated in Figure 1.12 (if for some reason the toolbar is hidden, click the pill-shaped button at the top right to reveal it). To return to the previous view, click the Split View button in the toolbar. Note that when you're in Browser mode, you can only switch between Grid and List views, not Filmstrip. If you're comfortable using keyboard shortcuts, press V to cycle among Viewer and Browser, Viewer only, and Browser only.

1.12 This is what Aperture looks like with Viewer hidden and Browser maximized, and note the Browser and Split View buttons in the toolbar that let you toggle layouts.

Genius

In Browser, you can use keyboard shortcuts to quickly scroll through your images. Press L to scroll forward, J to scroll backward, and K to stop scrolling. Press L and J multiple times to scroll faster in their respective directions. Make sure to click inside of Browser so that it has focus before using these hotkeys.

If you prefer to see your thumbnails in a vertical Filmstrip rather than a horizontal one, it's possible to rotate Browser by choosing View ⇨ Browser ⇨ Rotate Position (Shift+W). Like Inspector, it's also possible to swap which side of the screen Browser's on by choosing View ⇨ Browser ⇨ Swap Position (Option+W) as shown in Figure 1.13.

1.13 Aperture with Browser's position rotated and swapped.

Viewer

Viewer, the last key part of Aperture's interface, is where you see the full contents of your image (or selected images). When you select an image in Browser, Aperture will load the full contents of that version, displaying a "Loading" indicator while doing so, and display it in Viewer. Many different tools in Viewer help you examine your image in detail, from being able to zoom in to 1,000 percent to being able to quickly switch between seeing the original, master image, and the current version with your adjustments. We cover Viewer in depth in Chapter 3.

Aperture also has an excellent full-screen mode for Browser and Viewer that removes any distraction and lets you focus on your images. We explore this mode in depth in Chapter 3.

Managing files with Projects and Albums

As mentioned earlier, Projects are where your images and masters truly live. Making a new project is quite easy! To move a group of images into a new project, do the following:

1. **Select the images in Browser that you want to use for the new project.**

2. **Choose File ➪ New ➪ Project (⌘+N).** Aperture displays the New Project dialog, as shown in Figure 1.14.

3. **Type the project name.**

4. **Select the Move selected items to new project check box if you want to move your selected images into the new project.**

5. **Click OK.**

Project Name:	My Great Project
	☐ Move selected items to new project

Cancel   OK

1.14 The New Project dialog.

Another very common task in Aperture is to make a new, empty album at the project or library level and then move images into it. For example, we might make a *Submit to Agency* album and then drag whatever images we want to submit to our stock agent into that album. Another common task is to make a new album at the project level prepopulated with the images you've selected in Browser, such as if you select all the images of a certain subject and want to make a new album just for that subject. These tasks are straightforward and similar to making a new project.

1. **Choose one of the following options to begin creating an album:**

   ● **To make an empty album, select the project in the Library Inspector where you want the album to live.**

   ● **To make a new album from a group of images, select the images in Browser that you want to put into the album.** Aperture creates the new album at the same level as the currently selected item.

   ● **To make a library-level album, click on Library Albums instead of selecting a project in Library Inspector.**

2. **Choose File ➪ New ➪ Album.** Aperture displays the New Album dialog, as shown in Figure 1.15.

Album Name:	My Album
	☑ Add selected items to new album

Cancel   OK

1.15 The New Album dialog.

3. **Type the album's name.**

4. **If you are creating a new album from a group of images, select the Add selected items to new album check box if you want to add the selected items to the album.** If you are creating an empty album at the project level in the Library Inspector or at the library level in Library Albums, leave this check box unselected.

5. **Click OK.**

6. **If the album doesn't appear in the right place, drag and drop it to the right location in the Library Inspector.** To drag it to the library level, drag it out of the project and to the left until Aperture displays a black box around Projects & Albums and then drop it. To drag it into another project, drag the album until a black box appears around the right project. Note that this will not move the master files into this new project.

Where things get confusing is when you start to move images between albums and different projects. To move images (and videos and other items in your projects and albums) around, select them in Browser and drag and drop them to the desired destination. Holding down the Option key while dragging affects what Aperture does with the files in some cases. Table 1.1 explains the situations you can encounter.

Table 1.1 Effects of Dragging Images between Projects and Albums

Source	Destination	Effect	Effect with Option Key Held
Project	Different Project	Master and all versions are moved to the new project	Master and all versions are copied to the new project
Project	Album in Same Project	Image is copied into the album	Same
Project	Album in Different Project	Image is copied into the new album, but the master lives in the original project	Same
Album	Album in Same Project	Image is copied into the new album	Same
Album	Album in Different Project	Image is copied into the new album, but the master lives in the original project	Same
Album	Different Project	Master and all versions are moved to the new project	Master and all versions are copied to the new project

To quickly reveal which project an image is in from any album, select the image and choose File ⇨ Show in Project.

To remove an image from an album, select it and choose Photos ⇨ Remove from Album (or press Delete). However, removing an image from an album does not move the master to Aperture's Trash. To delete a specific version of an image, whether you're in a project or an album (and by delete we really mean move to Aperture's Trash), select it and choose File ⇨ Delete Version. If the version has an Aperture-created master file, it is deleted, too. If there is only one version of an image, then Aperture deletes the image's master file when you empty Aperture's Trash. However, if there are multiple versions of an image and you want to remove all of them, select the image and choose File ⇨ Delete Master Image and All Versions.

Also note that it's possible to delete an album, project, or folder by selecting it in the Library Inspector and choosing File ⇨ Delete Album, Project, or Folder, respectively. Deleting an album does not delete the contents of an album, but deleting a project (or folder that contains a project) does remove its contents, too.

Using special built-in views

We mentioned earlier that there is a special group at the top of the Library Inspector that lets you access library-wide collections. Specifically, they are Projects, Photos, Faces, Places, Flagged, and Trash. We discuss these views next with the exception of Photos, as this view is straightforward — clicking the Photos item displays every image in your library — and Flagged items, which is detailed in Chapter 4.

All Projects

Clicking the Projects item opens the All Projects view, as shown in Figure 1.16. In some ways this view is similar to the Events view in iPhoto, especially if you click the Group by Year button. Move your mouse over a project's thumbnail to scroll through all the images within a project. If there's a particular image you want to set as the project thumbnail, press the spacebar when the image is displayed.

Genius

A more direct way to set an image as a project's key photo is to Control+click on it in either the Browser or Viewer and choose Set Key Photo.

1.16 The All Projects view.

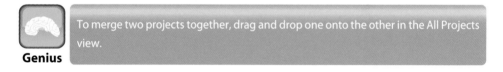

To merge two projects together, drag and drop one onto the other in the All Projects view.

Genius

Click the Info button to display the Project Info panel, where you can add a project description and assign its general location on a map. Double-click on a project's thumbnail to open the project in Browser view.

Faces and Places

Clicking the Faces item provides quick access to the Faces corkboard, with every face Aperture finds in your library. Clicking the Places item takes you to the Places map, with pins for every location you've assigned to a photo. We cover these features in depth in Chapter 5.

Aperture Trash

When you delete an item in Aperture, whether it's an entire project or a specific image, it's placed into the Aperture Trash, as shown in Figure 1.17. You can view the contents of Aperture's Trash at any time by clicking the Trash item in the Library Inspector and either retrieve something from it or empty it. To empty Aperture's Trash, choose Aperture ➪ Empty Aperture Trash.

1.17 Note how you view Aperture's Trash just like you would any other album.

Caution

Emptying Aperture Trash does not delete the image from your hard drive. To completely remove it, you must also empty the Trash in Finder. If you want to recover the file, open the Trash in Finder, and within the Aperture folder, there will be a folder for the image's project that contains the master file.

To restore an item from the Trash, either drag it back to the desired location or Control+click on it and choose Put Back.

Basic Customization Options

To open the Preferences panel within Aperture, choose Aperture ➪ Preferences. We discuss specific preferences throughout the rest of the book when they apply, but there are a few key options we want to point out for your initial Aperture setup.

Setting library location and other General preferences

The most basic setting under the General pane, shown in Figure 1.18, is which current Aperture library you're working with. In addition to the ways mentioned earlier to switch libraries (using the commands in File ⇨ Switch to Library), you can also switch libraries by clicking Change and browsing for the new library. Clicking Reveal opens a new Finder window with your current Aperture library selected.

1.18 The General pane of the Preferences panel.

We recommend selecting the Scroll to navigate photos in the Viewer check box so that using your mouse's scroll wheel in Viewer (as long as you're not zoomed in) enables you to go to the previous or next image.

The next option in the General pane is Enable Faces. We highly recommend deselecting this check box, unless you primarily photograph people and use Faces all the time. The reason we recommend disabling Faces is that it slows Aperture down, especially when importing images.

The last key option in the General pane is the Reset All Warnings button. Sometimes, a dialog has an Ask again next time check box or something similar. If you deselect that check box but decide that you really do want to be prompted again, clicking Reset All Warnings makes all the dialogs appear again.

Changing appearance preferences

The second Preferences pane is the Appearance pane, as shown in Figure 1.19. We recommend leaving the brightness levels at their default values, although you might prefer to set your Full Screen Viewer brightness to 18% (which is neutral gray) because the color surrounding an image can influence your perception of an image.

On the bottom half of the pane on the View Slideshows on pop-up menu, we recommend choosing Secondary Display instead of Main Display. That way, if you're presenting a slide show from your laptop while connected to a projector, the show appears on your projector's display.

1.19 The Appearance preferences pane.

We highly recommend selecting the Show "Loading…" indicator while full size photos load check box so that you know when the full version of your image is loaded into the viewer. We also recommend selecting the Badge referenced items check box so that you know which of your images are referenced and which are managed. This badge helps avoid accidentally making an image referenced or managed without meaning to and losing the master file. The other options are largely a matter of personal taste.

Changing default import behavior

The Import pane, shown in Figure 1.20, lets you modify the default import behavior. We cover importing in detail in Chapter 2, but the key option here is what you want to happen when a camera is connected. This setting allows you to pick between having a specific application open or doing nothing at all. Although you can set this preference within Aperture, it affects your entire system. We typically leave this set to Aperture, but if you sync an iPhone with your computer, we recommend using No Application so that Aperture doesn't open every time you plug in your iPhone.

1.20 The Import preferences pane.

Modifying preview preferences

Aperture automatically generates JPEG versions of all your images with all your adjustments applied so that other applications, like iWork or Apple TV, can access your adjusted images. However, these previews can take a *lot* of hard drive space if you're not careful. We cover them in depth in Chapter 10, but for now we recommend that you either disable them entirely by deselecting the New projects automatically generate previews check box or at least limiting the size to your screen resolution and selecting a medium quality, as shown in Figure 1.21.

1.21 The Preview pane.

Running in 32-bit or 64-bit mode

One of the great new features in Snow Leopard (Mac OS X 10.6) is that it's a 64-bit operating system, providing applications with some performance gains and allowing them to use more than 4GB of RAM at once. Aperture 3 is a 64-bit application, however, and occasionally you will need to use an older plug-in or such that's 32-bit only. By default, Aperture automatically detects if you're trying to use an older plug-in and automatically relaunches into 32-bit mode, but if you want to explicitly choose whether to run Aperture in 32-bit or 64-bit mode, follow these steps:

1. **In the Finder, go to your Applications folder and select Aperture 3.**

2. **Choose File ⇨ Get Info.**

3. **Select or deselect the Open in 32-bit mode check box depending on how you want to run Aperture.**

4. **Close the Get Info window and launch Aperture.**

How Do I Import Images?

©Ellen Anon

After you capture your images, the next step is downloading them onto your computer. The Import interface in Aperture 3 enables you to do far more than just copy the photos from the memory card to your computer's hard drive. It gives you a head start on organizing and optimizing your images as well. You determine where the images should be stored, whether to simultaneously create a backup copy of them, rename them or modify a time stamp, apply keywords or other metadata, and apply any adjustment presets. You can even view each image nearly full-screen to determine whether to import it.

We know that when you finish shooting you want to get your images into Aperture as quickly as possible so you can see the results and start editing. Aperture 3 offers lots of ways to import files, all designed to give you as much control of the process as possible while simultaneously making it as efficient and painless as possible. Most of the time, the files you want to import will be on a memory card. You can also import images that are already stored on your computer but that are not yet in Aperture, or that are on an external hard drive that's connected to your computer. You can even use Aperture to import video and audio clips in addition to your image files and keep them organized so they're easily accessible. Then you can play the video and audio clips in the browser and use them in Aperture-generated slide shows.

Note

Currently, you can't use Aperture to make adjustments to audio or video files beyond basic trimming.

If your files are on a memory card, you have the option to use a card reader attached to your computer or to directly attach your camera to the computer using the USB cable that comes with most cameras. Using card readers enables faster image downloading in many cases and means that you don't need to rely on the camera's battery. Some computers offer built-in card readers that are convenient and fast.

Touring the Import Panel

After you attach your memory card, camera, or hard drive to the computer, you're ready to use the import panel. We recommend that you set up Aperture Preferences to automatically open Aperture when a camera is connected by following these steps:

1. **Choose Aperture ⇨ Preferences to open the Preferences dialog.**
2. **Click the Import button.** The import-related preferences appear, as shown in Figure 2.1.

3. **On the When a camera is connected, open pop-up menu, select Aperture.** Aperture's import interface now will open automatically whenever you connect a memory card or camera.

2.1 Set Aperture Preferences to automatically open the Import panel whenever a camera or memory card is connected to the computer.

To access the Import panel manually, click the Import button at the top left of the main Aperture window, as shown in Figure 2.2.

The Import panel contains a lot of powerful options in a concise and well-laid-out interface that's divided into several major sections. You specify where to look for the images in the upper-left section of the interface, and the Viewer displays the images found on the card or the content of the hard drive that you selected. If you don't select a card, camera, or external drive, then the Browser appears beneath the Viewer and displays a directory to the files on your computer and any drives that are connected to the computer.

The Import Settings pop-up menu contains presets and options that determine how the files are imported, where they're stored, how they're named, and more. We cover those in detail later in this chapter. To the right of the Import panel and beneath the Import Settings pop-up is the Aperture Library area where you specify where to store the images when they're imported. At the bottom right, the number of files to import is indicated followed by buttons to initiate the import or to cancel out of the Import interface.

Import from options

Aperture Library options

Access Import panel button

Viewer

Import Settings pop-up menu

Grid view button

Browser

Cancel button

List view button

Thumbnail size slider

Import button

Viewer only button

Number of files to import

2.2 The Import interface is divided into well-organized sections.

Using the Different Views in the Import Panel

When you first open the Import panel, it displays thumbnails of your images. This is the Grid view. You can control the size of the thumbnails by using the slider beneath the Viewer panel.

There are three icons beneath the Viewer that you use to control how the images are displayed. Choose the Grid view (refer to Figure 2.2) to see the images displayed as a series of thumbnails, choose the List view, shown in Figure 2.3, to view basic information about each file as well as a tiny thumbnail, or choose the Viewer only mode, shown in Figure 2.4, to display a single image at a time so that you can inspect it more closely.

2.3 The List view displays information about each file.

Note If you're in Grid view, double-clicking any image changes the Import panel to the Viewer mode. Double-clicking the image in the Viewer again returns it to the Grid view.

2.4 The Viewer only mode displays a single image at a time.

Each image has a check box that contains a check mark by default to indicate that image should be imported. Selecting or deselecting the check box toggles the check mark on and off. You can quickly select or deselect all images by using the Check All or Uncheck All buttons at the top of the Import pane. While in Grid view or List view, to select or deselect a group of images, follow these steps:

1. **If the images are contiguous, select the first image, press and hold the Shift key, and click the last image in the group.**

2. **If the images are not contiguous, select the first image, then ⌘+click each subsequent image you want to select.**

3. **With the images selected, click the check box of one of the images.** All check boxes of the selected images will change accordingly, as shown in Figure 2.5.

2.5 Select a group of images and then toggle the check marks to choose the images to import.

Choosing Import Settings

In addition to selecting which images to import, you have a number of other choices to make about the import process, such as specifying a project for your images, choosing referenced versus managed files, renaming your images, changing the time stamp, applying presets, specifying what type files to import, how to handle RAW+JPEG pairs, running actions immediately after import, and automatically backing up the import. These choices help you to keep your images organized and increase the efficiency of your workflow as you customize the settings for your individual needs.

Configuring a destination project for your images

You need to decide whether you want to import the images into an existing project or to create a new project for them. If you set the default import location in the Import Preferences to New

Project, then by default the Destination pop-up will choose New Project even if you already have a project selected in the Library Inspector. However, if you specify Selected Item in the Import preferences, then by default the Destination pop-up in the Import panel will reflect whatever project you've selected in the Library Inspector. If you have not yet selected a specific project or album, then the Destination pop-up automatically chooses New Project.

You can override the default setting in the Destination pop-up by selecting a specific project or album to import the images there, or by selecting New Project, as shown in Figure 2.6.

Aperture Libra	New Project	
Destination	✓ 🖼 Anon	
	Recent Projects	ts
	🖼 S90	
	🖼 California (1)	
Store Files		

If you use a memory card to hold images that you take over an extended period of time, whether several hours, days, or weeks, the option Automatically split project is enabled in the Import interface.

2.6 Choose whether to import your images into an existing project or to create a new project.

Aperture can automatically split the import into several projects, one for each span of time. You can determine the time frame by choosing Preferences ⇨ Import ⇨ Autosplit Into Projects and choosing One project per day, One project per week, Two-hour gaps, or Eight-hour gaps, as shown in Figure 2.7.

As shown in Figure 2.8, the Viewer panel of the Import interface changes to show which images are in each project. The additional projects can be manually renamed in the Library panel after import.

Genius

If you opt to use an existing project for the import, you can create a new album within that project to further organize your images while in the Import panel by pressing ⌘+L. This opens a new dialog in which you name the new album by typing in the Album Name field. The images are imported within the selected project, but they are also visible within the new album, and that's very handy! To import your images into a new album within a *new* project, you must first create the new project in the Library by choosing New ⇨ Project and naming it before using the Import interface.

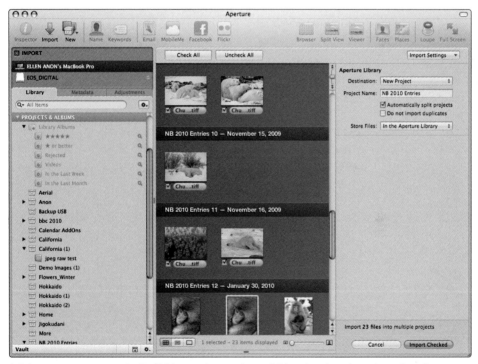

2.7 Set Preferences to split the import into new projects according to the time frame in which they were captured.

2.8 Aperture can automatically divide your images into additional projects based on when they were shot.

When you import into an existing project, select the Do not import duplicates check box to avoid importing multiple copies of the same file.

Using referenced or managed files

The next choice in the Aperture library section of the Import interface is one of the most important. You tell Aperture whether you want to use referenced or managed files. Before you choose the setting in the Store Files pop-up menu, you need to be certain that you understand the differences between referenced and managed files. Although we covered the differences between referenced and managed files in Chapter 1, the topic is important enough, and at times confusing enough, that we feel it bears a little repetition.

When you choose to store your files in the Aperture library, you are specifying that you want Aperture to *manage* your files. This means that Aperture will store the managed files within the Aperture library. In addition, any versions of the image that you create will also be stored in the library, which makes it easy to keep track of both your original masters and the versions. You choose the location of the library, which can be on your hard drive or on an external drive or even on a device such as a Drobo.

Note A Drobo is a type of external drive system containing two or more drives that creates automatic backups of each drive to protect against data loss in the event that a single drive fails. For more information, go to www.datarobotics.com.

If you opt to use referenced files, your master files are not stored within the Aperture library. Instead, they can be wherever you specify, such as the hard drive, an external drive, or a Drobo. Aperture imports thumbnails of the images and creates previews for the images and stores those within the Aperture library. In addition, any versions of the image that you create within Aperture are also stored in the Aperture library, including versions made using an external editor or plug-in. However, the masters will be in a separate location that you choose. As mentioned in Chapter 1, the primary difference is that you are in charge of organizing and keeping track of the masters. If you move them — for example, you decide to move the folder from your computer's hard drive to an external drive — Aperture won't know where to look for them, and you'll have to spend time helping Aperture find them using the Locate Referenced Files command, which we cover in Chapter 3.

Note Because Aperture creates thumbnails (and previews if you've set Preferences to automatically create them, as mentioned in Chapter 1) you can use referenced files and not have the drive containing the masters attached to the computer (after you finish importing them, of course).

If you opt to have Aperture not generate previews automatically, you can create previews later manually by choosing Photos ⇨ Generate Previews.

Most people find it a little easier to use managed files, unless their workflow requires referenced files. Both approaches work well, but referenced files require a bit more caution. In addition, sometimes it can be frustrating when you see a referenced file in the library but you can't export it or adjust it because the master isn't available.

Caution In an emergency, you can directly access your managed master files without using Aperture. Control+click on the Aperture library in the Finder and choose Show Package Contents. Then click the Masters folder and all the subfolders. Eventually you will find all the master files. *However, we don't recommend doing this except under dire circumstances because it's extremely easy to accidentally corrupt the library by moving or deleting a file.*

After you decide whether to use managed or referenced files, you specify that on the Aperture Store Files pop-up menu, as shown in Figure 2.9.

To use managed files, choose:

2.9 Use the Store Files pop-up menu to choose managed files or to specify where to store referenced files.

- **In the Aperture Library.** This moves the files into Aperture so that it keeps track of all master files as well as any versions of them.

To use referenced files, choose:

- **In their current location.** This leaves the files where they are and points Aperture to them.

- **Pictures.** This places the files in a subfolder there; use the radio button beneath the pop-up to either move the files or to create a copy of them. Then choose a name for the subfolder. We recommend choosing Project Name so it's easy to recognize which files belong to which projects.

- **Choose….** This places the files elsewhere on your hard drive or on an external drive. Specify whether to copy or move the files by selecting the radio button and then choose the name for the subfolder.

Renaming files on import

Most digital cameras assign filenames to your images that are a combination of letters and num-bers that don't offer any clues about the images, so it can be very helpful to rename your images as you import them. That way, when you see the filenames you have an idea which images they are. This is particularly true when working with referenced files.

To rename files as you import them, follow these steps:

1. **Click the Import Settings button in the upper right of the Import inter-face and choose Rename Files.** A Rename Files brick appears on the right side of the Import interface, as shown in Figure 2.10.

2. **On the Version Name pop-up menu, select one of the preset naming options that Aperture offers.** If you choose Custom Name with an option, such as Custom Name with Index, a Name Text field appears in which you add the text for Aperture to use.

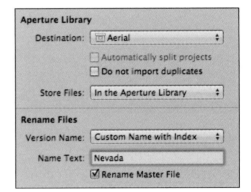

2.10 If you choose a preset with a custom field, add the text in the Name Text field.

3. **Select the Rename Master File check box if you want to rename the master files and not just the versions within Aperture.** This is optional. If you select this option and then export a master file, the exported file shows the name you gave it rather than the name assigned to it in-camera.

To create a custom preset name to use for renaming your files, follow these steps:

1. **On the Version Name pop-up menu, choose Edit from the preset options.** The File Naming dialog, shown in Figure 2.11, appears in which you create a custom preset.

2. **To add a new naming preset, click the plus button on the bottom left, and type a name for the preset over the highlighted name in the list of presets.**

3. **Drag buttons into the Format field to customize the format.** To remove a button from the format field, click and drag over it to select it, and press Delete on your keyboard. If you choose a custom button, a new field appears that you can leave blank or fill with text. If you add text, then that text automatically appears when you choose the preset in the Import options. If you leave it blank, you can add the text during the Import process.

4. **Click OK.**

![File Naming dialog box. Preset Name list on the left includes: Custom Name with Index, Custom Name with Master File Name, Custom Name with Index (no spaces), Version Name, Version Name and Date/Time, Version Name with Sequence, Version Name with Index, Image Date/Time, Custom Name with Counter. Example: Nevada [FileName]. Format: Custom Name, Master File Name. Include buttons: Version Name, Image Date, Current Date, Master File Name, Image Time, Current Time, Custom Name, Image Year, Current Year, Index #, Image Month, Current Month, Sequence #, Image Day, Current Day, Counter. Custom Name: Nevada. Incrementing counter starting at: 1. # of digits: Auto. Buttons: +, -, Reset Preset, Cancel, OK.]

2.11 Create a custom File Naming preset to meet your needs.

We commonly rename our files with a Custom Name plus Master Name. The Master File Name, which is the name assigned in-camera, provides a unique indexing number for the file as well as an easy way to identify the original filename in case you need to find it on a backup drive. The custom option enables you to add a meaningful name related to location or subject matter.

Note The same file naming presets are available when exporting images. So if you create a custom preset for use while importing, it will appear in the file naming presets for use when exporting files as well.

Fixing time zone settings on your images

Most digital cameras record the time that you captured the file. The problem is that some photographers, including us, rarely take the time to change the time setting in the camera when they travel and photograph in different time zones. Admittedly, the time stamp is more important for some types of photographers than others. For photojournalists, it may be imperative; whereas for family photos, it may be purely optional. However, you never know when having the information will be useful, and Aperture makes it so easy to correct the time stamp that there's no reason not to fix it.

To ensure that the correct time is associated with the image, assuming that the in-camera clock was accurately set for your home time zone, follow these steps:

1. **Click the Import Settings button in the upper right of the Import interface and choose Time Zone.** Two pop-up menus appear, as shown in Figure 2.12.

2. **Specify the time zone the image is currently in, which is normally your home time zone, using the Camera Time pop-up menu.**

3. **On the Actual Time Zone pop-up menu, choose the time zone to associate with the images.** It's that simple!

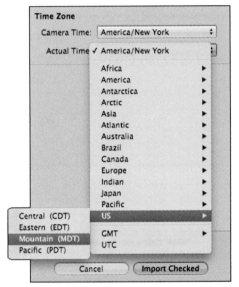

2.12 Use the Time Zone settings to correct the time associated with the image.

An introduction to presets

You can use presets in many places in Aperture, including the Import panel, Adjustment Inspector, the Metadata panel, and the File Naming dialog. In each case, presets enable you to apply a predetermined combination of settings with a single click. That saves time.

The Apple engineers have created some default presets that they think will be useful to many photographers, but you can create your own as well, and we show you how to customize them. By taking advantage of presets, you spend less time on the computer.

The first place you encounter presets is in the Import interface. You can apply metadata presets and/or adjustment presets while you import your images, which means your images are already partially optimized and contain metadata when you initially begin working with them, and that's efficient!

Setting up and applying a metadata preset on import

To apply metadata while importing, follow these steps:

1. **Choose Import Settings and select Metadata Presets.** This opens the Metadata brick in the right panel of the Import dialog, as shown in Figure 2.13.

2. **Choose None to apply no metadata.**

3. **Choose Basic Info to apply a default set of metadata options and then complete each field as you want.**

2.13 Use the Metadata Import Settings brick to choose a preset or to modify an existing one.

4. **Choose Edit to customize the fields in the Basic Info preset or to create an entirely new preset.** Although you can use the Basic Info preset at the default settings, it is even more useful if you take the time to customize it. That way you can prefill some of the fields that remain constant, such as your contact information, as well as choose which fields to display.

Choosing Edit will open the Metadata heads-up display (or HUD), as shown in Figure 2.14. On the left side is the list of current presets, and on the right are all the possible fields that you can include in the preset. Any field that you select is included in the preset and unselected fields are not visible in the preset. If you add text to any of the text fields, then the text becomes part of the preset. We fill in our personal information and any other fields that remain constant such as copyright so we don't have to retype them each time we import images. We select other fields such as Keywords so that the fields appear within the preset, but we leave them blank so we can add text during import. Note that you can add fields that enable you to rate, label, or flag images as they're imported.

Of course, it's up to you to decide which fields to include, but we recommend completing at least some of the IPTC contact information as well as the Copyright field in the IPTC Status section. It's important to include a way to reach you and information about the copyright with the file itself. Otherwise, it's all too easy for an image to be used without your permission and/or become "orphaned," meaning no one knows whose picture it is.

43

![Metadata preset dialog box showing Preset Name list with Basic Info, and fields including Email: ellenanon@mac.com, Website: www.ellenanon.com, IPTC Content section with Headline, Caption, Keywords, IPTC Subject Code, Caption Writer; IPTC Image section with Date Created: 3/26/2010 12:00:00 AM, Intellectual Genre, IPTC Scene, Location, City, State/Province, Country, ISO Country Code; IPTC Status section with Title, Job Identifier, Instructions, Provider, Source, Copyright: © Ellen Anon, Usage Terms: Clear Values; Cancel and OK buttons.]

2.14 Create custom metadata presets to use while importing images.

To type the copyright symbol, press ⌘+G.

Note

To create an entirely new preset, take these steps:

1. **Click the Action pop-up menu (gear icon) at the lower left of the Metadata HUD and choose New Preset.** A new preset appears called Untitled.

2. **Type a name for the preset.**

3. **Select the fields to include and fill in any fields that remain constant.** We created one called Contact and Copyright that contains just the copyright information and our contact information.

As shown in Figure 2.15, you can also duplicate or delete presets as well as import or export presets, which means you can create a preset on one computer and then export it for use on another.

To use a preset on another computer, take these steps:

1. **In the computer containing the preset you want to use, access the Metadata preset dialog from the Metadata HUD as just described, and choose Export.** A new dialog appears in which you choose a name for the preset (although most likely you won't want to change the name) and specify where to export the preset. We find it easiest to export to an external drive or thumb drive.

2.15 You can manage your metadata presets via the Action pop-up menu and even export them for use on other computers.

2. **Connect the drive to the other computer.**

3. **Open Aperture and access the Metadata HUD.**

4. **Click the Action pop-up menu and choose Import.** A new dialog appears containing a directory of your computer.

5. **Select the drive containing the exported preset.**

6. **Click OK.** Your preset is added to the list of presets. When you return to the Import dialog, your new preset or customized version of the Basic Info preset are available in the Metadata pop-up window.

Under the Metadata pop-up in the Import interface are radio buttons to Append or Replace the metadata. When you choose Append, the metadata is added to the existing metadata in the image, whereas Replace removes any metadata that already exists and replaces it with the information in the preset. Most of the time we opt to append the metadata.

You then need to add text to any blank fields. We often type the image location information as well as a few keywords that apply to all the images. You may want to add caption information, special instructions, or any other information you need, but not having to retype your contact and copyright information for each import session is very convenient. What's even better is the knowledge that every image in your library has the basic metadata applied as it's imported.

Setting up and applying an adjustment preset on import

RAW files often seem to be a little flat and may seem slightly less saturated, which can be a bit disconcerting when you first view your images and may make you hesitant to share your images with others until you've fully optimized them. At other times you may realize that your white balance is off in a series of images, or perhaps you want to view them as black and whites. Aperture 3's Import Panel offers access to the default Adjustment Presets as well as your custom adjustment presets by choosing Import Settings ➪ Adjustment Presets. Figure 2.16 shows the Adjustment Presets that are available from the Preset pop-up menu.

Adjustment Presets

Preset ✓ None

Auto Enhance	Quick Fixes ▶
Exposure (+1)	Color ▶
Exposure (+2)	White Balance ▶
Exposure (−1)	Black & White ▶
Exposure (−2)	Edit Presets...
Hold Highlights	
Brighten Shadows	

2.16 All the adjustment presets are available from within the Import panel although only one can be applied during the import process.

Only a single adjustment preset can be applied to each image during the import process, so often one of the Quick Fix presets such as Auto Enhance provides a good starting place for optimizing your images. You can apply additional adjustment presets after the images are imported by using the Adjustment panel.

You may prefer to create customized adjustment presets containing several of the adjustments you routinely use and have Aperture apply that preset during import. That way your images will look better when you're editing them and you'll have less work to do to optimize them. Keep in mind that you can create a variety of adjustment presets, each containing different combinations of numerous adjustments.

To modify an existing adjustment preset containing more than a single adjustment, do the following:

1. **Click the Edit Presets option on the Preset pop-up menu in the Adjustment Presets brick in the Import window.** Doing so will access the Adjustment Presets Manager shown in Figure 2.17.

2. **Select a preset.** The adjustments it contains will be listed in the panel on the right side of the dialog.

3. **Click the minus radio button by each adjustment to remove one or more of the adjustments within the preset.**

Adjustment Presets

Preset Name		
▼ Quick Fixes	Enhance	⊖
Auto Enhance	Levels (Auto Luminance)	⊖
Exposure (+1)	Edge Sharpen	⊖
Exposure (+2)		
Exposure (–1)		
Exposure (–2)		
Hold Highlights		
Brighten Shadows		
► Color		
► White Balance		
► Black & White		

Cancel   OK

2.17 The Adjustment Presets Manager enables you to manage and customize your adjustment presets.

Note Some sites such as www.maccreate.com offer numerous adjustment presets that you can download and then import. These presets emulate a variety of film effects — both color and black and white — as well as camera manufacturers' Picture Styles and more.

To create your own custom adjustment preset from scratch, follow these steps:

1. **Create an adjustment preset by clicking on an image that's already imported into Aperture.** Choose an image that has only the adjustments applied that you want to use for your preset, or even better, an image with no adjustments applied at all.

47

2. **Apply the adjustments you want as part of the preset.** For example, we often apply a combination of a Curve adjustment to add a small amount of midtone contrast, along with some Definition and some Edge Sharpening. It's a good idea to be fairly conservative as you set the sliders, although all adjustments that are applied via a preset can be tweaked by adjusting the sliders later in the Adjustments panel.

3. **Go to the Presets pop-up menu that's in the Adjustments panel, as shown in Figure 2.18, and choose Save as Preset.** The Adjustment Presets dialog appears.

4. **Assign a descriptive name in the Adjustment Presets dialog so that later you remember exactly what the preset does.** Your customized presets will appear in the list of adjustment presets in the Import panel in addition to the default presets.

2.18 Create customized adjustment presets from scratch within the Adjustments panel in Aperture and apply them in the Import panel.

If you make a series of your own presets, or download and import custom presets, you can group them together by doing the following:

1. **Choose Presets ➪ Edit Presets.** This displays the Preset Manager.

2. **Click the Action pop-up menu and choose New Preset Group.**

3. **Drag as many presets into the new group as you want.** That way you can keep your presets organized and easy to find.

By taking advantage of the metadata and adjustment presets in the Import panel, you'll have considerably less work to do later.

Configuring what types of files to import

Because many digital cameras now include options to capture video and audio files as well as photos, Aperture 3 gives you the option to exclude certain types of files or to only include specific types of files while importing from your memory card. That way only the types of files that you're interested in appear in the Import Viewer, making it easier to quickly choose the files that you want to import. You don't have to wait while files that you're not interested in are imported, or spend time individually deselecting files in the Import panel.

To limit the types of files that Aperture imports, choose Import Settings ⇨ File Types. In the File Types brick that appears, as shown in Figure 2.19, select any file types you want to exclude, or select the option to only include files that were flagged or locked in the camera.

File Types
- ☐ Exclude photos
- ☐ Exclude videos
- ☐ Exclude audio files
- ☐ Exclude audio attachments
- ☐ Only include files flagged/locked in camera

2.19 Use the File Types options to control which type files are imported from your memory card.

Working with RAW + JPEG pairs

Some cameras offer the option to shoot in RAW+JPEG pairs so that each image is recorded as both a JPEG file and a RAW file. Aperture now offers more flexibility in how to deal with these image pairs.

Shooting in RAW+JPEG can be helpful in several types of circumstances. For example, if you've purchased a newly released camera and Apple has not yet updated Aperture to support that camera's RAW file you can still view and work with the files by using a RAW+JPEG workflow. Or perhaps you've applied a Picture Style in-camera to your JPEG files and want to view your images using those settings. You might also opt to shoot using both file types if you need to work extremely quickly initially to output files and want the convenience of using JPEG files, but you want the flexibility and power of RAW files to use later.

Begin by choosing Import Settings ⇨ RAW+JPEG. A new RAW+JPEG Pairs brick appears in the Import dialog. As shown in Figure 2.20, there are a variety of options for instructing Aperture how you want to import the image pairs.

RAW+JPEG Pairs

Import ✓ Both (JPEG as Master)
Both (RAW as Master)
Both (Separate Masters)
JPEG files only
RAW files only

Matching RAW files

2.20 Aperture 3 offers choices of how to import RAW+JPEG pairs as well as options to import just one type of file.

The first three options allow you to import both file types of each pair, while the other options import only one type of file.

- **Both (JPEG as Master).** Both files are imported, but you actually see the JPEG file in the Viewer. Adjustments are applied to the JPEG version.

- **Both (RAW as Master).** Both file types are imported, but you actually see the RAW version in the Viewer, and any adjustments are applied to the RAW file. This is the system Aperture 2 used when working with RAW+JPEG pairs.

- **Both (Separate Masters).** This third option imports both the JPEG and the RAW files and treats each one as a master file. The advantage of this method is that you can easily remove either type of file later to save space. The disadvantage is that adjustments applied to one member of the image pair are not automatically applied to the other. Instead, you need to use the Lift and Stamp tools that we cover in Chapter 6.

- **JPEG files only** or **RAW files only.** This is self-explanatory. If you choose one of these options and want to keep the mate, you need to store those files manually and remember where you put them.

- **Matching RAW files.** This is a good option if you initially import just the JPEG files and do your editing based on them, and later you want to import the RAW files associated with just the JPEGs that you've kept.

Matching RAW files is a fantastic new feature because it enables you to automatically import just the RAW files that match the JPEGs that are in the project; the other RAW files are ignored without your having to manually select the files individually or re-edit the project. In addition, you can specify whether you want to import all matching files that Aperture finds, just those files that are unrated or better (so Aperture doesn't reimport images you've rejected but not yet deleted), or only the mates to the images that are visible in the project using the current filter. So if what you really want are the RAW files associated with just your five-star images, for example, those are the only RAW files that Aperture imports.

Note When you use either of the first two options, you can access the other files after you import them by selecting the file and choosing Photos ⇨ Set RAW as Master or Set JPEG as Master. Any adjustments you apply to one file type are applied to the other file type.

Caution Unfortunately, there isn't a way to delete just the JPEGs or just the RAW files from the pairs when they are imported as Both (JPEG as Master) or Both (RAW as Master). When you delete one, you delete the other, which means that if you're looking to conserve storage space at a later time, you can't delete just one type of file for image pairs.

Caution

Currently, when importing Matching RAW files you must select the project that contains the JPEG images rather than a specific album.

Running actions automatically after importing

In addition to being able to apply adjustment and metadata presets while importing, you can instruct Aperture to run custom AppleScripts immediately after importing your images. Although many users will never need this feature, for others it can be a huge advantage, particularly for those with customized workflows using repetitive tasks. You can create custom actions using AppleScript so that your images can be uploaded to FTP servers automatically on import, sent to the Web, inserted into a Keynote presentation, and so on. AppleScript can be used to automate just about any actions that you do repeatedly.

To apply an action, choose Import Settings ⇨ Actions. Then, as shown in the Actions brick in Figure 2.21, choose the AppleScript to use.

Setting up an automatic backup on import

2.21 Use Actions to apply custom AppleScripts to your images immediately after import to save time.

One of the disadvantages of digital images is that the media used to store them can fail. In fact, every hard drive will fail at some point, including the one in your computer. The hope is that day is far away, long after you no longer need that particular hard drive. But the harsh reality is that a hard drive failure can occur at any time. To protect against losing your images, you need to store them on at least two separate drives. We talk more about creating backups for your Aperture library in Chapter 10. However, you can create a backup of the files that you're importing during the import process. That way when you reformat the memory card to reuse it, you still have your files stored in two places. We strongly recommend that you take advantage of this feature.

To automatically back up your files on import, take these steps:

1. **Connect a backup drive to the computer and choose Import Settings ⇨ Backup Location.** The drive appears in the Backup To pop-up menu, as shown in Figure 2.22.

2. **Select the backup drive.**

3. **Use the Subfolder pop-up menu to create a folder for the backups on that drive.** We recommend using the Project Name for the subfolder to make it easier to identify, but you can choose any of the presets, or click the Edit option to create a custom name for the folder. Aperture not only imports the files into

Backup Location

Backup To: FreeAgent640

Subfolder: Project Name

2.22 It's smart to create a backup copy of your files on an external drive as you import them into Aperture.

the Aperture library, but simultaneously creates an external backup. That's efficient!

When you finish choosing your import settings, click Import Checked. The Import interface disappears, and you see your images in the Viewer and/or Browser, ready for you to begin editing.

Accessing Images from iPhoto

If you've been using iPhoto and have decided it's time to move up to Aperture 3, you can import your entire iPhoto library or just import certain images. You can also use your Aperture library within iPhoto.

Importing your iPhoto library

To import the entire library, in Aperture choose File⇨Import⇨iPhoto Library. A new dialog appears (see Figure 2.23) in which you instruct Aperture how to import the library and where to store it.

To create a duplicate copy of your iPhoto library, choose In the Aperture Library from the Store Files pop-up menu. Your original iPhoto library remains in iPhoto and a copy of it is stored in the Aperture library. This doubles the amount of hard drive space used because you have two libraries as opposed to one. One of the cool features of having duplicate libraries is that any change you make to an image in Aperture is reflected in the iPhoto library. (Of course, images that you import directly into Aperture don't appear in the iPhoto library unless you import them there separately.)

Because storage space is often an issue, many photographers prefer not to maintain duplicate libraries in Aperture and iPhoto. After importing the iPhoto library into Aperture, you can delete your iPhoto library. You still are able to use iPhoto with all your Aperture images in case you want to take advantage of some of the output features, such as calendars or greeting cards. To use

Aperture images in iPhoto, open iPhoto, then choose File ⇨ Show Aperture Library. You can browse through your Aperture library and select the images to import into iPhoto.

2.23 Use this import dialog to copy or move your iPhoto library into Aperture 3.

It's also possible to import your iPhoto library into Aperture as referenced files. That way Aperture doesn't duplicate the master files but can access them to create versions. You see the files within both Aperture and iPhoto, but behind the scenes the master files are still stored in the iPhoto library. To create a referenced version of your iPhoto library, open Aperture. Choose File ⇨ Import iPhoto Library. In the dialog shown earlier in Figure 2.23, choose In Their Current Location in the Store Files pop-up menu.

You can also opt to create a referenced copy of the iPhoto library that is stored within Pictures or any other location that you choose. That creates a duplicate copy of the iPhoto library that is referenced by Aperture, so the master files are stored outside Aperture as discussed earlier in this chapter.

To create a referenced duplicate copy of your iPhoto library, follow these steps:

1. **Choose Store Files ⇨ Pictures or Store Files ⇨ Choose.**

2. **Specify a Subfolder name from the Subfolders pop-up menu.** Any name that includes a / (forward slash) will create a hierarchy of nested folders.

3. **To customize the subfolder name and structure, choose Edit.** A Folder Naming dialog appears, as shown in Figure 2.24. For example, you would choose Project Name/ Image Date to create a folder with the project name and subfolders for each date.

4. **Click OK when done.**

5. **Click Import.**

2.24 Create a custom folder structure for referenced images using the Folder Naming dialog.

When you import your iPhoto library using any of the approaches we've covered, the organization of your iPhoto images and albums is maintained in projects in the Library Inspector. All the adjustments you've made in iPhoto as well as any keywords, ratings, and so on are also maintained.

Importing select images from iPhoto

If you prefer to use Aperture with only certain images, it's possible to import as many or as few images as you desire from your iPhoto library without having to import the entire library. To import select images from iPhoto, follow these steps:

1. **Open Aperture and choose File ⇨ Import ⇨ Show iPhoto Browser.**

2. **Navigate through the iPhoto Browser to select the images you want to import into Aperture, and ⌘+click on them or click and drag the cursor over a group of images.**

3. **Drag the images onto the desired item in the Library panel in Aperture.**

Alternatively, you can preselect the destination in Aperture by clicking it, then drag the images you've selected in the iPhoto Browser directly into Aperture's Viewer or Browser. The images will be imported into Aperture.

Dragging and Dropping Files into Aperture

There are times when you may be looking through your Finder or your desktop or other place on your computer and come across one or more files you want to import into Aperture. Although you can choose File ⇨ Import ⇨ Files or use the Import interface, it may be more efficient to select the images and drag them directly onto the Viewer, Browser, or a specific item in the Library. Aperture will import image, audio, and/or video files this way. This can be particularly helpful with files that didn't originate within your camera. It's also helpful if you use third-party software that functions as a freestanding program rather than a plug-in within Aperture, or if you accidentally choose Save As rather than Save when working on a file in your external editor. Dragging and dropping is a quick and easy way to get the files into Aperture.

Moving to Aperture from Bridge

If you've been using Photoshop for your image editing and organizing, it's likely that you've developed your own system for storing your images. For most photographers, this means they have a system of folders, most likely within Picture, but possibly elsewhere. Some photographers have elaborate setups of folders nested within folders. It's possible to import those folders into Aperture and maintain the same organization. However, you can't use the Import interface to import folders; you must choose File ⇨ Import ⇨ Folders As Projects. When you do, a new dialog appears, as shown in Figure 2.25.

2.25 Import folders as Projects and Albums using this dialog.

From the Import Folders As pop-up menu, choose Folders and Projects to have Aperture create an overall Folder in which there are Projects for each folder that you're importing. Or choose Projects and Albums from the same pop-up menu to have Aperture import the folder as a project containing albums for each subfolder.

No matter which you choose, the overall result is similar to what is shown in Figure 2.26. Use the remaining options in the dialog to create subfolders if you choose, and to name any subfolders as well as to rename the images and specify how to handle JPEG+RAW pairs.

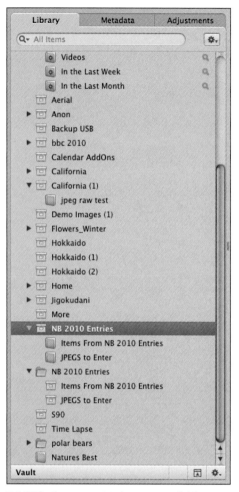

2.26 Whether you opt to import your folder structure using Folders and Projects or Projects and Albums, the original organization is maintained within Aperture.

What Methods Can I Use to See My Images?

© Ellen Anon

As you work with Aperture, there are times that you want to focus on a single image at a time, while at other times you need to compare two or more images or even to peruse all the images in an album or project. Sometimes you need to take a closer look at the image and at other times you'll want to see certain information about the images. In this chapter, you learn how to customize the way you see your images.

Customizing the Interface

Aperture's engineers realize that you may prefer to organize the interface differently in order to work more efficiently, so there are many ways to customize the interface. This section covers rearranging library items, using different Viewer modes, using the Viewer with multiple monitors, using multiple Browsers, and showing hot and cold areas (clipping) in images.

Rearranging and grouping library items

Chapter 1 covered several ways to filter what you see in the Library panel, but the more you shoot and use Aperture, the more cluttered the Library panel becomes. There are several ways you can organize and rearrange your albums and projects so that you can easily find them. By default, Aperture organizes the items by name. If you'd rather it organize items by kind, go to the Action pop-up menu at the top right of the Library panel shown in Figure 3.1 and choose Kind.

Library	Metadata	Adjustments

Q▾ All Items   ⚙▾

- 🗂 Projects
- 🖼 Photos
- 📷 Places
- 🏴 Flagged

Add to Favorites

Keep Projects & Albums Arranged By ▶   ✓ Kind

Export Album as New Library...   Name

Maintain Previews   Manual

3.1 Choose how to organize your projects and albums.

To manually order the projects and albums, select the project, album, or folder to move, and then click and drag it to the desired location.

Another way of organizing the albums and projects is to add folders to the structure. Using Folders is similar to taking a pile of papers that are sitting on your desk and putting them in a folder — the papers are still in the same order they were while sitting out on your desk, but your desktop looks cleaner and more organized. To use folders to help organize your Projects as shown in Figure 3.2, do the following:

1. **Click in the empty gray area of the Library panel to remove any selections, and then click the New button and choose Folder to create a new folder at the same level as projects.** A new untitled folder appears at the bottom of the list of projects. (If you have a project selected, the new folder is added within that project.)

Note

Select a Project and then click the New button and choose Folder to create a folder within a project to organize any albums, books, or slide shows within it.

2. **Name the folder.** If you've opted to organize the Library by Name, the folder moves to the correct alphabetical location. If you've organized the Library by Kind, the new folder is added alphabetically to the other folders, following projects.

3. **Drag the folder wherever you want it.**

4. **Drag projects and albums into the folder.**

5. **Toggle the disclosure arrow by the folder to display or hide the projects and albums.**

Using Viewer modes

You might think there's only one way for Aperture to display your images in the Viewer, but in fact, Aperture offers a number of choices by choosing View ⇨ Main Viewer, as shown in Figure 3.3.

Choose one of the Main Viewer options as follows:

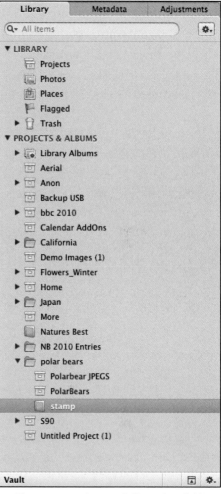

3.2 Move some projects and albums into folders to simplify the Library panel.

- **Show Multiple.** This is the default setting, and allows the Viewer to display from one to 12 images at a time.

- **Show One.** This option allows the Viewer to display only one image, no matter how many images are selected in the Browser.

- **Three Up.** This option displays the image you select as well as the one immediately before it and after it in the Browser.

- **Compare.** This option helps you select the best image from a group of similar images.

- **Stack.** This option helps you select the best image within a stack. We cover that in more detail later in this chapter.

To use the Compare option or mode, follow these steps:

1. **Select two images and choose View ⇨ Main Viewer ⇨ Compare.** Both images appear in the Viewer; the one on the left has a green border in both the Viewer and the Browser and the one on the right has a white border, as shown in Figure 3.4. The image that has the green border is the "keeper so far" and the one with the white border is the one you're comparing to it.

2. **To compare the next image to the keeper, press the right arrow on your keyboard.**

Browser	
✓ Split View	
Viewer	
Cycle View Mode	V
Faces	⇧F
Places	⇧P
Full Screen	F
Show Projects	
Main Viewer ▶	
Secondary Viewer ▶	
Browser ▶	
Inspector ▶	
Zoom to Actual Size	Z
Zoom In	⌘=
Zoom Out	⌘-
Quick Preview	P
Show Master Image	M
Show Focus Points	⌥F
Highlight Hot & Cold Areas	⌥⇧H
Show Loupe	`
Loupe Options ▶	
Metadata Display ▶	
Hide Toolbar	⇧T
Customize Toolbar...	
Onscreen Proofing	⌥⇧P
Proofing Profile ▶	

Submenu for Main Viewer:

✓ Show Multiple	⌥U
Show One	⌥R
Three Up	⌥H
Compare	⌥O
Stack	⌥T

3.3 Choices for the Main Viewer.

3.4 Use the Compare mode to help choose your favorite image from a series.

3. **If you decide you want the image with the white border to be the new keeper, press Return.** That image moves to the left in the Viewer and now has a green border, and the next image in the Browser automatically appears with a white border.

4. **When you're happy with the image you've chosen, ⌘+click the image you don't want to remove.** Then add stars, a label, or a flag to the image, as covered in Chapter 4, to identify your favorite image from the group.

Using the Viewer with multiple monitors

If you're fortunate enough to have multiple monitors, Aperture is designed to take advantage of them. As you might expect, you have choices as to what's displayed on the second monitor. Access these choices by choosing View ⇨ Secondary Viewer, as shown in Figure 3.5.

Choose one of the Secondary Viewer options as follows:

- **Mirror.** This allows each monitor to display the same thing. You might use this option if you're doing a live demonstration and have a large monitor set up for your audience.

- **Alternate.** This displays the currently selected image only in the secondary Viewer. That way you can have multiple images visible in the main Viewer and a single image on the other monitor.

3.5 Choices for what to display on a secondary monitor.

- **Span.** This extends a single Aperture window across both monitors. We rarely find this helpful.

- **Blank.** This leaves the other monitor blank so that it's not distracting.

- **Desktop.** This enables you to see the contents of your desktop displayed on the secondary monitor.

Using multiple Browsers

Sometimes you want to select images from multiple projects or albums; for example, if you're creating a slide show or a book or entering a contest and you know the task would be easier if you could view two projects or albums at a time. To open two Browsers, select the first project or album as usual. Then hold the Option key and click on another project or album. This divides the Browser into two panes, as shown in Figure 3.6. You can then select images from each Browser to copy or transfer to another item in the Library.

3.6 Divide the Browser into two panes to access images from two projects or albums.

Click the Close (X) button on the top left of the Browser pane tab to close one of the Browsers.

Showing hot and cold areas of an image

Some of your images may have highlights that are quite bright (hot) and/or shadows that are quite dark (cold) in which no details are visible. We refer to these areas as *clipped*. This can happen both while taking the shot in-camera, particularly in contrasty conditions, and/or while you're optimizing your images. Aperture can display these areas with a color overlay so that it's easy to see where the image is losing detail. That way you can set the adjustments to restore as much detail as possible.

To set Aperture to display the hot and cold areas, choose View⇨Highlight Hot & Cold Areas, or press Option+Shift+H. Aperture displays clipped shadows with a blue overlay and clipped highlights with a red overlay, as shown in Figure 3.7.

By default, Aperture places the overlay on pixels in which at least one channel is completely clipped. To change the sensitivity of the

3.7 Aperture can place a red or blue overlay on any highlight or shadow areas that are losing detail due to clipping.

threshold so that the overlay covers areas that are quite dark, but not completely clipped, or that are extremely light but not completely clipped, follow these steps:

1. **Choose Aperture ⇨ Preferences to open the Preferences dialog.**

2. **Click the Advanced icon.**

3. **Adjust the Hot Area threshold slider and the Cold Area threshold slider as desired.**

To change the clipping overlay to monochrome, which can be easier to see on images with areas of saturated reds and blues, choose Monochrome in the Clipping overlay pop-up menu in the same Advanced Preferences dialog. That way the overlay appears as a shade of gray.

Taking a Closer Look

At times when adjusting your images, just seeing the image filling your monitor isn't enough; you need to look closely at parts of the image at increased magnification. For example, when you apply sharpening, check for chromatic aberration, remove a dust spot, and so forth, viewing the image at 100 percent magnification or even more is important so that you work as accurately as possible. That way you can check details to make certain you're not accidentally adding (or leaving) artifacts. In this section, we show you how to use the Zoom tool and the Loupe tool to readily see the details in your pictures.

Zooming and scrolling in Viewer

The Zoom tool increases the magnification of the entire image in the Viewer. There are several ways to access the Zoom tool.

3.8 Use the Zoom Viewer button to increase or decrease the magnification of the image in the Viewer.

- **Click the Zoom Viewer button, shown in Figure 3.8, to magnify the image to 100 percent focused on the center of the image.**

- **Choose View ⇨ Zoom to Actual Size to accomplish the same thing.**

● **To zoom in centered on a specific part of the image, place your cursor on that area, and then press Z.** Aperture increases the magnification to 100 percent and the area under the cursor is visible. We find this the most efficient way to zoom.

● **Press ⌘+± to zoom in/out incrementally centered on the part of your image under the cursor.**

After zooming in using any of the preceding methods, you see the Zoom Scroll tool appear displaying the current magnification in the image, as shown in Figure 3.9. As you hover your cursor over it, it increases in size and displays a tiny thumbnail of the image with a small white rectangle. Click and drag the rectangle to navigate through the image so that different areas are displayed at the increased magnification.

Zoom Scroll tool

3.9 Use the white rectangle in the Zoom Scroll tool to navigate through the magnified image view.

To zoom out to see the entire image, press Z again or choose View ⇨ Zoom to Actual Size and click to toggle it off. To decrease the magnification incrementally, press ⌘+−.

Note
Although you can press the spacebar and hold it while dragging in the Viewer to navigate through the image, in most cases we find it far easier to use the Zoom Scroll tool.

Genius
To increase or decrease the magnification of the image to any amount from 25 percent to 1000 percent, click and drag the cursor over the field displaying the current magnification on the Zoom Scroll tool or click and hold the arrow to the right or left of the numerical display. The magnification will change accordingly.

Using and customizing the Loupe

If you'd rather see a small part of your image in detail but still see the overall image, as shown in Figure 3.10, you can use the Loupe tool. You can also use the Loupe tool to view the thumbnails in the Browser at increased magnification.

3.10 Use the Loupe tool to view a small section of the image at increased magnification while still seeing the entire image.

To access the Loupe tool, do one of the following:

- **Click the Loupe tool button at the top right of the interface.**
- **Choose View ➪ Show Loupe.**
- **Press the ~/ˆ key.**

To use the Loupe tool, click in the dark area near the bottom right and drag it over the part of the image you want to see magnified.

Control+click on the Loupe tool and a dialog appears, as shown in Figure 3.11, in which you can customize the Loupe tool as follows:

- **Choose Focus on Cursor to change the behavior of the Loupe tool so that you can leave the Loupe tool in one place and have it display whatever is under your cursor.** Some people prefer to use it this way so that the Loupe doesn't block part of the image.
- **Choose a magnification from 50 percent to 1600 percent.**

3.11 Use this dialog to customize the Loupe tool.

- **At magnifications greater than 200 percent, choose Pixel Grid to display a grid within the Loupe tool.**

- **Choose Color Value to add a readout to the Loupe of the Red, Green, and Blue channel values as well as the luminosity value of the point under the Loupe.**

- **Select Use Centered Loupe to toggle off this option and return to the older style Loupe that was introduced in the original version of Aperture.** The Loupe will change shapes slightly and whatever is shown under the small circle will appear magnified in the larger part of the Loupe. Some people find this more convenient, but we prefer to keep Use Centered Loupe selected and use the newer Loupe.

Viewing in Full-Screen Mode

Although the default workspace is very usable, some people prefer an interface with the least amount of distractions possible. Full-screen mode hides your desktop completely, and you control what parts of the Aperture interface are visible.

To access full-screen mode, press F or click the Full Screen button in the toolbar, as shown in Figure 3.12. The display changes to full-screen mode, as shown in Figure 3.13. To exit full-screen mode, press F again, the Escape key, or click the Exit Full Screen button in the Full Screen toolbar.

In this section, we show you how to work with the Viewer and Browser in full-screen mode, as well as how to work with the filmstrip and toolbar and the heads-up displays (HUDs).

3.12 Click this button to enter and exit full-screen mode.

3.13 Full-screen mode showing the Viewer and the optional toolbar.

Using Browser and Viewer in full-screen mode

In full-screen mode, you can view a single image or multiple images (if you've set the Viewer mode to Multiple) in the Viewer with an optional filmstrip Browser or just the Browser showing a grid of thumbnails, as shown in Figure 3.14. To toggle between the two views, press V.

3.14 The Browser in full-screen mode.

Caution

Initially, the full-screen background is black, which is dramatic against your images. If you're using full-screen mode to show your images to others, you may want to keep the background black. But if you're using full-screen mode to make adjustments to your images, it's a good idea to change the background to a shade of gray. That way your eyes won't be fooled by the increased contrast of the background, and you'll be more able to accurately adjust the contrast and saturation of your images.

Genius

Whether in full-screen mode or the regular interface, double-click an image in the Viewer to toggle between the Viewer mode and the Browser mode.

To change the color of the background in full-screen mode, take these steps:

1. **Choose Aperture ⇨ Preferences to access the Preferences dialog.**

2. **Click Appearance.**

3. **Drag the Full Screen Viewer brightness slider to the right.** We suggest setting it to 18 percent, which is the default setting for the Viewer in the regular interface.

Working with the filmstrip and toolbar

To navigate through the images while in the Viewer mode in full screen, you need to use the film-strip. If the filmstrip is not visible initially, it's hiding. To see it, move your cursor to the left edge or the bottom edge of the interface and it will appear, as shown in Figure 3.15.

Click and drag the Always Show Filmstrip control to the locked position to make the filmstrip always visible. When the filmstrip is locked, the image decreases slightly in size to make room for it without any overlapping. When you unlock the filmstrip, the image reverts to full size with the filmstrip overlapping it. When you move the cursor away from the filmstrip, it disappears.

To position the filmstrip at the left, bottom, or right edge of the interface, unlock it and drag it to the desired location.

Use the search field in the filmstrip to filter the display so that only certain images are visible in the filmstrip. For example, you can set it to show the four-star or better images, or the flagged images. To show all the images again, click the small X at the right of the search field.

To filter using more complex rules, click the Filter button to the left of the search field. This elicits the Browser Filter panel that we cover in Chapter 4.

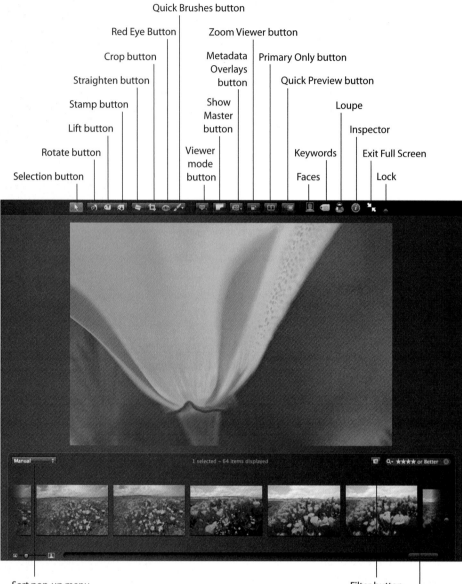

Quick Brushes button

Red Eye Button   Zoom Viewer button

Crop button   Metadata   Primary Only button
                     Overlays
Straighten button   button   Quick Preview button

Stamp button   Show   Loupe
                     Master
Lift button   button   Inspector

Rotate button   Viewer   Keywords   Exit Full Screen
                     mode
Selection button   button   Faces   Lock

Sort pop-up menu   Filter button

                                              Search field

3.15 The filmstrip is always available even if it's not initially visible.

To control the order in which the images are displayed, click the Sort pop-up menu shown in Figure 3.16 and choose the criteria to use to organize the images and whether they should be in ascending or descending order.

To adjust the size of the thumbnails in the filmstrip (and thus the size of the filmstrip as well), drag the small slider that's near the top of the filmstrip (or at the left if the filmstrip is at the bottom of the screen).

Drag the large slider to quickly scan among the images in the filmstrip.

| Date |
| Rating |
| Label |
| Version Name |
| File Name |
| Keywords |
| File Size |
| Orientation |
| Pixel Size |
| ✓ Manual |
| ✓ Ascending |
| Descending |

3.16 The Sort order options.

Hovering your cursor near the top center of your monitor reveals the toolbar as shown earlier in Figure 3.15. The key commands and tools you need are all right there. Just as with the filmstrip, slide the lock to make the toolbar always visible while in full-screen mode. Otherwise, it disappears when you move your cursor. When the toolbar is locked, the image decreases slightly in size and moves out of the way so nothing is hidden.

Working with heads-up displays

In addition to the toolbar and filmstrip, you can use a heads-up display version of the Inspector or the Keywords HUD, as shown in Figure 3.17. To access the Inspector HUD, click the Inspector button in the toolbar or press H. An Inspector appears that floats over your image. If you slide the lock, the HUD moves to a vacant side of the interface, and the image decreases in size to accommodate it. The Inspector HUD has all the same controls and options as the Inspector does in the regular Aperture interface that we covered in Chapter 1. To hide the Inspector, press H or click the icon again.

3.17 The Inspector HUD.

73

If you hold down the Shift key while dragging any slider in the Adjustments HUD, everything in the HUD disappears except the slider so that you can see most of your image while making the adjustment, as shown in Figure 3.18. We love this feature!

To access the Keywords HUD, choose the icon in the toolbar or press Shift+H. A floating HUD appears to use for creating and assigning key-words. We cover using the Keyword HUD in detail in Chapter 4. To hide the Keyword HUD, press Shift+H or click the icon again.

Additional Viewer Options

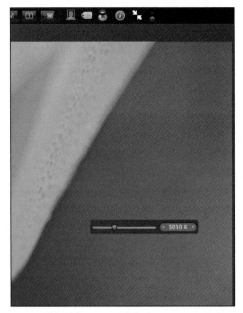

3.18 Hold the Shift key while dragging a slider to make the rest of the HUD disappear.

Regardless of whether you're using full-screen mode or the regular interface, there are three more Viewer options that you need to know: Primary Only, Quick Preview, and Viewing Masters, which we cover in this section.

Using Primary Only

When you have multiple images selected that are visible in the Viewer, any changes (other than adjustments) that you make are applied to all the selected images. So if you assign a star rating or apply a label and so forth, you won't affect just one image, you modify all of them. But the reality is that at times while working you're likely to want to make changes to just one of the images. To do that, click the Primary Only button. Notice that when you select multiple images, one of them has a wider white border. That's the one that will still have a white border when you click Primary Only, as shown in Figure 3.19.

74

Primary Only button

3.19 Use the Primary Only button to apply changes to just one of several images that are selected.

Using Quick Preview

After you've downloaded your images, if you're like us, you're impatient to start seeing them and perhaps making some preliminary edits. Although images load pretty quickly in Aperture 3, if you're

uploading a lot of images, it will still take time for Aperture to complete the download and generate previews. If you try to go through the images too quickly, you may discover that the spinning beach ball appears while Aperture creates a preview for that image. If you hate waiting and are willing to go through your images having Aperture use the initial previews (that are often JPEG files embedded within the RAW file), use Quick Preview mode.

To engage Quick Preview mode, click the Quick Preview button in the toolbar, as shown in Figure 3.20. A yellow border appears around

3.20 Use Quick Preview to view your images quickly.

75

the images you select. You won't be able to make any adjustments while you're in Quick Preview mode, and we suggest you not make any decisions about the final sharpness or exposure because the Quick Preview version may differ considerably from the actual file.

Still, it's a good way to quickly get a sense of the images you've captured. To exit Quick Preview, click the Quick Preview button again.

Viewing the master image

While you work in Aperture, as long as you're not using Quick Preview mode, the image preview in the Viewer updates to reflect all your edits. Although you can toggle any particular adjustment off and on using the check boxes in the Adjustments panel, sometimes it's helpful to glance at the original image to make sure you're heading in the right direction. The fastest way to do that is to click the Show Master button shown in Figure 3.21.

Show Master button

3.21 Click the Show Master button to see the master file with no adjustments.

The image in the Viewer reverts to the original before you applied any adjustments, although all your adjustments are still intact. To return to edited view, click the Show Master button again.

Configuring and Using Metadata Overlays

Most of the time, you'll want to be able to see certain information about your images at a glance. For example, you'll want to see any ratings, labels, or flags that you've applied, whether you've assigned keywords, whether you've edited the image in a plug-in or external editor, and so forth. But some of the time you may want to just see the image without any distractions, and at other times you may want to see even more information about the files. You can use the Metadata Overlays pop-up menu in the tool strip, shown in Figure 3.22, to control the display of metadata in the Viewer and the Browser as follows:

Browser & Viewer Metadata Overlay button

3.22 Click the Browser & Viewer Metadata Overlay button to apply metadata overlays.

- **Under Viewer, choose Show Metadata to have Aperture display a metadata overlay.** By default, the display uses the Basic View unless you choose Switch to Expanded View, and shows basic information such as ratings, labels, flags, and badges. (Aperture uses badges to convey a variety of information about the file such as if it's a referenced file, if the master is available, if you've assigned keywords to it, and so on. We cover this in detail in Chapter 10.)

- **Under Viewer, choose Switch to Expanded View to see more information such as any keywords that you've applied, the version name, the date the file was created, even whether you've e-mailed the image or used it in a book.** Once you choose this, the option in the pop-up menu changes to Switch to Basic View. Choose that to return to an overlay with less information.

- **Under Browser, choose Show Metadata to see a metadata overlay in the Browser with each thumbnail.** By default, the display uses the Basic View unless you choose Switch to Expanded View, and shows basic information such as ratings, labels, flags, and badges.

- **Under Browser, choose Switch to Expanded View to see more information.**

Caution If the Browser is set to filmstrip, it may only show some, but not all, of the information in the overlay. To be certain the overlays show exactly the information you expect, use the Grid view or the List view in the Browser. Because the Browser has only limited area to display information, we suggest you only use the Expanded View in the Browser metadata overlay if the Browser is set to List view.

To specify what information is included in the Basic and Expanded View overlays in both the Viewer and the Browser, do the following:

1. **Choose Edit in the Metadata Overlays pop-up menu.** A new dialog appears, as shown in Figure 3.23.

2. **Choose which view to configure from the View pop-up menu.** The items that will be displayed are listed on the right under Display Order.

3. **To remove any items, click the minus (–) button next to the item in the Display Order list.**

4. **To choose additional items to include, use the expansion arrows next to the items on the left under Metadata Fields.** Select the check box next to that item and that field then appears on the right under Display Order.

5. **Select the Show metadata below image check box (at least in the Viewer) and the show metadata labels check box.** We recommend choosing these options, otherwise the metadata blocks some of your image. The metadata labels help organize the metadata that you're seeing. A metadata label is a word such as *Keywords* that appears before the list of keywords in the overlay.

6. **Click OK to apply the changes.**

3.23 Customize the data that appears in the metadata overlay using this dialog.

Switching between RAW + JPEG Masters

If you've imported RAW + JPEG pairs with either the RAW or JPEG set as Master, you only see one member of the pair in the Viewer. However, any metadata or adjustment changes you make to one are applied to the other as well.

Note To switch an entire album of RAW + JPEG pairs to use the other format as master, or if you have an album or project that contains JPEG + RAW pairs, some with RAW as master and some with JPEG as master, select the Album or Project in the library, then choose Photos ⇨ Switch Album/Project to use RAW Masters or Switch Album/Project to use JPEG Masters.

To change the format that is used as the master, choose Photos ⇨ Set RAW as Master. If the master was already a RAW file, the option automatically appears as Set JPEG as Master, as shown in Figure 3.24. This enables you to change master formats on an image-by-image basis.

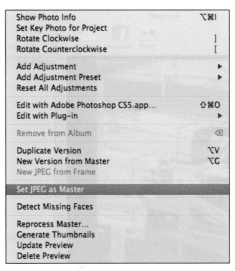

3.24 You can toggle between the JPEG as Master and RAW as Master options to check metadata and changes.

Working with Referenced Images

In earlier chapters, we talked about importing images as referenced files. As you already know, referenced files are convenient in some cases because you can store your master files outside the Aperture Library where other programs can access them as well, and you can store the images on external drives so that you don't run out of room on your computer. However, working with referenced files requires a bit more attention on your part. This section covers identifying and managing the master images for referenced files as well as reconnecting missing masters and relocating images.

Identifying and managing referenced images

Anytime you import a referenced image, Aperture places a badge on it, as shown in Figure 3.25, so that you can readily tell it's referenced. The badge is visible in the metadata overlay, as discussed earlier in this chapter. If the badge is green, the drive containing the image is connected, but if it's red, the master is offline.

Once you identify an image as a referenced file, you need to make sure that the drive containing the master file is connected if you want to make any adjustments to the image or output it. Otherwise, you may be left wondering why the Adjustments panel is grayed out and why Aperture suddenly won't export an image.

If you use more than one drive to store your master files, the chances are that you won't remember which drive you need. To have Aperture jog your memory, select a file and then choose File ⇨ Show in Finder. If the drive containing the image is connected and online, the Finder appears with the path to the file selected. If the drive is offline, Aperture tells you that, but it also shows you the name of the drive, as shown in Figure 3.26. All you have to do is find that drive and connect it. Aperture automatically sees it, and you're good to go.

Referenced file badge

3.25 The badge clearly identifies files that are referenced.

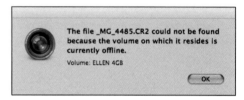

3.26 Use the Show in Finder option to see where your master files are stored.

Reconnecting a missing master

If you accidentally move the master file from where it was when you imported the image as a referenced file or changed it in some way, Aperture may not know how to find it. We've noticed that Aperture 3 is far more able to locate files by itself than earlier versions, but it's still possible that it may not be able to locate the master. In that case you have to tell it where to look. To reconnect one or more missing master files, do the following:

1. **Reconnect the hard drive containing the referenced masters.**

2. **Select the Project or Album containing the referenced files.**

3. **Choose File ⇨ Locate Referenced Files.** The dialog shown in Figure 3.27 appears. On the left is a list of the names of hard drives where you're storing referenced masters, as well as how many masters were found and any that weren't located. The next column tells you the specific location of the master file for each referenced file.

4. **Click Show Reconnect Options if they are not already visible.**

5. **Select the file at the top that you want to reconnect with its master.** A thumbnail of the image and some identifying metadata appear next to it.

6. **In the bottom section of the dialog, navigate to the location of the referenced master and select the master.** A thumbnail of the image and some identifying metadata appear next to it so you can compare it to the image selected above and be sure that you're connecting the right master.

7. **Click Reconnect to reconnect a specific image.** Alternatively, you can select a group of images to reconnect and click Reconnect All.

3.27 Use the Locate Referenced Files option to reconnect referenced files and their masters.

Relocating referenced masters

If you decide that you need to move the masters for some (or all) of your referenced files, for example, to place them on an external drive, there's a way to do it so that Aperture knows exactly where to look for them. Then you won't have to spend time later trying to reconnect the masters and referenced files. To relocate the masters for referenced files, follow these steps:

1. **Select the referenced images in the Browser.**

2. **Choose File ➪ Relocate Masters.** A dialog appears, as shown in Figure 3.28.

81

3.28 Use the Relocate Masters option to move master files.

3. **Choose a location to store the images.** We often create a new folder in Pictures, but if you're moving the files to an external drive, you may just need a folder on that drive. Be sure to use a name for the folder that alerts you that it contains referenced masters. Consider putting the letters RM after the name or any other convention that works for you.

4. **Choose None from the subfolder pop-up menu to store each file individually within the folder you just selected in Step 3.** If you want Aperture to organize the images into subfolders, then choose one of the subfolder presets or create your own by choosing Edit and following the prompts to configure a custom preset.

5. **Specify a naming convention to use.** Choose Master Filename to use the current master filename. This is the format we recommend so that you can easily identify the images. However, you can use any of the other formats such as Version or Custom.

6. **Click Relocate Masters.** Aperture moves the masters to their new location.

Note

You can relocate masters that are managed as well. In that case, they become referenced files. To relocate managed files, follow the same steps you use to relocate referenced files.

Caution

Although relocating masters is usually a very quick process, depending on how many masters you're moving it could require some time. Be sure to leave the external drive connected while Aperture moves the masters to it. If you're not sure whether the masters have all been moved, choose Window ⇨ Show Activity. If Aperture is still in the process of moving the masters, the task appears in this window.

Converting referenced masters to managed masters

You may find that you have a number of referenced files that you want to convert to managed files. For example, if you are traveling with a laptop and leave the external hard drives that contain all your referenced files at home, you might want to be able to make adjustments or export some files while you travel. To change referenced files into managed files, follow these steps:

1. **In the Browser, select the files you want to convert to managed files.**

2. **Choose File ⇨ Consolidate Masters.** In the dialog that appears, choose whether you want to move the files into the Aperture library or make a copy of them that is managed in the library.

3. **Click Continue.**

Deleting referenced files

When you delete a referenced file, you follow the same steps we covered in Chapter 1 to delete files. However, when you press Shift+⌘+Delete to empty the trash, a dialog appears as shown in Figure 3.29.

3.29 The Empty Trash dialog.

To delete the referenced master file as opposed to just deleting the version within Aperture, select the Move referenced files to System Trash check box. If you want to leave the master file intact but remove the version that's in Aperture, leave that check box unselected.

Working with Stacks in Browser

As mentioned in Chapter 1, you can organize groups of related images into stacks. These can be images that are very similar, part of a panorama, part of a High Dynamic Range (HDR) series, different versions of the same image, or any images that you want to group together for any reason. Stacked images have a dark-gray box around them and a number in the upper-left corner of the first image indicating the number of images in the stack, as shown in Figure 3.30. Stacks can contain as many images as you want.

3.30 Stacks can organize groups of related images.

Aperture can auto-stack all the images in a project based on the time sequence in which you took them. To auto-stack images based on time, follow these steps:

1. **Select a project or album.**
2. **Choose Stacks ➪ Auto-Stack.**
3. **Adjust the Auto-Stack Images dialog slider to the desired time frame from 0 seconds to 1 minute.** As you do, the images are organized into stacks.
4. **Choose Stacks ➪ Close All Stacks.**

Aperture automatically creates stacks whenever you create a new version of an image, including when you use a plug-in or external editor such as Photoshop, so the files stay together. You can change this behavior by deselecting the Automatically stack new versions option in General Preferences, but we recommend you leave it selected.

To manually create stacks, select the images to include and then press ⌘+K, or choose Stacks ⇨ Stack.

When stacks are open, all the images are displayed. When they're closed, only a single image — the one farthest to the left — is visible. By closing stacks you reduce the number of files you have to visually sort through in the project or album, and that can save time.

Note

Stacks work in both the regular mode and full-screen mode.

You can drag the images around within a stack to reorder them as well as drag images in and out of existing stacks. To divide a stack, place your cursor on the thumbnail that you want to begin a new stack and choose Stacks ⇨ Split Stack.

To open and close a stack, click on the number in the first image. Alternatively, choose Stacks ⇨ Open All Stacks or Close All Stacks to open or close all the stacks within the album or project.

To set the image that appears on the top of a stack (called a stack pick), do one of the following:

- **Select the image and then choose Stacks ⇨ Pick.**
- **Select the image and press ⌘+\.**
- **Drag the image to the farthest left position in the stack.**

If the stack appears in multiple albums, such as one for a book and one for a Web page or slide show, you may want different pick images for each album. To set an image as the album pick, select the image and choose Stacks ⇨ Set Album Pick. You can use a different image in each album.

To unstack a group of images, select the stack and choose Stacks ⇨ Unstack.

You can use the Compare mode within stacks to help you compare the images in the stack. This is similar to comparing individual images using the Compare mode, which we discussed earlier in the chapter. To compare images within a stack, follow these steps:

1. **Select a stack.**
2. **Choose View ⇨ MainViewer ⇨ Stack, or press Option+T.** The stack pick is automatically set as the currently chosen image and has a green border.

3. **Proceed comparing images within the stack to the stack pick, and press Return if you want an image with a white border to become the new stack pick, which changes its border to green.** The next image in the stack appears for you to compare until you have reviewed all the images in the stack.

4. **Use the keyboard up and down arrows to move from stack to stack.**

Creating and Working with Light Tables

As great as it is to work with digital images, sometimes it feels like it would be easier if you could spread the images out in front of you and arrange then as if you were dealing with prints or slides. Using Light Table enables you to work with your digital images in a very similar way with the advantages that you can resize the images as well as the Light Table itself. A Light Table can be particularly helpful when trying to organize images for a slide show or book, or when color correcting many related photos, or when creating a collage. To create a Light Table, take these steps:

1. **In the Library panel, choose the project or album where you want the Light Table to appear.** Then select the images you want to view in the Light Table. You can select more images than you ultimately need because the images you select initially only appear in the Browser for the Light Table.

2. **To create the new Light Table, click the New button in the toolbar and choose Light Table.** A dialog appears in which you give the new Light Table a name.

3. **In addition to typing a name for the Light Table, select the Add selected items to new light table option.**

4. **Click OK.** The new Light Table appears in the Library panel. The interface changes slightly as shown in Figure 3.31. The Viewer is now a Light Table with a grid, and there are some different buttons above it and above the Browser.

5. **To add additional images to the Light Table, choose any image or images in the library and drag them onto the Light Table in the Library panel.**

To begin arranging your images, select one or more in the Browser and drag them onto the Light Table. As long as the group of images is selected, they all move as a unit on the Light Table. To move a single image, click anywhere on the Light Table except on an image. Then click the image. You'll see the image has a thick white border, as shown in Figure 3.31.

Light Table Zoom Navigator button

Light Table Put Back Selected button

Light Table Scale
to Fit button

Light Table Uncover button

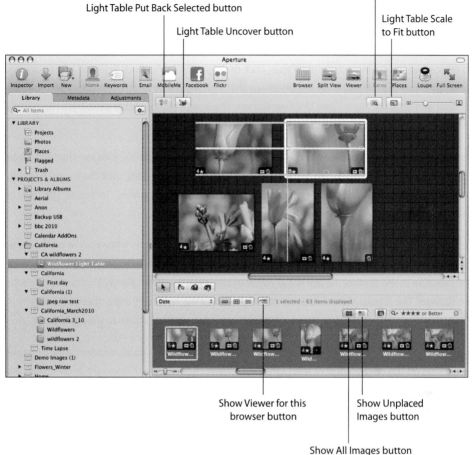

Show Viewer for this
browser button

Show Unplaced
Images button

Show All Images button

3.31 Use the Light Table to arrange groups of images.

Drag the image wherever you want. As you do, the yellow alignment lines appear to help you align the image with the other images. In addition, small square handle boxes appear along the edges of the image. Click and drag these handles to resize the image. If necessary, use the slider in the top right of the interface to resize the Light Table or click the Light Table Scale to Fit button. Click the Light Table Zoom Navigator button to magnify a portion of the Light Table.

To have Aperture automatically arrange the images, Control+click on the Light Table next to the images and choose Arrange All from the pop-up menu. To restore an image to its previous size, Control+click the image and choose Reset Selected Size from the pop-up menu.

Metadata is data about a file that helps describe the contents of the file. Aperture provides powerful tools to manage the metadata attached to an image, whether it's entering IPTC Core contact information, adding keywords to help you quickly find an image, or setting an image rating so that you can easily pull your top images from your library. This chapter helps you explore how to use metadata in Aperture to make it easier to manage your library.

Using Ratings to Sort Images

One of the key fundamental pieces of metadata that you can set on an image is a rating. When you first started to shoot, a keep/delete system was probably more than sufficient, but as you became a better photographer and your image collection grew, you most likely realized that keep or delete wasn't enough to separate your best images out. Ratings are incredibly useful because they let you quickly pull the best images from your library, separate the best from the good-enough-to-keep images, and identify the worst images that you can delete first when you're running low on space.

Each image can have either no rating or a rating from one to five stars. Table 4.1 illustrates the system we use, which has proved rather useful over the years.

Table 4.1 Our Image Rating System

Rating	Meaning
5 Stars	These are your absolute best images. Post them to your Web site, include them in slide shows, and show them to clients. Absolutely back these up.
4 Stars	These images are above average, and you will most likely include some of these in a slide show or Web gallery. While they are not quite as good as your five-star images, you don't want to lose them and will back these up, too.
3 Stars	These are your average images. You keep them to submit for various, specific image requests, even if you don't typically show them to clients. You back up three-star images, too.
2 Stars	Two-star images are images that you're keeping for some particular reason, even though they're not good enough to show to a client. An example would be a below-average quality photo of a rare animal that you're keeping because it's a photo of a rare animal. You don't back them up because it doesn't really matter if these get erased.
1 Star	One-star images are your lowest-quality images. Typically, you keep these for a specific part that you might consider compositing into another image, but they're not important enough to back up. If you're running low on hard drive space, these are the first images that you delete.

Setting ratings

Setting a rating on an image is quite straightforward. Select the image and choose the appropriate rating by choosing Metadata ➪ Rating. Assuming you have your metadata overlays (which we discussed in Chapter 3) configured to show a rating, you see the rating appear as a badge on the image, such as in Figure 4.1. Alternatively, use the keyboard shortcuts 1-5 to set a rating of one to five stars on the selected images (note that you don't press the ⌘ key, just press the number). Use the minus (–) and equals (=) keys to decrease or increase the selected image's rating. Pressing 0 clears the rating and makes the image unrated, and pressing 9 gives the image a special *rejected* rating, which we discuss shortly.

Badge indicates an image's rating

4.1 Aperture can display an image's rating as a badge in both Browser and Viewer.

> **Note** In the Library Albums group within the Library Inspector, there's a 5-Star Smart Album that shows you all of the five-star images in your library. This is a great way to quickly display your best images.

The control bar, as shown in Figure 4.2, also provides buttons to reject an image, lower its rating, raise its rating, or to mark it as a five-star select. If the control bar is not visible, choose Window⇨Show Control Bar.

4.2 The control bar.

Working with rejected images

How often have you finished a shoot, started looking through your images, and become unhappy with what you shot, suddenly feeling the urge to just throw away everything? Fortunately, by marking images as *rejected* rather than just deleting them, Aperture gives you a second chance to recover it so that if you change your mind, it's easy to restore your image.

If there's an image that you want to get rid of, choose Metadata ⇨ Rating ⇨ Rejected or press 9 on your keyboard. This command displays an X in the ratings badge, and when you move to the next or previous image, the rejected image disappears from the Browser (later in this chapter, when we discuss searching for images, we show you how to see your rejected images within an album or project).

Under the Library Albums group in the Library Inspector, there's a Rejected Smart Album, shown in Figure 4.3. Clicking it shows all your rejected images in Browser, just like any other album. If you want to unreject an image, select it and set its rating to something other than rejected, be it unrated or one to five stars. If you really want to get rid of these images, click inside Browser and choose Edit ⇨ Select All. Then choose File ⇨ Delete Master Image and All Versions.

4.3 The Rejected Smart Album in the Library Albums group and its contents.

Caution

It's a good idea to periodically click on the Rejected Smart Album to see if there are any images that you can delete to free up hard drive space.

Prior to Aperture 3, choosing Delete Master Image and All Versions would have removed the images from Aperture and moved the master files to your system's trash. However, as discussed in Chapter 1, this command instead moves your images to Aperture Trash in Aperture 3.

If you realize that you made a mistake deleting one of these images, follow these steps to retrieve it:

1. **Select Trash in the Library Inspector.**

2. **Select the image you want to retrieve.**

3. **Control-click on that image and choose Put Back.**

To empty the Trash, choose Aperture ⇨ Empty Aperture Trash. Empty Aperture Trash moves the images to your system trash, but the images aren't actually removed from your drive until you empty your system trash.

Using Flags and Labels to Further Organize Images

While ratings are a great way to start organizing your images, you will most likely quickly find that you want another level of organizing. For example, if you come back from a trip with 75 five-star images, you probably don't want to upload all 75 to your Web site. Wouldn't it be great if Aperture had a way to say "flag these images for my Web site"? If you work with a stock agency, perhaps you'd also like to be able to flag some images to send to your agent? Thankfully, Aperture 3 provides two new levels of organization, flags and labels, which allow you to handle both of the previous examples, and it's also possible to customize the label names to be more applicable to your workflow.

Setting flags and labels

Flagging images is quite easy. Select the appropriate images and choose Metadata ⇨ Flag. When you do so, assuming you have your metadata overlays enabled and set to show flags, Aperture displays a flag icon in the top-right corner of the image (in Viewer) or thumbnail (in Browser), as shown in Figure 4.4. To unflag an image, select it and choose Metadata ⇨ Unflag.

Note To quickly flag and unflag an image in Browser, first make sure your metadata overlay is on for Browser and set to display flags. When you mouse over your image, you will see a ghosted flag icon appear. Click on that icon to flag your image; click on the solid flag icon to unflag it.

As you might have guessed, there's a special item in the Library Inspector under the Library group at the top for flagged images called, you guessed it, *Flagged*. This album shows all flagged images in your library.

Genius If you need to pull images from your entire library for some purpose and want to do so by flagging your selected images, we recommend first going to the Flagged Smart Album, selecting all the images in there, and choosing Metadata ⇨ Unflag so that you don't end up with previously-flagged images in your new selection.

4.4 Flagged images in Browser.

While flagging provides an extra level of organization, it's a fairly straightforward and simple one—is this image flagged or not? While that's great for direct questions, such as "Which images should I post to my Web site?" it doesn't provide the flexibility you need when really working with your images. That's where labels come in. Labels let you tag images with specific status, such as "send all images with this label to my agent" in addition to the separate rating and flagged metadata.

Aperture has seven labels that you can apply to an image (as well as a "No Label" label). As you probably have come to expect from Aperture, it's easy to add a label to an image. Select the image and from the Metadata menu, move your mouse over the Label section shown in Figure 4.5.

Label:

4.5 The Label section of the Metadata menu.

After you pick the label you want, let go. Control+clicking on an image displays a context menu with a similar Label control, too.

If you have Viewer or Browser set to display metadata overlays, you'll see one of two types of indicators for your image's label. Viewer's basic and expanded metadata overlays and Browser's basic overlay shows the label as a small, colored circle on the right side of the image. Browser's expanded overlay shows the label color behind the version name, as shown in Figure 4.6.

4.6 Labels in Browser with the expanded metadata overlay.

Selecting an image and setting its label to *No Label* removes the label.

Customizing label names

Unfortunately, Aperture doesn't let you customize your label colors, but there's a good reason for that. The label colors within Aperture match the uncustomizable label colors within the Finder. When you export a version of your image, as we cover in Chapter 8, Aperture labels the file it creates with the same color it has in Aperture in the Finder. This is a wonderful feature because it means that if you use a label to indicate an image status in Aperture, that status is preserved when you export your image outside of Aperture.

You are able to customize the label name, though, so rather than saying something useless like *Green*, the label has the status name like *needs sharpening*. To customize a label name, follow these steps:

1. **Cho0ose Aperture ⇨ Preferences.**
2. **Click the Labels tab shown in Figure 4.7.**
3. **Click in the text field next to the appropriate label and type the new label text.**

4.7 Custom label names allow you to adjust label meanings for your specific workflow.

Now when you select the label color from the Metadata menu, rather than seeing the color name below the label color you see your label name.

Using the Metadata Inspector

While ratings, flags, and labels are powerful pieces of metadata within Aperture, there are other types of metadata automatically associated with an image, starting when you first press the shutter button on your camera. Exchangeable Image File (EXIF) data consists of information that the camera records about the image, from shutter speed to GPS location (if available), into the file. Typically, you can view but not modify this data. International Press Telecommunications Council

(IPTC) metadata is the next type of metadata. Consisting of fields like keywords, captions, and copyright, this is data that you will modify (and often will even set at import, as we discuss in Chapter 2). No matter which type of metadata you're working with, Aperture's Metadata Inspector is the central place to view and edit image metadata. It's even possible to create preset metadata values, such as your contact info, that you can quickly apply to an image.

To view the Metadata Inspector, make sure the Inspector is visible; if it's not, choose Window ➪ Show Inspector. Next, click the Metadata tab in the inspector or choose View ➪ Inspector ➪ Metadata.

At the top of the Metadata Inspector is the Camera Info panel, as shown in Figure 4.8. If it's not visible, select Show Camera Info from the Inspector's Action pop-up menu. The Camera Info panel is very useful because at a quick glance, it gives you access to essential EXIF information, such as shutter speed and ISO, as well as Aperture metadata, such as

Canon EOS-1Ds Mark III			AWB	PSD
EF16-35mm f/2.8L II USM				⊚
ISO 400	16mm	0 ev	f/5.6	1/1000
⊙▾	× ★★★★★			⚑

4.8 The Camera Info panel provides an easy way to see key image metadata.

your image rating. Additionally, each of the Aperture metadata displays (label, rating, and flagged) is also a control that you can click on to adjust each item's respective value.

Caution Although selecting multiple images in Browser and using the commands under the Metadata menu affect all the selected images, using the commands in the Metadata Inspector only affects the primary selection (the one with the bolder outline).

Another neat feature in the Camera Info panel is the focus points display. Mouse over the Focus Points button, which looks like a diamond made up of rectangles in the top-right part of the panel, and Aperture displays the selected focus point for the selected image (if it's available), like in Figure 4.9. Clicking this button makes the display stick so that you always see your focus point superimposed on the image, and clicking it again turns the focus point display off. Choosing View ➪ Show Focus Points also toggles focus points on and off.

At the very bottom of the Metadata Inspector is the Maps pane (note that the Maps pane isn't available in the Metadata heads-up display [HUD], only in the windowed Metadata Inspector). If it's not visible, click the Reveal button to open the pane, and you'll see a map of the United States. If there's GPS information with the image, Aperture displays it on the map. Use the Action pop-up menu to switch map types (such as satellite or terrain). We cover working with place information in depth in Chapter 5.

4.9 An image with its focus points superimposed on top.

Switching and customizing metadata views

In the middle of the Metadata Inspector, you find a bunch of different metadata fields and values, from caption information (which you can edit) to file size (which you can't edit). The collection of metadata fields displayed in this area is called a *metadata view*. Aperture ships with a number of default metadata views, but it's also possible to customize these views and to create your own.

The default view is called General. It contains a mix of Aperture, EXIF, and IPTC metadata, including rating, version name, shutter speed, aperture, and copyright notice. To switch views, use the pop-up menu at the top of the Metadata Inspector. Many of the metadata views are self-explanatory, such as *Caption Only*, but there are two special views toward the bottom of the list worth mentioning:

● **IPTC Core.** This is a special metadata schema that the IPTC group created to be widely compatible between different programs, and Aperture 3 supports it completely. The IPTC Core metadata view displays all the fields in this schema, and you can set values for all these fields.

● **Large Caption view.** Sometimes, if you're spending hours organizing your images, Aperture's small font can be tiring on your eyes. To make things easier, the Large Caption view, shown in Figure 4.10, has only one field in it, Caption, but the text and field sizes are larger.

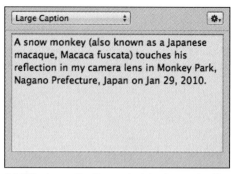

Fortunately, these metadata views are not locked in stone and are quite customizable. The easiest way to customize them is to rearrange the items. Perhaps, for example, you want the File Name field to appear next to the

4.10 The Large Caption metadata view makes it easier on the eyes.

Version Name field in the general view. To do so, move your mouse over the File Name label so that it's highlighted. Then drag and drop the field wherever in the list you want it to appear. The other fields animate out of the way to help you tell where you will drop the field.

However, Aperture's metadata view customization goes far beyond just rearranging preexisting fields. It's also possible to add and remove fields from views as well as to create a completely custom view. Here's how to get started:

1. **From the Metadata Views pop-up in the Metadata Inspector, choose the Edit item at the bottom of the menu.** The Metadata Views dialog opens, as shown in Figure 4.11. On the left side of this dialog is a list of your metadata views, and on the right side is a list of all possible metadata fields that Aperture knows about. When you click on a view in the list on the left, you'll see that certain fields become checked in the right list. A check mark next to an item means it's part of the metadata view.

2. **From here you can do the following:**

   ● **Add or remove a field from a preexisting metadata view.** Select the view on the left and select or deselect the field's check box on the right.

   ● **Rename a view.** Double-click its name on the left and type a new name.

   ● **Create a new view.** Click the Action pop-up menu on the bottom left of the window, choose New View, type its name, and select fields to include from the right.

   ● **Edit a copy of an existing view.** Select the view and choose Duplicate View from the Action pop-up menu.

4.11 The Metadata Views customization dialog helps you create exactly what you need.

- **Delete a view.** Select the view and choose Delete View from the Action pop-up menu or press Delete on your keyboard. *Be careful*, as Aperture does not prompt you about whether you're sure you want to delete this view.

- **Rearrange the views so that ones you use more frequently are at the top of the list.** Select the appropriate item in the Metadata Views list and drag and drop it to wherever you want it to be ordered.

3. **Click OK when you finish customizing your metadata views.**

Setting metadata

While some values, like image ISO, are read-only, it's possible and necessary in most cases to set most values manually. For example, the camera and computer can't automatically guess what the image caption should be. To set a value, simply click in the appropriate metadata field in the Metadata Inspector and start typing. When you finish, either press Tab to go to the next field or click outside the current text field.

There are a couple special fields where you don't type a value. To set a value for the Rating, Flag, and Label fields, click on the desired value. For the IPTC Core date created field, even though it's prepopulated with the image date, it's possible to change this value by either clicking on the date and typing a new date or by using the stepper buttons on the right side of the field to adjust the date and time up or down.

Caution Although Aperture lets you type long values for any metadata field, the IPTC Core specification limits certain fields. For example, a title can be at most 64 characters long, each keyword phrase can be at most 64 characters long, and instructions can be at most 256 characters long.

To quickly clear all IPTC metadata from an image, select the image and choose Clear IPTC Metadata from the Metadata Inspector's Action pop-up menu.

Genius If you're using referenced files and use another program such as Adobe Photoshop to update an image's metadata outside of Aperture, select the image and choose Metadata ⇨ Update from Master to import the image's new metadata back into Aperture.

Managing and applying presets

As you start to work with metadata, you might find yourself typing certain values (such as your contact information) over and over again. To avoid always having to retype these values, it's possible to create a metadata preset containing multiple values that you can apply when needed, even on import.

To start creating a preset, choose Aperture ⇨ Presets ⇨ Metadata or choose Manage Presets from the Metadata Inspector's Action pop-up menu. Aperture opens the dialog shown in Figure 4.12.

Notice how this dialog is very similar to the Metadata Views dialog, but on the right-hand side there are fields for setting values. Let's create a Contact metadata preset.

1. **In the Metadata Presets dialog, choose New Preset from the Action pop-up menu.**

2. **Type its name, *IPTC Contact Information*, into the table row on the left that Aperture automatically makes editable.**

3. **Select the check box next to each contact field on the right that you want to use, and type a value for each field.**

4. **Click OK when you finish.**

4.12 The Metadata Presets dialog.

Now when you select an image and click the Action pop-up menu in the Metadata Inspector, you see your IPTC Contact Information preset under the Append with Preset and Replace with Preset menus. Selecting IPTC Contact Information from the Append with Preset menu adds the preset's information to whatever values you set for the image. Be careful — as if you manually typed a field like your e-mail into the image's metadata — because choosing Append with Preset will leave you with duplicate values in your image's metadata. Choosing Replace with Preset will clear out the image's values for all the fields in the preset, replacing them with the values in the preset.

If you type values onto an image and want to use those values to set up a new preset, select the image and choose New Preset from Version from the Action pop-up menu in the Metadata Inspector. Aperture opens the Presets dialog with this new preset selected and ready for you to rename.

A unique feature of the Presets dialog is that it's possible to export and import presets, making it easy to share them between multiple computers. To export a preset, do the following:

1. **In the Metadata Presets dialog, select the preset in the list.**

2. **Choose Export from the Action pop-up menu.**

3. **Choose a folder to export the preset to.**

4. **Give your preset a unique name.**

5. **Click Export.** Aperture will create an *.apmetadata* file that you can share with another computer.

Similarly, to import a preset, open the Metadata Presets dialog and choose Import from the Action pop-up menu. Find the *.apmetadata* file within the Import dialog, select it, and click Import.

Genius

If you already have the *.apmetadata* file selected in the Finder, drag and drop the file onto the Import panel. Aperture will automatically go to its folder and select it.

Adjusting Date and Time after Import

One of the most annoying pieces of metadata to work with is image date and time. It's very useful to figure out when a shot was taken and if it's a sunrise or sunset, and you've probably set the date and time on your camera, but what happens when you shoot outside your normal time zone or forget to update the time for daylight saving time? Fortunately, Aperture lets you adjust an image's capture date and time both while importing (see Chapter 2) and after the fact.

To adjust an image's date and time, follow these steps:

1. **Select either a single image or group of images.**

2. **Choose Metadata ➪ Adjust Date and Time.** Aperture displays the dialog shown in Figure 4.13.

4.13 The Adjust Date and Time dialog makes it easy to fix your images' time stamps.

3. **Enter the desired time into the Adjusted field.**

4. **Select the Also change master file check box if you want Aperture to adjust the creation date on the masters as well as the image time within Aperture.**

5. **Click Adjust.** Aperture adjusts the primary selection to the displayed time and adjusts any other selected images relative to how you changed the primary selection. For example, if you set the time to be an hour earlier, Aperture subtracts an hour from all the other selected images.

Working with Keywords

While many of the different metadata fields are simple and straightforward, keywords deserve special attention. Keywords are special identifiers that you put on an image to help describe it, from the scientific name of an animal in the photograph to a word to describe the image's overall mood. Keywords make it easy to search for an image or to make a Smart Album, Web page, book, or more based on a particular keyword.

Aperture provides a number of tools to help you add keywords to your images, including the Metadata Inspector, Keyword control bar, and Keywords heads-up display (HUD), as well as a central keyword library that stores your custom keyword hierarchy. Later in this section, we cover how to export your custom keyword library to another computer.

Let's start with the simplest tool to set keywords and work our way up. In the Metadata Inspector, switch to the General view or some other view that shows the keywords field. Click in that field and start entering a comma-separated list of values that describe your image, such as *Pacific ocean, surf, stormy sky*. When you finish, press the Tab key to move to the next field or click outside the keywords field to confirm the values you entered. To remove a keyword, delete it from the keywords field.

> **Note**
>
> We recommend selecting the Check Spelling While Typing option when typing keywords and captions. To enable it, Control+click on the keywords (or caption) field and choose Spelling and Grammar ⇨ Check Spelling While Typing if it's not already selected.

When you start typing keywords for the next image, assuming you start with the same few letters, Aperture's AutoFill feature fills the rest of the keywords field with the same keywords you typed the first time. For example, if you typed *Pacific ocean, surf, stormy sky* for the first image and start typing *Pac* for the second image, Aperture by default suggests auto-completing the keywords with *Pacific ocean, surf, stormy sky*. This is useful when keywording very similar images because it can help save you typing. But it can also be frustrating if there's a typo in the suggested keywords, because Aperture continues to suggest that you auto-complete your typing with the typo. Fortunately, Aperture provides a way to edit the AutoFill values.

1. **Choose Metadata ⇨ Edit AutoFill List.** Aperture displays the AutoFill Editor dialog, as shown in Figure 4.14, containing all the values you've ever typed for each metadata field.

4.14 The AutoFill Editor dialog allows you to edit the autofill values that Aperture uses when you enter metadata.

2. **To adjust the keywords AutoFill values, scroll down until you see the IPTC Keywords group, and open the group.** Each table row represents a set of keywords that Aperture tries to auto-complete as you type.

3. **To edit a row, double-click on it and type any adjustments.**

4. **To remove a row, select it (or multiple rows), and click the Remove button.**

5. **Repeat this process as needed, adjusting values for other fields such as IPTC Caption as well.** This dialog also lets you add new AutoFill values for some fields, though not IPTC Caption or Keywords. To do so, select the field name, click the Add button, and type a new value.

6. **Click Save when finished.**

The Keywords control bar

Another way of adding keywords to images is to use the keywords controls in the control bar. To show the keyword controls, first make sure the control bar is visible by choosing Window ⇨ Show Control Bar. Then show the keyword controls by choosing Window ⇨ Show Keyword Controls. You see the area indicated in Figure 4.15.

Action	Landscape	Outdoor	Headshot	Group	Silhouette	Day	Add Keyword
Portrait	Indoor	Close-up	Full body	Conceptual	Still life	Night	Photo Descriptors ⬍

4.15 The keyword controls in the control bar.

There are three main controls in this area. The first control is the Add Keyword text field. Select an image, type a new keyword into this field (Aperture will auto-complete it if you've used the keyword before), and press Return to add the keyword to the selected image. To remove a keyword from an image, select the image, type the keyword into this field, and press Shift+Return.

The next control is the group of keyword buttons on the left. Select an image and click one of these buttons to assign that keyword to the image. The first eight (going top to bottom from left to right) are also assigned the keyboard shortcut Option+Keyword Number 1-8. The Metadata ⇨ Add Keyword menu shows the same values as the keyword buttons with the hotkeys, and selecting a keyword in that menu also adds it to an image.

If you have multiple images selected, then by default Aperture adds the keyword to every selected image. If you have Primary Only (which we cover in Chapter 3) enabled, then Aperture only adds the keyword to the primary selection.

To remove a keyword, hold down the Shift key while clicking the keyword button or pressing the keyboard shortcut, or choose Metadata ⇨ Remove Keyword. To remove all keywords, select the image and choose Metadata ⇨ Remove Keyword ⇨ Remove All Keywords.

The last control is the Keyword Preset Group pop-up menu. A keyword preset group is a collection of related keywords, such as the People and Snapshots presets that Aperture ships with. This pop-up menu contains a list of presets, and switching presets changes the keywords assigned to the keyword buttons as well as the contents of the Metadata ⇨ Add Keyword and Metadata ⇨ Remove Keyword menus. Use the comma (,) and period (.) keys to switch between keyword preset groups.

Editing button sets and keywords

While the default keyword preset groups cover a wide range of common keywords, you'll more than likely want to create your own groups. To begin, choose Edit Buttons from the Keyword Preset Group pop-up menu. Aperture displays a dialog that looks like Figure 4.16.

4.16 The Edit Button Sets dialog.

The left side of this window contains controls to manage your preset groups, which are called Button Sets in the dialog. The right side of this dialog is the Keywords Library, which contains every keyword you've ever assigned to an image as well as some preinstalled keywords.

Keywords Library

Before we can discuss creating new preset groups, we need to take a short detour to talk about the Keywords Library. The Keywords Library, which is also accessible via the Keywords HUD that we discuss in the next section, is where you manage all your keywords. Here, you can add, remove, and change keywords as well as create hierarchy among keywords.

The first button on the left, Lock/Unlock Keywords, lets you lock your Keyword Library so that you can't make any changes. At first it might seem odd that you'd want to lock your Keyword Library. However, often photographers use a standard keywording vocabulary for their images. If you take the time to enter that vocabulary into Aperture, locking your keywords ensures that you don't accidentally use a keyword not in the keyword vocabulary. If you try to type a new keyword when your Keyword Library is locked, Aperture prompts you to either cancel or unlock the library.

To find an existing keyword, either scroll through the list to find it or start typing the keyword in the Search field at the top to filter the list. Once you find the keyword you're looking for, double-click it to change it; for example, to fix a typo. Note that this is a live update, and if you're using that keyword in any image, Aperture prompts you to make sure you want to update that keyword in every image to which it's applied.

To delete a keyword, select it and click the Remove Keyword button or press the Delete key. Again, if this keyword is in use, Aperture prompts you to confirm that you truly want to delete it, as deleting it removes it from any image to which it's applied.

Adding a keyword is slightly complex because keywords in Aperture are hierarchical. For example, let's say that you create a *bird* keyword, and you have a bunch of shots of parrots to tag. Rather than having to apply *bird* and *parrot* keywords to each image, wouldn't it be great if you could make *parrot* a child of *bird* so that any time you applied *parrot* to an image, it automatically was also tagged with *bird*? Aperture's keywording structure lets you do this. Let's look at how.

1. **Click the Add Keyword button indicated in Figure 4.17.**

2. **Type *bird*.**

3. **Make sure *bird* is selected, and click the Add Subordinate Keyword button.** Notice how a disclosure triangle appears next to *bird*.

4. **Type *parrot*.**

5. **Select *parrot*, and click the Add Subordinate Keyword button.**

6. **Type *eclectus*.**

7. **Select *bird* again.**

8. **Click the Add Keyword button.**

9. **Type *eagle*.** Notice how it's added at the same level as *bird*.

10. **Click and drag *eagle* onto *bird* so that *bird* becomes highlighted.** When you let go, Aperture makes *eagle* a child of *bird*.

4.17 The Add Keyword and Add Subordinate Keyword buttons.

What we just did was to make a new parent keyword, *bird,* with two children, *parrot* and *eagle*. Furthermore, we added a child to *parrot, eclectus*. Now, any image we tag with *eclectus* will also have the *parrot* and *bird* keywords, and any image we tag with *eagle* will also have the *bird* (but not *parrot* or *eclectus*) keyword. However, any images tagged only with *bird* will not be tagged with *eclectus* or *eagle*.

Genius

You can drag and drop keywords onto and above other keywords to easily change their hierarchy.

Any hierarchy updates you make are also live. If you make a keyword that's in use (*hawk*) or the child of another keyword (*bird*), Aperture prompts you to make sure you really want to do so. After you make the change, the images will adjust accordingly (all the images you tagged with *hawk* are also now tagged with *bird*).

If you create a keyword hierarchy such as *bird/parrot* and then create another hierarchy, such as *parrot/eclectus/male* and *parrot/eclectus/female*, at the top level it's easy to merge the two together. Click and drag the top-level *parrot* onto *bird*. Aperture warns you that there's a keyword with the same name at the destination hierarchy level and asks if you want to merge hierarchies. Click Merge, and now you have *bird/parrot/eclectus/male* and *bird/parrot/eclectus/female* keyword hierarchies.

Customizing button sets

Under the Button Sets group are two columns: Name and Contents. The Name column represents the different groups of keywords you see in the pop-up menu. To temporarily disable a group so that it still exists but doesn't appear in the pop-up menu, deselect the check box by the group's name. The Contents column lists all the keywords that are part of each group.

Underneath the Name column are four buttons: Add (+), Remove (–), Import, and Export. To create a new keyword preset group, click the Add button and then give your preset group a name. Next, you need to add contents to this group. To do so, either find an existing keyword or add a new one. Once you find the desired keyword (which can be anywhere in a keyword hierarchy, too!), drag and drop it from the Keywords Library to the Contents column.

Rearrange items in the Contents column by dragging and dropping them to the desired location, and delete an item by selecting it in the list and either pressing the Delete key or by clicking the Remove button below the Contents column. Remember, you will be able to use the keyboard shortcut Option+1 through 8 to assign the first eight keywords to an image.

Once you're happy with your keyword preset group, click OK to close the dialog. Note that you can also export the keyword preset group by selecting it in the Name column and clicking Export. Aperture exports it as a .plist file that you can import into Aperture on another computer by opening the Edit Button Sets dialog, clicking Import, and selecting the exported .plist file.

The Keywords heads-up display

The last way to apply keywords to an image is by using the Keywords heads-up display (HUD) shown in Figure 4.18. Open the Keywords HUD by choosing Window ⇨ Show Keywords HUD (Shift+H) or by pressing the Keywords button in the toolbar. The contents of the Keywords HUD should look very familiar to you — they're identical to the Keywords Library that was covered in the previous section. Rather than having to use the Edit Button Sets dialog to access your Keywords Library, the Keywords HUD provides direct access, including all the features (add/delete/reorganize keywords) we described previously.

Genius

Use the Export and Import buttons in the Keywords HUD to share your custom keywords between computers.

To assign a keyword to an image, drag and drop the keyword onto the image, either in Browser or Viewer. As described before, if you have a hierarchy of keywords such as *bird/parrot/eclectus*, dropping *eclectus* onto your image also tags it with *bird* and *parrot*.

If you have multiple images selected, dropping a keyword onto one image adds it to all selected images. However, if Primary Only is selected, then Aperture only adds the keyword to the primary image.

Keywords

bicolor cleaner wrasse
bicycle
big bird
Big Island
Big Island lava
big sur
biking
billboard
Billy Parker
birch
▶ bird
Bird

Import... Export...

4.18 The Keywords HUD.

Adding Custom Metadata

While there are many standard metadata tags, sometimes you really want to add a custom field to an image. For example, we add a *Stock Agent* field to our images to keep track of which agency represents which images. There are two parts to adding custom metadata: creating the field and adding it to a view. To create a new field, follow these steps:

1. **Open the Metadata Inspector.**

2. **Select Manage Custom Fields from the Action pop-up menu.** Aperture displays a dialog like you see in Figure 4.19.

3. **To add a new field, click the Add (+) button and type its name.**

4. **To delete a field, select it and click the Remove (–) button.** Aperture prompts you to confirm this deletion if you've set a value for this field in any image.

Custom Metadata Fields
Label
Photomatix
Stock

+ −   Cancel   OK

4.19 The Custom Metadata Fields dialog.

5. **Click OK to close the dialog.**

Use the techniques described earlier in this chapter regarding switching and customizing metadata views to add this new field to a metadata view.

Applying Batch Metadata Changes

While you will have to set some metadata values per image, such as *Caption*, there are others, such as *Copyright Notice*, which you'll want to set on a group of images. Aperture provides two ways to apply metadata in bulk: the Batch Change tool and the Lift and Stamp tool.

Using the Batch Change tool

To use the Batch Change tool, open the images whose metadata you want to change and choose Metadata⇨Batch Change. You will then see the Batch Change dialog, as shown in Figure 4.20. There are three main sections in this tool that allow you to adjust your images' time zone, to change your image's filename, and to add or remove metadata from your presets.

To adjust the time zone, select the Adjust Time Zone radio button. Then pick the time zone that your camera's set to from the Camera's Time Zone pop-up menu and the time zone you shot the image in from the Actual Time Zone menu. When you click OK, Aperture adjusts the time zone settings for your images.

The second block lets you rename your images using a naming preset (we cover naming presets in Chapter 2). Note that renaming a version only renames your image within Aperture. If you also want to rename your master files on the hard drive with this new name format, select the Apply to Master Files check box.

4.20 The Batch Change dialog allows you to adjust many images' metadata at once.

The last block is where you can change specific fields. Rather than giving you access to every possible field, Aperture displays a pop-up menu with your metadata presets. To set a new value, start by picking a preset that contains your desired field. Then choose whether you want to append the new value to the existing value or replace the existing value completely, select the fields for which you want to set values, type the value, and click OK. If you choose to replace the existing value, select a field and leave its value empty. Aperture clears the specified field from the selected images.

We've found that the built-in Basic Info preset has the fields we use most of the time (keywords, image city/state/country, and copyright notice) with batch change.

Using the Lift and Stamp tool

The other way to set metadata values in bulk is with the Lift and Stamp tool, which lets you literally lift values from one image and stamp them onto other images. Lift and Stamp is quite powerful because in addition to lifting metadata values like keywords and ratings, it also allows you to lift some or all of the adjustments you made to one image and to stamp those adjustments onto a group of images. We cover how to set adjustments in Chapter 6, and the procedure to lift and stamp them is identical to lifting and stamping metadata.

1. **Select the source image whose values you want to lift.**

2. **Choose Metadata ⇨ Lift Metadata and Adjustments.** Aperture opens the Lift & Stamp dialog, as shown in Figure 4.21.

3. **Select the check box next to each metadata value you want to lift.** For metadata groups, like IPTC in the previous figure, where Aperture only has a check box next to each group rather than each line, if there are fields that you don't want to lift, select the line with that value and press the Delete key.

4.21 The Lift & Stamp dialog.

4. **Using the pop-up menu in the bottom left of this dialog, choose whether you want to add or replace the metadata on the destination images.**

5. **Select each image that you want to stamp these values onto, and click Stamp Selected Images.**

Searching for Images

Throughout this chapter, we've talked a lot about how to add metadata to your images, but we've yet to talk about how to use that metadata to find images. There are two primary ways to search for an image in Aperture: using Browser's search field and filter HUD to search within Browser's contents or making a new Smart Album that searches either within a project or your entire library. These two methods are quite similar and, in fact, use the same filter HUD to create a search query. The main difference is that using Browser's search field and filter HUD to search is a temporary operation. Typically, you'll search within Browser for a few particular images and then clear the search query. Smart Albums are more permanent, offering a way to essentially save a search query. The way Aperture searches within stacks isn't always obvious, and we'll clarify what happens for you after we explain basic searching.

Searching within Browser

In Chapter 1, we quickly pointed out the search field and filter button but largely glossed over them. As a reminder, you'll find them in the upper-right corner of Browser, but if they're not visible, choose View ⇨ Browser ⇨ Show Sort & Filter Controls.

Browser's search field is more than just a simple text search, though, providing easy access to common searches. When you click its pop-up menu, Aperture opens the menu as shown in Figure 4.22, which has commands like Three Stars or Better and Rejected. Select one of these commands to filter Browser's contents, and click the clear button that appears in the search field to clear the filter.

Earlier in this chapter, we mentioned how rather than deleting an image right away it's best to mark it as a rejected image first. If you look in the search field, you'll notice that it's set to *Unrated or Better* by default. This means

Unrated or Better	^`
★ or Better	^1
★★ or Better	^2
★★★ or Better	^3
★★★★ or Better	^4
★★★★★	^5
Show All	^6
Unrated	^7
Rejected	^8
Flagged	^/

Label:
○ ● ○ ○ ○ ○ ● ○

4.22 Browser's search field's pop-up menu.

that by default, Browser filters out and hides your rejected images. If you want to also see your rejected images, either change the search field to show only your rejected images or set it to show all your images to see every image within Browser's scope.

If you type some text into the search field and press the Return key, Browser also searches your image's metadata for the specified text.

To specify more complex search criteria, click the filter HUD button to the left of the search field and Aperture opens the HUD you see in Figure 4.23. There are five key areas to this HUD. The title bar is the first, as it tells you the scope of this filter, whether it's a project, album, or library. The second significant area shows the controls at the top left that let you switch between matching all the selected criteria (meaning the results will meet every piece of criteria) or any the selected criteria (meaning the results match one or more criteria). Near the top right is the Add Rule pop-up menu, which you use to add search criteria. The main, middle area of this HUD contains all your criteria. The last main area are the buttons at the bottom of the HUD that let you create a new collection, whether it's an album, book, or other, from the search results.

4.23 The Filter HUD.

Note If the Stack picks only check box is selected, Aperture only examines the top image in a stack to see if it matches your search criteria. If it's not selected, Aperture searches within the whole stack.

Using the filter HUD is fairly straightforward. Pick whether you want to match all or any of the selected rules, add rules as needed by using the pop-up menu, select the rules that you want to be active, and specify the criteria for each rule, such as images with a yellow label and a four-star or higher rating. However, there are a few key rules that we want to point out to you.

- **Aperture Metadata.** Use this rule to search for custom metadata. Your custom metadata field appears in its field pop-up menu.

- **Attachment.** If your camera is capable of recording audio files, Aperture imports it as an attachment to an image (there's more on this in Chapter 9). The Attachment rule explicitly filters images that either have or don't have an attachment.

- **File Status.** This rule lets you search for managed, referenced, offline, online, or missing master images.

- **File Type.** The File Type rule allows you to find files that are video files, specific types of files (including RAW as a generic reference for all RAW files), and externally edited files.

- **Text.** While the Text rule should be fairly obvious, as it's a search for whether an image has a specific piece of text in its metadata, there's an option in the text field that we want to point out. If you click the pop-up menu in this rule's text field, you see the following useful options:

  - **Full text search.** This is the default; it searches all of an image's metadata.

  - **Limited text search**. This is faster, especially when searching a large collection of images, but it only searches caption, creation date, filename, keywords, project name, and version name.

If you want to save your search results as a regular album, meaning the contents won't be dynamically updated as you change your image's metadata, open the filter HUD and click New Album With Current Images. If you want to save this search as a new Smart Album, whose contents will be dynamically updated as you change your images' metadata, open the filter HUD and click the New Smart Album button. When you finish searching in Browser, click the Clear (X) button in Browser's search field to clear the current search query.

Creating Smart Albums

To create a new Smart Album, start by selecting its scope in the Library Inspector. Specifically, if you want that Smart Album to only search within a project, select the project. If you want it to search within your whole library, either clear your selection in the Library Inspector by clicking in an empty area or select a preexisting library-level album. Next, choose File ⇨ New ⇨ Smart Album, and Aperture opens Smart Settings HUD, as shown in Figure 4.24, which looks very similar to the Filter HUD.

4.24 The Smart Settings HUD.

The Smart Settings HUD works almost exactly the same way as the Filter HUD, where you add rules and set criteria. The main difference is that it includes a Source row that tells you what scope the Smart Album's looking at. If you drag your Smart Album into a different scope within the Library Inspector, such as from the library level into a project and vice versa, the new scope's name appears in the Smart Settings HUD for that Smart Album. Click the new scope's name to switch the Smart Album to only look at that scope.

The other difference is that the Smart Settings HUD doesn't have buttons on the bottom to create a new Smart or normal album because you're already creating a Smart Album when you see it. In fact, when you click New Smart Album within the Filter HUD, Aperture automatically closes the Filter HUD and opens the Smart Settings HUD for this new Smart Album with the exact same rules and criteria you selected in the Filter HUD.

Searching with stacks

Searching for images always gets a little confusing when you work with stacks, and we wanted to explicitly mention what happens.

By default, Aperture searches each image in the stack for a matching image. If it finds a match, it only displays the matching images from within a stack. However, it still displays a stack badge label and dark area around the image, as shown in Figure 4.25, indicating that the image is part of a stack.

If you open the Filter HUD and select Stack picks only, Aperture will only see if the top image in a stack matches the criteria. If a three-star image is your stack pick but your stack contains a five-star image and you tell Browser to only display five-star images, it won't display this stack at all.

4.25 The default search behavior in Browser when one image within a stack matches the search criteria.

Writing IPTC Information to a Master

One frequent question people have is what happens to all their metadata if Apple stops support-
ing Aperture down the road? Aperture 3 provides a command that lets you embed your IPTC
metadata into a master file. To use this command, select your images and choose Metadata ⇨ Write
IPTC Metadata to Master.

Caution

Write IPTC Metadata to Master requires Mac OS X 10.6. It has no effect on OS X 10.5.

You might be wondering why you shouldn't use this command on all your images. While it should
work fine most of the time, put simply, RAW was meant to be a read-only type of file. There's a
chance that writing this metadata into the master will make the RAW file unreadable by other
programs. While chances are that you'll be fine, we recommend testing this command with your
RAW files and then making sure you can open that RAW file in another RAW converter before
using this command on multiple images.

How Do I Use Faces and Places to Categorize My Images?

Faces and Places, new to Aperture 3, take advantage of cutting-edge face detection and face recognition technology as well as GPS information and Google maps, even if your camera lacks these technologies. You use Faces and Places not only to identify people and places in your images but also as a way to organize your images so you can see all the images you have of a particular person and/or all the images you took in a certain location without having to keyword each one.

Using Faces

Faces is designed to make it easy for you to assign names to people in your photos and then to find photos of each person with a minimum of fuss. If you take advantage of Faces, years from now you'll be able to look at these photos and still know who's who. When you assign a name (or place) to a photo, Aperture automatically adds it to the keywords that are exported. If you've ever looked at old photos and wondered who you were looking at, it's easy to see why this feature is a huge advantage. In this section, we cover enabling Faces, using the interface, searching for photos of certain people, and changing names.

Enabling Faces

Aperture is set to scan every photo that you import as well as every image in your library if you update a library from an earlier version of Aperture for any and all potential faces. This is because the preference to enable faces is selected by default. This search runs in the background but may slow some operations such as the initial import as well as the processing for extensive adjustments.

If you don't need to identify the people in your photos, or want to speed up your import or adjustments, you can turn off Faces. Your downloads will be faster, and you can turn on Faces whenever you want to use it. To turn off Faces (or to turn it back on) follow these steps:

1. **Choose Aperture ⇨ Preferences.** The Preferences dialog opens.

2. **Click the General tab and select or deselect the Enable Faces check box.**

3. **Click the Appearance tab and select or deselect the Show corkboard background for Faces check box as desired.** This is completely a matter of personal preference, but we like the corkboard because it makes it obvious that we're in the Faces view.

4. **Close the Preferences dialog.**

Caution If you enable Faces after a period of having it disabled, Aperture automatically scans all your projects looking for faces. This occurs as a background task with minimal interruption to your activities unless you're trying to make image adjustments at the same time.

Using the Faces interface

There are two main ways to use the Faces interface: via the Faces button and via the Name button. We cover using the Name button shortly. Keep in mind that the Faces interface is a Viewer mode like Split View, Viewer, Browser, and Places. The Faces View displays the photos with faces that Aperture detects, including those that you've named as well as those that are still unnamed. Images that you've named appear on the corkboard where the Viewer normally appears, and images with unnamed faces appear on the bottom where the Browser normally sets.

Do one of the following to access the Faces view via the Faces icon, as shown in Figure 5.1:

- **Select a specific project, album, or folder in the Library panel to show the faces just for that entity and click the Faces icon.**

- **Select the Faces icon in the Library Inspector to display all faces in the entire library.**

5.1 Use the Faces view to add names to images.

Genius

If you prefer shortcuts, press Shift+F to enter Faces.

Assigning names using Faces

You can assign names to images from within Faces or from within the Browser by clicking the Name button. We begin by showing you how to use Faces to name your photos.

To assign names using Faces, follow these steps:

1. **Click the unnamed overlay on an image.** The overlay changes to type name, and then you do so. Aperture tries to use the information in your Contacts to auto-fill the information. In Figure 5.2, Michael's name is added to his photo.

5.2 Click the unnamed overlay and type a name.

2. **Click Return and the image appears on the corkboard with the name you assigned.**

3. **As you mouse over the thumbnail on the corkboard, a small *i* appears in the lower right of the thumbnail, as shown in Figure 5.3.** Click the *i* to reveal the dialog also shown. Choose how much information you want to include such as the person's address and phone number, e-mail address, and so forth.

4. **Click View Photos to see other photos that you've identified (as Josh in this example) as well as any pictures that Aperture thinks might contain the same person, as shown in Figure 5.4.**

5.3 Hover the cursor over the image until the *i* appears in the lower-right corner, then click the *i* to fill in information about the person in the resulting dialog.

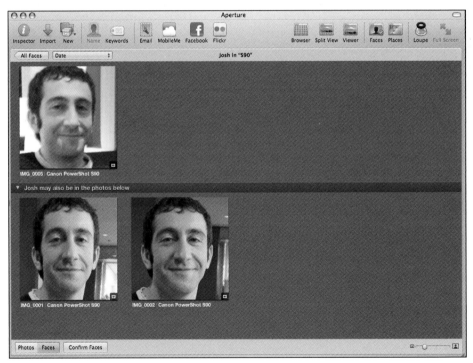

5.4 Use this dialog to see all the pictures of this person that you've named so far and any images that Aperture thinks might be that person.

5. **Click Confirm Faces at the bottom of the interface, then select the images to confirm as sharing the same name, as shown in Figure 5.5.** Those images join the original in the top part of the interface.

- To reject an image, click the thumbnail at the bottom so that it says Not the person.

- If you mistakenly confirm a photo that's not identified correctly, click the name to reject it. The overlay changes to click to reject, as shown in Figure 5.6.

5.5 Click Confirm Faces to verify the name on the photos.

5.6 Click the name to reject the name if you make a mistake.

6. **Click Done, and then click All Faces to return to Faces to identify more photos.** To exit Faces and return to editing images, choose Split View, Viewer, or Browser.

Sometimes Aperture misidentifies an image as having a face or if there is a face, it's not someone you want to identify. In that case, as you hover the cursor over the thumbnails in the bottom of the Faces view, the option Skip appears as an overlay on the thumbnail, as shown in Figure 5.7. Click Skip to remove it from Faces.

5.7 Hover the cursor over the thumbnail and click Skip to remove an image from Faces.

Assigning names using the Name button

If while going through your images in the Viewer and/or Browser you discover images with faces that Aperture missed or images to which you haven't assigned names yet, make sure Faces is enabled in Preferences.

Then click the Name button in the toolbar as shown in Figure 5.8 to add face labels and assign a name.

To assign names using the Name button, follow these steps:

1. **Select the image in the Browser.**

2. **Click the Name button.** An overlay appears that you use to assign a name, as shown in Figure 5.9.

5.8 Click the Name button to assign names while in Viewer mode.

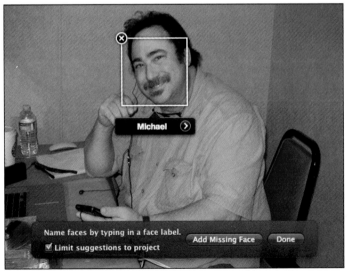

5.9 Use the overlays to assign names to individual images.

3. **Click Add Missing Face if necessary**. A rectangle appears that you drag and resize to frame the face. Then click the Click to Name button and type the name. If there's more than one person in the photo, click the button again and repeat the process.

4. **Click Done to exit and continue viewing your images, or click the right arrow next to the name to enter Faces.** Doing the latter opens Faces showing all images of that person that have been identified on top and images that might be that person on the bottom. Continue as described earlier to confirm or reject these other images.

Renaming a person

If you discover you've given someone the wrong name, you can easily correct it by taking these steps:

1. **While in the Viewer or Split View mode, select the image with the incorrect name.**

2. **Click the Name button in the toolbar.**

3. **Click the name, and then type the correct name in the text field.**

4. **To delete the name entirely, click the X in the upper-left corner of the positioning box overlay that's over the person's face.** The image becomes unnamed and is not included in Faces. To leave the image in Faces but have it become unnamed, click the X to the right of the text field containing the name.

5. **Click Done when you've renamed or unnamed the image.**

Finding people using Faces

One of the purposes of adding names to your photos is so that you can easily find pictures of that person. To find images of a certain person that you've already named using Faces, follow these steps:

1. **Open the Faces dialog.**

2. **Type the person's name in the search field at the top right.** Aperture limits the corkboard display to that person.

3. **Click the small *i* in the lower right corner of the person's photo on the corkboard.** A new dialog appears as shown in Figure 5.10.

5.10 Use this dialog to add information about the person as well as to see all the photos you've named of that person.

4. **Click View Photos or mouse over the thumbnail to see the various photos of the person, as well as photos that Aperture thinks might be that person.**

5. **To add additional photos to the named photos, choose them in the Browser and drag them into the Viewer.** Aperture will automatically add the Faces information.

6. **Double-click to open a particular photo in the Viewer.**

Another approach is to create a Smart Album for each person. To create Smart Albums for people, do the following:

1. **Name a photo in Faces as described earlier.**

2. **While in Faces, drag the thumbnail of the named photo to the library, project, album, or folder to create a new Smart Album containing just images of that person, as shown in Figure 5.11.** If the Smart Album is at the library level, it will contain all images of that person and will update when you import new images of that person (and confirm the identity of the person in Faces). If the Smart Album is at a more specific level, then it will update only when new images are added at that level.

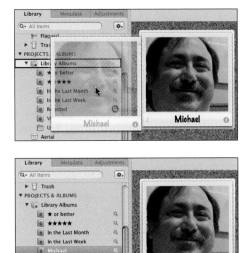

3. **To search for photos of a person, choose the appropriate Smart Album.** It doesn't get easier than that!

5.11 Drag an image onto the Library Inspector to automatically create a new Smart Album.

Genius

Using Places

Knowing exactly where you took an image, or choosing a location and quickly seeing all the photos you made there can come in handy. Places uses the built-in GPS information that some cameras offer to automatically plot where you took the images. But if your camera doesn't offer GPS data, you can still take advantage of Places. You can use GPS data from an iPhone or other GPS tracking device, or assign location information manually. In this section, we cover how to enable Places, how to assign locations to images regardless of whether your camera has a GPS feature, as well as how to search for images by location.

Enabling Places

By default, Aperture's Preferences are set to enable Places. *However, you must have Internet access for Places to work.* If you want to disable (or reenable) Places, follow these steps:

1. **Choose Aperture ➪ Preferences.** The Preferences dialog appears.

2. **Click the Advanced tab.**

3. **In the Look up Places pop-up menu, choose Never to disable Places and Automatically to enable it, as shown in Figure 5.12.**

4. **Close Preferences.**

5.12 Set Preferences to enable or disable Places.

Assigning locations to photos

There are a variety of ways to assign locations to your images depending on your situation. If your camera embeds GPS data into the files, Aperture automatically assigns locations to each file as long as Places is enabled, as shown in Figure 5.13. (As you increase the magnification of the map, more individual pins appear.)

5.13 If your camera is GPS enabled, Aperture will automatically display the locations of all your shots.

In addition, click any of the sections of the Places bar at the top of the interface to see a list of all the locations that you've assigned so far. Then click any of the places to see the images you took at that location, as shown in Figure 5.14.

If your camera doesn't have a GPS feature, you can drag images to a location on a map, use a search feature within Places to assign a location, or use the search feature on the map located in the Metadata panel. You can also use GPS information from a handheld device. We cover all of these methods next.

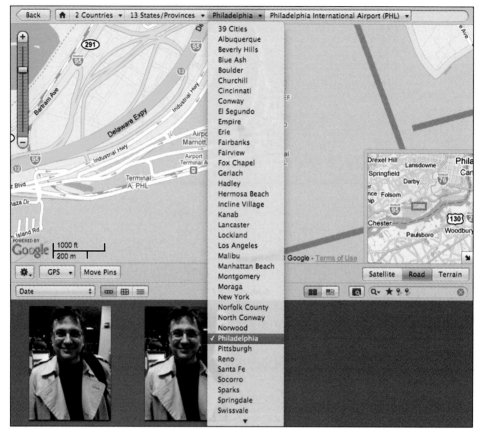

5.14 Use the Places navigation bar to display photos taken at specific locations and to see where you've taken shots.

Dragging images onto the map using Places

One of the easiest ways to assign locations is to just drag the images onto the map. To use this approach, do the following:

5.15 Click the Places icon to open Places.

1. **Open Places by clicking the Places icon in the upper-right part of the interface, as shown in Figure 5.15.**

2. **Click and drag the +/- slider to increase the magnification to see the area in as much detail as you need.**

3. **Select one or more images in the Browser and drag them onto the map.** A pin appears on the map with the name of the location and the number of images assigned to that pin, as shown in Figure 5.16.

4. **Choose the Viewer, Split View, or Browser to return to the regular Aperture interface.**

5.16 Drag one or more images to the map to create a new pin and assign the images to that location.

If a pin already exists at a certain location and you want to add more photos to it, select the photos and drag them onto the existing pin. Initially, it may appear as though Aperture is trying to create a second pin, but if you superimpose the pins, the images will be added to the initial pin.

Using the Metadata panel map to assign a location

If you prefer to assign locations while still using one of the regular viewing modes, use the map on the Metadata panel to assign locations to one or more images at a time. To assign locations using the Metadata panel map, follow these steps:

1. **Select one or more images in the Browser.**

2. **Click the Metadata tab in the Inspector.**

3. **Click the Show/Hide Map button at the bottom of the panel, as shown in Figure 5.17.** A small version of the Places map appears.

4. **Type the location in the search field.** A list of possible locations appears. Choose the best one. The map zooms in to that location, as shown in Figure 5.18. Click the +/- buttons as needed to increase or decrease the magnification of the map.

Show/Hide Map button

5.17 Click the Show/ Hide button to reveal the map in the Metadata panel.

133

Note If you create multiple pins that are close together, as you decrease the magnification of the map, Aperture merges the pins together to keep things more orderly. As you increase the magnification, the number of pins expands to show all the pins that you've created.

5. **Click the check mark to assign the location or click the X to cancel.** If you click the check mark, Aperture assigns the location to the images.

Using the search option in Places to assign a location

At times it can be awkward to manipulate the map to show you the precise location that you need. For those times you can use the search feature in Places to have Aperture suggest a list of possible places.

To use the search feature to find and assign locations, do the following:

1. **Click the Places icon to open Places.** The Viewer changes to a map.

2. **Select one or more images in the Browser.**

3. **Type the location in the search field.** A list of possible locations appears. Choose the best one. The map zooms in to that location, as shown in Figure 5.19.

4. **Click Assign Location at the bottom of the pop-up menu.**

5.18 Use the map in the Metadata panel to assign locations.

134

5.19 Use the search field to set the map and assign the selected images to a specific location.

Creating and assigning custom locations

If you take a lot of photos in a certain area, you may want to be very detailed about the locations you assign and/or you may want to create a custom name such as "Home" or "Joe's House" and so forth. To create and assign custom locations, do the following:

1. **Select the image or images to assign to the new location in the Browser.**

2. **Choose Metadata ⇨ Assign Location from the main menu bar, as shown in Figure 5.20.** A new dialog appears.

3. **Type a location in the search field.** In some areas, this can even be a local landmark or a National Park and so forth, although in other areas you may be limited to the name of a town. A list of possible locations appears under Google Results on the left.

135

4. **Choose the nearest location.** The map changes to a highly magnified view centered on that location with a large blue circle indicating the area included in that location, as shown in Figure 5.21. Click and drag the double blue arrows on the edge of the circle to expand or limit the area. If necessary, drag the blue circle precisely where you want it. Note that you can choose a satellite view, road view, or terrain view for the map.

5. **In the Place Name text field, type a custom name if desired.** This is where you can rename a place "Home" or anything else.

6. **Click Assign to create a pin with that name for the images that you selected.** When you return to this dialog at any time in the future, all the custom places and names appear initially.

Metadata	View	Window	Help
Rating			▶
Label:			
○ ○ ◉ ○ ○ ○ ○ ○			
Unflag			/
Add Keyword			▶
Remove Keyword			▶
New Keyword			⌥`
Attach Audio File...			
Assign Names			N
Adjust Date and Time...			
Assign Location...			
Remove Locations			
Manage My Places...			
Update from Master			
Write IPTC Metadata to Master...			
Batch Change...			⇧⌘B
Edit AutoFill List...			
Lift Metadata			
Lift Adjustments			
Lift Metadata & Adjustments			⇧⌘C
Stamp			⇧⌘V

5.20 Choose Assign Location from the Metadata menu to assign custom locations.

Genius

If you discover you've assigned the wrong location to a group of images, select those images and use the Assign Location dialog to reassign a new location to those images.

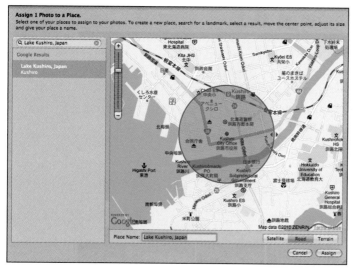

5.21 Modify the size and location of the blue circle to define the precise location you want, then add a custom name.

Assigning locations using iPhone GPS information

One of the really cool features in Places is that if your camera doesn't record GPS information but you have an iPhone, you can use the GPS information from the iPhone and assign it to the rest of your photos. You don't even have to upload the images from the iPhone!

To use the GPS location from your iPhone to assign a location to your images, do the following:

1. **In the field, take a quick shot with your iPhone.** Be sure you photograph something that you'll easily recognize as being a shot of the location. If you take a close-up of a person, you may not recall that you intended to use the GPS information from that shot!

2. **After you upload the rest of your images into a project or album, click Places from the toolbar.**

3. **Connect your iPhone and then choose the GPS pop-up menu beneath the map.** Choose Import GPS from iPhone Photos. The display changes to show photos that are on your iPhone, as shown in Figure 5.22.

137

5.22 Use your iPhone to import GPS data for images from another camera.

4. **Select the photo or photos that have the GPS information you need, and click OK.**
   Aperture adds each of the GPS points to the map.

5. **To assign photos to the points, select one or more images and drag them to the desired point.**

Caution

You must actually attach the iPhone. You can't download iPhone pictures and then try to retrieve the GPS information directly from them to apply to other photos. If the iPhone isn't available, create a new location using the images from the iPhone and then drag the other images to that location.

Assigning locations using GPS receivers

If your camera doesn't support GPS but you have a separate GPS unit, use the GPS unit to record your locations while you're out shooting. It's helpful to make certain that the time setting in your camera matches the time settings on the GPS unit because Aperture can use the time information to determine which photos should be assigned to which locations. Otherwise, you'll need to manually assign images to the various locations. After you download your images into a project and the GPS tracks from the GPS unit, you need to import the GPS track file into Aperture.

Caution

Some GPS receivers allow you to download the GPS tracks directly, while others require that you use third-party software such as Garmin Training Center, Rubitrack, and so forth, to download the files to the computer first.

To import the GPS track files and assign images to waypoints, do the following:

1. **Select the project that needs the GPS file and then click Places in the toolbar to open the Places interface.**

2. **Click the GPS button and then select Import GPS Track.** A dialog appears showing your GPS tracks.

3. **Click the Choose Track File to navigate to the GPS track.** When the track is imported into the project, it appears as a purple line on the map when you're in Places view.

4. **In the Browser, select the image or images that you want to assign to a location.**

5. **Control+click the waypoint that you want to use as a location for the images, then choose Assign Photos from the shortcut menu that appears as an overlay on the waypoint.** The waypoint's location information is assigned to the images.

To have Aperture automatically assign locations based on time information in the GPS track, do the following:

1. **Select a project containing a GPS track.**

2. **Select an image in the Browser and drag it onto a waypoint in Places.** A dialog appears at the bottom of Places asking if you want to assign location information to other images in your project based on time.

3. **Click Assign Locations to have Aperture automatically match the time stamps from the GPS files with the time stamps on the camera so that your images are automatically assigned to their correct locations on the map.**

Assigning location information using Projects view

If you shot all the images in a project at the same location, the fastest way to assign location information to them is to use the Projects view. To assign a single location to all the images in a project, do the following:

1. **Choose Projects in the Library Inspector to change to the Projects view.**

2. **Click the info button on the lower right of the project thumbnail, as shown in Figure 5.23.** The Info HUD appears.

3. **In the Info HUD, click Assign Location.** The Assign Location interface appears, as shown in Figure 5.24. Choose a location from the list of custom places you've created under My Places, or type a location in the text field and then choose the closest match from the list that Google generates. To give the location a custom name, fill in the Place Name text field.

4. **Click Assign.** Each image in the project is assigned to that location.

5.23 Click the info (*i*) button that appears over the project thumbnail while in Projects view to access the Info HUD.

5.24 Use the Info HUD to assign a location as well as to add any other notes about the project.

Moving a Pin

If you notice that a pin is not in precisely the right location as you zoom in, you can move the pin, and all the images that are assigned to that pin will move as well. To move a pin, do the following:

1. **While in Places view, click Move Pins.** A small overlay appears, as shown in Figure 5.25, and the pins change to purple.

2. **Use the +/- slider on the left to zoom in as far as necessary.**

3. **Move the pin to the more accurate location, and then click Done in the overlay.** All images move to the new location and the pin returns to red.

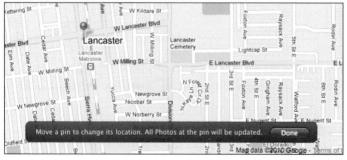

5.25 Click Move Pins to fine-tune the location of the pins.

Removing location information from an image

It's conceivable that you might want to remove location information from some images, particularly if you're sending an image to a client or contest or similar situation where you might prefer to keep the precise location confidential. To remove location information, do the following:

1. **Select the image in the Browser.**

2. **Open the Metadata inspector, and click the Map pane button at the bottom of the panel to reveal the map.**

3. **Choose Remove Location from the Map Pane Action pop-up menu, as shown in Figure 5.26.**

5.26 Use the Remove Location option to delete the place assigned to an image.

Finding images using Places

After you assign locations to your images, you can locate all the images you've taken at specific locations using Places or using the Smart Settings HUD and the Filter HUD. To find all your images at a specific location using Places, do the following:

1. **Click Places in the Library Inspector.**

2. **Type the location in the search field.** Any locations you've created whose names match the text appear at the top of the search results, while additional results generated by Google appear in the Google Results at the bottom.

3. **Select the correct location.** Places view changes to display the pin for that location and the bar across the top.

4. **Click the pin to have Aperture select those images within the Browser.** The pin turns yellow, as shown in Figure 5.27.

5.27 Aperture can display all the images you've taken at a specific location.

5. **Alternatively, click the location from the bar at the top to limit the images displayed in the Browser to just the images at that particular location.** This step automatically creates a Smart Settings filter in the Filter.

You can also search for images using the Smart Settings HUD and then create an album or Smart Album populated with images sharing a certain location. This can be helpful if the images from that location are currently stored in a variety of projects and/or albums and you want to create a book, slide show, or other project using those images. To use the Smart Settings HUD to search for images, do the following:

1. **From the Split View or Browser view or the filmstrip in full-screen mode, click the Smart Setting Filter button as shown in Figure 5.28.** A new dialog appears.

Smart Setting Filter button

5.28 Use the Smart Setting Filter to create a smart filter to show images by locations.

2. **Click the Add Rule pop-up menu and choose Place.** A new rule appears at the bottom of the dialog for Place.

3. **Select the Place rule, and from the includes pop-up menu, choose the desired category, then complete the text field with the location.** Aperture filters the current view to display only those files meeting the criteria.

4. **Click New Smart Album or New Album with Current Images to create albums containing the images that meet your criteria.** That way you can continue to work with those images and not have to search for them again. Click the X in the top-left corner to close the Filter. Note that the filter text field reflects your search criteria. To return to seeing all the images, click the small X at the right of the filter text field.

Using Places and Faces gives you unparalleled power to organize your images and retrieve them in ways that would have been nearly impossible — and certainly cumbersome — before Aperture 3.

Although it's always wise to take the time to make the best photos possible while shooting, Aperture has a lot of tools that you can use to make your images even better. With a click of a button, setting a few sliders, or applying a few brushstrokes you can optimize your shots and add impact without spending excessive amounts of time on your computer. That way you can make the most of your images and still have time to go about your life!

Reprocessing Masters for Aperture 3

Apple modified the algorithms it uses in Aperture 3 for better noise processing, sharpening, and highlight recovery with RAW files. However, anytime algorithms change, the appearance of images you've already processed may change when you update them to the new algorithms. Apple realizes that even though the new algorithms enable you to perform some great new functions including selectively brushing adjustments in or out, you may not want the appearance of all your images to change when you upgrade to Aperture 3. Therefore when you upgrade your Aperture or Aperture 2 libraries, the images use their original algorithms by default, so that their appearance remains the same. You then have the option to upgrade images one at a time, or to update groups of images, projects, or the entire library. Of course, all new images that you import into your Aperture 3 library automatically use the new algorithms.

Note

If the image has already been reprocessed or was imported new into Aperture 3, the Reprocess Master option will not appear in the Adjustments panel.

To upgrade a single image from an older library that you converted to an Aperture 3 library, choose the image and choose the Adjustments panel, as shown in Figure 6.1, then click Reprocess.

To reprocess a selection of images or an entire project, album, book, slide show, and so on, do the following:

1. **Select the images or project, album, book, slide show, and so forth, that you want to reprocess.**

2. **Choose Photos ➪ Reprocess Masters.** A new dialog appears, as shown in Figure 6.2

6.1 If an image was processed using an earlier version of Aperture, the Reprocess option will appear in the Adjustments panel.

3. **In the new dialog, specify whether to reprocess all the images or only those with or without adjustments, and whether you want to create a new version for each image or just reprocess the original version.**

4. **Click Reprocess Photos.**

Reprocess Photos

Reprocessing photos allows you to take advantage of Aperture's new adjustments and imaging technology. You cannot undo this action.

Which photos do you want to reprocess?

- ⦿ All photos
- ◯ Only photos with adjustments
- ◯ Only photos without adjustments

Do you want new versions created for the reprocessed photos?

- ⦿ Reprocess existing images
- ◯ Keep existing versions and reprocess new versions

(Cancel) (Reprocess Photos)

6.2 Specify the criteria to use while reprocessing images including whether to create a new reprocessed version while retaining the original version.

You can opt to reprocess the entire library by following the same steps just described but choosing Photos in the Library Inspector initially.

Caution Reprocessing images takes time, so the more images you select to reprocess at once, the longer it will take. We find it more efficient to reprocess images on an as-needed basis than to try to do all our older images. If we need to reprocess a lot of images, we let Aperture work on it at night or when we're away from the computer.

Straightening an Image

With digital images, there's just no excuse to show pictures with a crooked horizon. Whether you're handholding or carefully composing a shot on a tripod, it's all too easy to accidentally hold the camera at an angle. Then when anyone looks at your photos, the first thing they notice is the tilt rather than the subject you want them to see. Fortunately, it's easy to fix crooked images in Aperture.

To straighten an image, follow these steps:

1. **Click the Straighten tool from the group of tools beneath the Viewer, as shown in Figure 6.3, or press G to use the keyboard shortcut.** The cursor changes to a double triangle.

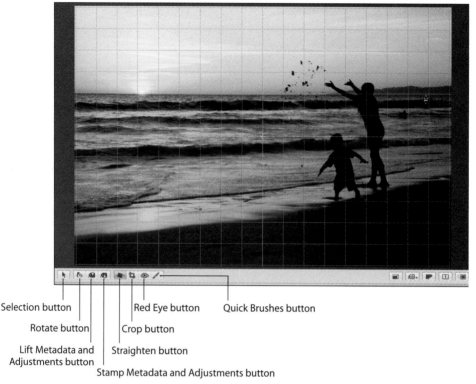

Selection button   Red Eye button   Quick Brushes button

Rotate button   Crop button

Lift Metadata and   Straighten button
Adjustments button
                 Stamp Metadata and Adjustments button

6.3 Use the Straighten tool to quickly correct tilted horizons.

2. **Click on the image.** A yellow grid appears superimposed over your image.

3. **Drag the cursor to rotate the image using the yellow grid as a guide to align any vertical or horizontal items.** Aperture simultaneously straightens the image and crops it.

Cropping Images

Sometimes you need to crop an image, whether to remove distracting items around the edges, to help emphasize the subject, or because you need to output the image at a specific aspect ratio that's different from the one your camera uses. Aperture enables you to crop images while maintaining the same aspect ratio your camera uses, to apply other preset crop sizes, or to create a custom crop. To crop an image, follow these steps:

1. **Click the Crop tool (see Figure 6.3) or press C to use the keyboard shortcut.** A new dialog appears, as shown in Figure 6.4, in which you choose the aspect ratio for the crop.

2. **Initially, the Aspect Ratio pop-up menu is set to Maintain Aspect Ratio.** To use a preset ratio or to create a custom crop, click the pop-up menu and choose a preset or click Do Not Constrain. The Crop dialog displays the aspect ratio.

3. **To toggle the height and width aspect ratios, click the double arrow that's between the height and width displays.**

4. **Select the Show Guides option to superimpose a Rule of Thirds grid while you drag out the crop.** This grid can help you place the crop for the best composition following the basic Rule of Thirds principles.

5. **Click and drag on the image to establish the crop.** Click and drag in the center of the crop area to reposition the crop. Click and drag any of the rectangular handles on the edges of the crop to change the size of the crop. When you're satisfied with the results, press Return to crop the image. A Crop brick appears in the Adjustments Inspector.

✓ Do Not Constrain

Master Aspect Ratio
Main Display Aspect Ratio
Second Display Aspect Ratio

2 × 3 (4 × 6)
3 × 4
4 × 5 (8 × 10)
5 × 7
8.5 × 11
16 × 9 (HD)
Square

Custom

6.4 Use the Crop dialog to set an aspect ratio for the crop or to create a custom crop.

You can modify the crop at any time by clicking the Crop tool again and repositioning the crop. To remove the crop entirely, deselect the Crop brick check box in the Adjustments Inspector.

Caution

The size of the cropped image appears at the bottom right of the Crop dialog. Be careful to leave enough pixels that you can still create high-quality output. If you crop too aggressively you may find that there are only enough pixels to create a very small print or to put on the Web.

Reducing Red Eye

Sometimes when taking pictures of people and using a flash, you may find that their eyes look red. The people aren't really possessed by the devil! Instead what happens is that the pupils of their eyes are at least partially dilated because the surroundings are a bit dark. When the camera sets off the flash, it lights up the blood vessels in their eyes, which appear red. Many cameras now incorporate a preflash to help constrict people's pupils. But if you have images of people with a red eye effect, it's easy to correct. To remove red eye, do the following:

1. **Click the Red Eye removal tool by clicking the icon beneath the Viewer, or by going to the Adjustments pop-up menu.** A new dialog appears and a Red Eye brick is added to the Adjustments Inspector.

2. **Click on a red eye and the red eye disappears.** A yellow circle with centering lines appears, as shown in Figure 6.5. Use the radius slider to adjust the size of the circle. Be sure to cover the entire pupil and possibly a little extra. You don't need to make it the exact size of the pupil but you need to err on the large side.

6.5 Cover the pupil with the Red Eye tool to remove the red.

Caution

For the most natural looking results, you usually won't want to make the pupils appear overly black.

3. **Move the cursor to any other red eyes and repeat.**

4. **Use the sliders in the Red Eye brick to refine the corrections.** You can modify the size using the radius slider or the opacity of the correction by using the sensitivity slider.

Using the Adjustments Inspector

Aperture offers a comprehensive set of tools to optimize your images that we cover individually and in depth in this section. But there are also some commonalities among all the adjustments that we cover first, such as setting the preferences for clipping, creating new versions for adjustments, working with histograms, controlling which adjustments appear in the inspector, and brushing adjustments in and out of an image.

Setting Preferences for making adjustments

Before we look at using the actual adjustments, we need to set some preferences that control several aspects of the adjustment tools. To do this, follow these steps:

1. **Open the Preferences dialog by choosing Aperture ➪ Preferences ➪ Advanced Tab.**

2. **Specify the Hot and Cold area threshold settings.** These settings determine what areas Aperture will show as clipped (so dark or light that there are no visible details) when you choose View ➪ Highlight Hot and Cold Areas. (Hot areas — highlights lacking detail — appear with a red overlay; Cold areas — shadows lacking detail — appear with a blue overlay as shown in Figure 6.6.) Highlighting the clipped areas that way makes it easy to see if an adjustment is too extreme and is causing the image to lose important details. The numbers that you set in Preferences establish whether the highlights and shadows must be completely clipped before they appear as Hot or Cold areas, or whether the overlay warning appears when an area is almost clipped. We prefer to set our Hot Area threshold at 100 percent and our Cold Area threshold at 0 percent, but for some outputs such as slide shows, you might prefer to set those numbers to be less extreme so that you don't run the risk of the image appearing too contrasty.

3. **Set the Auto Adjust Black Clip and Auto Adjust White Clip settings.** We prefer to set the Black Clip to 0.01 and the White clip to 0.00 rather than the default settings of 0.10.

That way, if we use an auto adjustment it introduces only minimal clipping in the shadows, which is just enough to add some shadow definition and no clipping in the highlights.

4. **Leave the option for the Clipping Overlay to appear in Color because for most images it's easy to see that way.** If the image has a lot of pure red or pure blue, you may prefer to select the Monochrome option so clipped areas appear as a medium gray.

6.6 Highlighting Hot and Cold areas makes it obvious where an image is losing detail.

5. **Leave the option to create new versions when making adjustments unselected.** If you select it, then every time you make a new adjustment, Aperture creates a new version, which is quite cumbersome. We find it preferable to manually create new versions when we want them. Be sure that in Preferences ⇨ General you select the option to automatically stack new versions so that it's easy to keep different versions of an image together.

- **To create a new version from the Master, choose Photos ⇨ New Version from Master.** Aperture creates a new version based on the master file without any adjustments you may have added.

- **To create a new version from a version, choose Photos ⇨ New Version from Version.** You can continue to add new effects while keeping a copy of the image with the initial adjustments.

Note

Creating versions of a master file this way requires only minimal memory space because the original pixels are not duplicated. Each version just contains a series of instructions of what adjustments to apply to that version. However, versions that are created for use with plug-ins or external editors require considerably more space because they are new master files and contain pixels. We cover plug-ins and external editors later in this chapter.

Working with the histogram

One of the advantages of working with digital files is being able to use histograms. Histograms show the distribution of the tonal values in an image and can be set up to show individual channels, a combination of the Red, Green, and Blue channels (RGB), or the luminosity information. This enables you to see factually whether an image is taking advantage of the complete tonal range or whether it's lost a lot of information in the highlights or shadows, and more. A complete discussion of histograms is beyond the scope of this book

To specify the type of histogram you want Aperture to display on the top of the Adjustments Inspector, do the following:

1. **Select an image, and then choose the Adjustments Inspector.**

2. **Click the Action pop-up menu beneath and to the right of the histogram, as shown in Figure 6.7.**

3. **From the pop-up list, scroll to the bottom and choose the type histogram you prefer.** We prefer to use an RGB histogram for the overall image histogram because it provides the most information.

6.7 Choose the type of histogram to appear in the Adjustments Inspector.

When making a Curves adjustment you can choose a different type histogram to appear superimposed on the curve by going to the Action pop-up menu in the Curves brick. In Levels, you can choose RGB or Luminance from the Channel pop-up menu to control the type of histogram that appears in the dialog.

Commonalities of all the adjustment bricks

No matter which type adjustment you use, they share some common features, as shown in Figure 6.8.

- **Disclosure triangle.** Use this to expose or hide the settings for each adjustment. We normally leave the adjustments exposed but that means we have to scroll through them; hiding the controls means less scrolling. That's strictly a personal preference.

- **Check box.** When selected, the adjustment is applied to the image. To see the image without the effect, deselect this box. It's an easy way to be sure you're heading in the right direction with your improvements, then toggle it back on again. All sliders can be continuously readjusted.

153

Sliders. Most adjustments contain sliders that can be directly adjusted, but double-clicking the knob resets that slider back to the default setting. In addition, many have a scrubby number field in which you can type a specific number or click and drag the cursor to quickly set the slider.

Curved arrow. Use this to reset an adjustment to the default settings.

Action pop-up menu:

Add New...adjustment. To add an additional brick of the same type, click the Action pop-up menu in the brick and choose Add New ... adjustment. This is helpful when you want to brush the adjustment in one way to parts of the image and use the same controls to make a different adjustment to affect other parts of the image.

Add to Default/Remove from Default. To add an adjustment to the default series of adjustments that appears for each image, choose Add to Default from the Action pop-up menu. Normally this would apply to adjustments that are not in the default set of adjustments but are available from the Adjustments pop-up menu, as shown in Figure 6.9. Similarly, to remove an adjustment that you don't use often, choose Remove from Default Set.

6.9 Any of the additional adjustments can be added to or removed from the default set of adjustments that appear in the Adjustments Inspector.

6.8 All the adjustment bricks share some common features.

154

Brushing adjustments in or out

Most (but not all) adjustments have the option to be brushed in or out from the Action pop-up menu as shown earlier in Figure 6.9, while some also contain a brush icon to directly access the brush in or out of the dialog. The ability to brush the effect in or out without needing to make a separate selection is a huge addition to Aperture 3. To brush an adjustment in (or out), do the following:

1. **Apply an adjustment.** Initially it affects the entire image.

2. **Choose Brush adjustment In or Away from the Action pop-up menu at the top right of most adjustment bricks.** A new, small dialog appears, as shown in Figure 6.10. If you opt to brush the adjustment in, the brush is selected and the effect disappears from the entire image preview, whereas if you opt to brush it out, the eraser is selected and the effect remains.

6.10 This dialog contains a lot of powerful controls to help you make localized adjustments.

3. **Set the brush parameters in the dialog.**

   - **Choose the size of the brush.** Normally, we work using a magnified view so that we can work accurately

- **Choose the softness of the brush.** The softer the brush, the more the changes blend into the background; the harder the brush, the more discrete and obvious the edges are. Usually, we work with a soft to mostly soft brush.

- **Specify the strength of the adjustment.** The setting you use here controls the initial strength of the change, but you can modify it after the fact in most cases by adjusting the settings in the adjustment brick. In addition you can vary the strength setting for each brushstroke to apply the effect in differing intensities.

- **Choose Detect Edges to have Aperture automatically limit your brushstrokes to certain areas.** That way you can quickly modify one or more discrete areas of the image without having to use an external editor and make a selection. When you use Detect Edges, the size of the brush is smaller than it would be otherwise.

4. **Choose from several other controls located in the Action pop-up menu in the upper right of the small dialog to control how the effect is applied.**

   - Choose whether to apply the effect to the entire image, clear the effect completely, or invert which areas show the effect.

   - The next group of options controls whether to apply an overlay to make it easier to see where you've applied the effect.

   - The last group of controls limits the brush to applying the effect to just the highlights, middle tones, or shadows.

When you take advantage of the option to brush an effect in or out, be sure to zoom in and work carefully so you don't accidentally leave sloppy edges around the effect. Remember that you can apply an effect in one area and then open another adjustment of the same type, with slightly different settings, and apply that adjustment to a different part of the image by choosing Add New adjustment from the Action pop-up menu in the adjustment brick. The ability to brush adjustments in and out to create localized adjustments gives you a huge amount of control over your images without ever having to leave Aperture and without having to make difficult and time-consuming selections.

Genius
Press ⌘+Z to undo previous adjustments. Repeating the keystroke combination continues to step the adjustments back in time if you discover you're heading in the wrong direction. You can also use the curved arrow near the top right of each of the bricks to reset the brick to its default settings.

Making basic adjustments

In this section, we cover the basics of using each adjustment including those that appear by default in the Adjustments Inspector and the additional adjustments that are available from the Adjustments pop-up menu. Of course, no image needs *every* adjustment. Before you begin adjusting your image, we highly recommend that you take a minute to assess the strengths and weaknesses of the image and develop a game plan for what you need to do to make the image pop. That way you won't waste time floundering, randomly trying different adjustments, and instead will select only the adjustments you need for each image.

One of the really convenient things about using Aperture to optimize your images is that every edit you make within Aperture (not a plug-in) can be modified at any time in the future. It's all nondestructive. As mentioned earlier, you can create multiple versions of an image using different adjustments or crops. These versions require only minimal additional hard drive space, and that means you can feel free to create and experiment while creating multiple renditions of an image.

Note The order that the adjustments appear in the Adjustments Inspector is the order in which Aperture applies them to your image. You cannot rearrange the order they appear in the brick, but you can select them and work on them in any order you choose. However with some processor intensive adjustments such as the Retouch brush, you may find that your computer works better if you apply those adjustments before making other adjustments.

Adjusting the Raw Fine Tuning

The Raw Fine Tuning brick appears automatically for all RAW files but is unavailable if the file is not a RAW file. It contains controls that let you further customize the algorithms used to decode the RAW file. Aperture uses algorithms that Apple has developed for each supported camera as well as DNG files, but your individual camera may differ from the one the engineers used and you may want to modify the settings used for specific types of shots, such as those with higher ISOs, or individual images. The available sliders are:

- **Boost.** This slider controls the amount of overall contrast by making the lighter tonalities lighter at its default setting of 1.00 and reducing the brightness of the middle and lighter tones when the slider is moved left toward zero. In most images, the darkest tones are minimally affected at most.

● **Hue Boost.** This slider controls some color shifts that may appear when the Boost slider is used. At settings of 0.00, the original hues are preserved, whereas at 1.00 some color shifting is applied. The Hue Boost may make it possible to see more color differentiation and seems to work best with nature photographs. We find that settings of 1.00 often reveal additional hues in bright sunsets or highly saturated subjects such as sunsets as shown in Figure 6.11. You may need to experiment with various Boost settings as you modify the Hue Boost slider.

6.11 Setting the Hue Boost slider to the far right often reveals additional colors, particularly in areas with highly saturated reds and yellows. The image on the left has a Hue Boost of 0, whereas the image on the right has a value of 1.0.

● **Sharpening.** This slider controls the amount of sharpening applied to the image during the RAW decode. This is to counter the small amount of softening that occurs as digital images are captured.

● **Edges.** This slider controls how different two pixels have to be before Aperture considers them an edge. It applies the sharpening to areas it defines as being an edge.

Note

View your image at 100 percent magnification before adjusting the Sharpening and Edges sliders. Experiment with a variety of combinations of settings but keep in mind that the Sharpening slider essentially controls the amount of sharpening to add to the edges, and the Edges slider controls where that sharpening is applied. Remember that this sharpening is not intended as output sharpening; there are other specific Adjustments for output sharpening.

● **Moire.** This slider controls the anti-aliasing correction applied to control some high-frequency issues. In plain language, that means that it can be used to correct some digital artifacts that occasionally appear in images with certain types of linear repeating details such as window screens. If it looks like a silk moiré pattern (and thus the name) appears somewhere it shouldn't in your image, try adjusting the Moire slider. However, most of the time you won't need to touch this slider at all.

- **Radius.** This slider is used in conjunction with the Moire slider to determine what areas of the image are considered to be high frequency and thus control where the Moire correction is applied.

- **De-noise.** This slider controls the amount of smoothing applied to the image to reduce noise. At 0.00, no noise reduction is applied. Because the smoothing is likely to reduce any fine details in the image, we recommend against using this slider whenever possible. We prefer to apply noise reduction only where needed and use the De-noise adjustments or plug-ins for this. However, in certain images shot at high ISOs or with very long exposures, especially with older digital cameras, the De-noise slider may be helpful. As with sharpening, be sure to view the image at 100 percent magnification to accurately see the effect.

Note With files from some cameras, an Auto Noise Compensation option may appear rather than the De-noise slider.

If you adjust the sliders and create a group of settings that you want to save to apply to other images shot with the same camera under similar conditions, do the following:

1. **Click the Action pop-up menu in the top right of the brick and choose Save as Camera Default**. A new dialog appears.

2. **Assign a descriptive name for the new preset so that you easily recognize it in the future.**

3. **Click OK to save the preset and have it appear in the Camera pop-up menu at the top of the brick.** When you want to use that series of settings for one or more images, select the images and choose the preset. The RAW decode for the images changes accordingly.

Setting the white balance

Many photographers leave their cameras set to auto white balance, which usually does a good, but not always perfect, job of balancing the light so that the colors in your image appear the way you expect. Some photographers use white balance presets such as daylight cloudy, shady, fluorescent, and so on, offered in their camera presets. These settings often do a good job as long as the lighting conditions don't change without your changing the preset. Still other photographers set a custom white balance setting in-camera that works perfectly…as long as the lighting remains identical to the conditions in which they created the preset. The bottom line is that no matter which approach to white balance you take in-camera, you may want to tweak the white balance settings on the computer. In Aperture 3, there are two places to adjust the white balance settings — in the White Balance brick and in the White Balance presets.

If the overall color of your image appears too cool or too warm, or is just off in some way that you can't quite identify, one way to fix it is to try the White Balance presets to see which one does the best job of balancing the colors. To use the White Balance preset, follow these steps:

1. **Click the Presets pop-up menu and then choose White Balance.** A list of six preset white balance settings appears.

2. **Hover the cursor over a preset and a thumbnail of the image appears with that white balance setting, as shown in Figure 6.12.** Being able to preview the results of each preset makes it easy to select the best one.

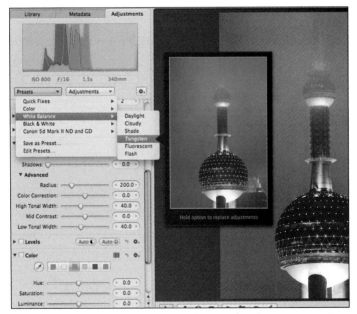

6.12 Use the White Balance presets to choose the best white balance settings.

3. **If the result is not perfect, continue on to the White Balance adjustment brick to fine-tune the Tint and Temperature sliders.**

Whenever you want to tweak the white balance of your image, you can adjust the Temperature and Tint sliders in the White Balance adjustment brick. Use the Temp slider to warm or cool the image by dragging it toward the blue or yellow side. This is a common adjustment. Some images also benefit from adjusting the tint, making it more magenta or more green, but in most cases we find we make fewer adjustments to the tint and when we do, the adjustments are usually smaller than those we make to the Temp slider.

If you aren't sure what combination of settings the image needs, Aperture can give you some help if there's something in your image that should be neutral gray. By neutral, we mean something that should be gray, whether light gray or dark gray or somewhere in between, but pure gray without a colorcast. This might be a gray rock, a gray card, an item of clothing, a road, a bird, or whatever is in your image that should be neutral gray. If there is something in your image that should be neutral gray, take the following steps to have Aperture customize the white balance settings for the image:

1. **Click the Eyedropper tool in the White Balance brick.** The cursor changes to an eyedropper and the Loupe tool appears, as shown in Figure 6.13. As you move the cursor, the area appears magnified in the loupe to help you choose the pixels that should be neutral gray.

2. **Click to have Aperture adjust the white balance to make those pixels neutral gray and to readjust the rest of the image accordingly.** If you don't like the results, press ⌘+Z or manually tweak the sliders.

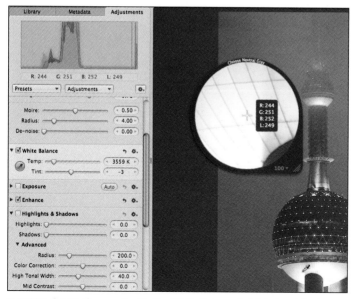

6.13 Use the Eyedropper tool in the White Balance brick to have Aperture automatically set the Temp and Tint sliders.

161

Using the Exposure controls

The Exposure brick has four sliders that enable you to adjust the overall exposure of the image as well as to recover detail in some of the lightest areas of the picture, to set the black point, and to adjust the overall brightness of the image.

Begin by setting the Exposure slider so that most of your image is exposed correctly. Before you set the other sliders, it's possible that the overall image may still be a little too bright or too dark, and in some cases there may be a small amount of highlight clipping. The idea is to get the bulk of the image correctly exposed using this slider in such a way that you can use the other sliders to refine the results and improve the exposure of the image, as shown in Figure 6.14.

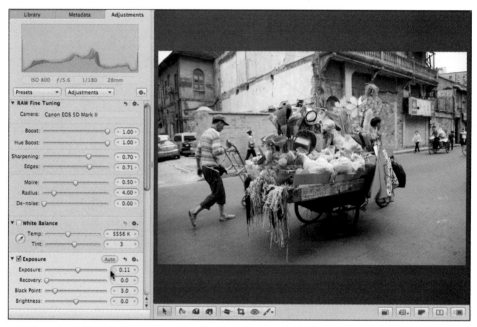

6.14 Begin by setting the Exposure slider so that most of the image is properly exposed.

Genius

While adjusting the Exposure, Recovery, and Black Point sliders, hold down the ⌘ key to have the image temporarily replaced by a grayscale version. This makes any clipping more obvious as well as helps you see precisely which pixels are being set to black or white. That can help you set the sliders more accurately. After you release the ⌘ key, check the results visually on the image and make any refinements that are needed.

If there is some highlight clipping, use the Recovery slider. In some cases, highlight detail has been recorded by the sensor, but that isn't currently visible, as shown in Figure 6.15. This is the information that you use the Recovery slider to access. Adjusting the Recovery slider also makes some of the brightest pixels slightly darker in order to enable more highlight details to become visible.

Note Use the Recovery slider to access highlight information that isn't currently visible but that was recorded by the sensor. Use the Highlight adjustment when you want to make the highlight details that are just barely visible darker and therefore more apparent.

6.15 Adjust the Recovery slider to reveal highlight detail that was captured on the sensor.

Use the Black Point slider to determine which pixels will be pure black, as shown in Figure 6.16. (This is called setting the black point.)

Adjust the Brightness slider to change the overall brightness of the image, as shown in Figure 6.17. This makes the majority of the pixels lighter or darker but has less effect on the lightest and darkest pixels.

6.16 Holding down the ⌘ key can make it easier to see where there is clipping, particularly when setting the black point.

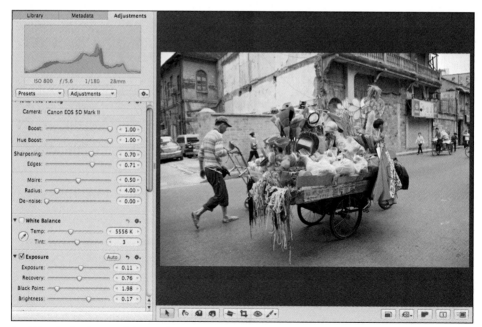

6.17 Use the Brightness slider to adjust the bulk of the pixels to be lighter or darker while maintaining the black point.

Genius

You can also set the black point using Curves or Levels, but doing so darkens more of the pixels. Setting the black point using the Black Point slider affects less of the tonal range. Which way is better depends on the particular image. If an image just needs some true blacks for definition and pop, then use the Black Point slider. If the image feels too light and needs to be darker or denser, then set the black point in Curves or Levels.

By using the four sliders in the Exposure brick you should be able to set an acceptable exposure level in the overall image even though you may still need to use other tools to add (or reduce) contrast or to improve highlight and/or shadow detail.

Taking advantage of the Enhance tools

The Enhance brick contains four sliders as well as tint controls that enable you to modify aspects of the color and contrast of the image, thereby increasing the impact of many images. As we describe each control, we suggest you experiment by pulling the sliders to their extreme positions in both directions. That way you'll visually see the effect each control has and can then set the slider to the best position for the particular shot.

The first slider is the Contrast slider that enables you to increase or decrease the overall contrast within the image. Increasing the contrast this way spreads the pixels across a wider tonal range, but primarily increases the range of darker tonalities that are included. You can see the change not only in the image, as shown in Figure 6.18, but also in the histogram. Notice that the white point is only minimally modified. With images that are overly contrasty, try slightly reducing the overall image contrast.

Note

For most images, we find we rarely use the Contrast slider, preferring instead to use Levels and Curves adjustments where we can increase the contrast in particular parts of the tonal range such as the midtones.

6.18 Increasing contrast by using the Contrast slider moves the black point more than the white point but can be used to boost the contrast of overly flat images.

The next slider is the Definition slider. We use this adjustment on many of our images to increase the pop of the image. Increasing the definition increases midtone contrast as well as adding some saturation and sharpness, as shown in Figure 6.19. Although it can be tempting to use this slider aggressively, as we have done here, we suggest you use it carefully and check the results at 100 percent magnification to ensure you don't accidentally add artifacts.

The Definition slider is very similar to the Clarity slider in Adobe products such as Camera Raw.

Genius

6.19 Use the Definition slider to add pop to your images.

The Saturation slider increases or decreases the saturation of all the colors in the image, as shown in Figure 6.20. If you want to modify the saturation of a particular color, use the Color controls instead. Although you can convert an image to black and white by completely decreasing the saturation, we find it's better to use the Black and White Adjustment or presets that we cover later in this chapter.

6.20 Using the Saturation slider increases (or decreases) the saturation of all the colors in the image. This can result in unnatural skin tones.

The Vibrancy slider increases (or decreases) the saturation of some of the colors in the image, but is geared toward helping skin tones remain more natural looking while increasing (or decreasing) the saturation of other colors. This means that some yellow and orange tones are less affected by adjusting the Vibrancy slider, while the blues and greens will be noticeably modified, as shown in Figure 6.21. You can take advantage of the Vibrancy slider not only with photos of people, but with any photo where you want to increase or decrease the saturation of the greens and blues while having less impact on the yellows.

6.21 Using the Vibrancy slider increases (or decreases) the saturation of colors in the image while trying to protect skin tones.

Genius

With some images you may want to use the Saturation and Vibrancy sliders in opposite directions to create different effects on the colors in your image. Don't hesitate to experiment in order to create just the right balance for each particular picture.

The Tint controls enable you to modify the colorcast of the highlights, midtones, and shadows separately. To access them, click the disclosure arrow to reveal three tint wheels, as shown in Figure 6.22.

Think of these controls as joysticks. To use them, click the center white circle and drag it to the desired position. To reset the wheel, double-click the white circle; it snaps back to its default setting.

Alternatively, to have Aperture help set the wheels for you, use the eyedropper beneath the wheel and click the corresponding pixels

6.22 The Tint wheels enable you to alter the colorcast of the highlights, midtones, and shadows separately.

in the image. So with the Black eyedropper, click on the darkest area in the image that you want to be a neutral black. Similarly, use the White eyedropper to correct the colorcast of anything that should be white by selecting it and then clicking on anything white in the image. Use the Gray dropper to balance the colorcast in areas that should be a shade of gray without a colorcast. As you use each eyedropper you'll see the position of the center point on the Tint wheels move as well as see the color change in the image. Of course, you can still manually drag the position of the Tint wheels to suit your taste.

Although we don't use the Tint wheels often, we do find them helpful for modifying the colorcast of shadows or highlights, especially when we want to warm the highlights slightly. The Tint wheels can also be helpful if your image was shot with a mix of lighting types such as fluorescent, tungsten, and daylight.

Using the Highlights & Shadows adjustments

The Highlights & Shadows controls enable you to reveal more detail in the highlights and/or shadows of your image. We find the Highlights & Shadows adjustments very helpful with contrasty images where detail has been recorded in the highlights and shadows, but was initially too light or too dark to easily see, as shown in Figure 6.23.

6.23 Use the Highlights & Shadows controls to reveal more detail in the lightest and darkest areas of your image.

We recommend that for best results you use the expansion arrow to reveal the Advanced controls, as shown in Figure 6.24.

To use the Highlights & Shadows controls, do the following:

1. **Set the Highights or Shadows slider for the amount of lightening for the shadows and/or darkening for the highlights**. You may need to modify the setting after you adjust the other controls.

2. **Set the High Tonal Width slider for the Highights and/or the Low Tonal Width slider for the Shadows to the minimum position (as far left) as possible while still creating the desired effect.** The idea is to affect the least amount of the tonal range as possible while revealing the detail in the extreme dark and light parts of the image. That way you preserve more of the midtone contrast within the image and create more natural-looking results. As you decrease the tonal width, you may need to increase the amount slider.

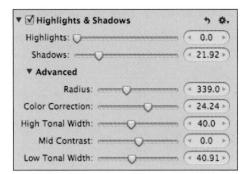

6.24 For best results, take advantage of the Advanced Highlights & Shadows controls.

3. **Adjust the Radius slider to control how far out the effect extends.** With many images you may leave the Radius slider at, or very close to, its default position; however, if initially the results don't look natural, try moving this slider.

4. **Use the Color Correction slider to restore the intensity of the color in the pixels that are affected by the Highlights & Shadows adjustment.** With some images you won't need to use this slider, while with others it will help maintain the saturation of color in the brightest and/or darkest areas of the image.

5. **Use the Mid Contrast slider to try to restore the midtone contrast within the image.** The wider the tonal width that you affect with the Highlights and/or Shadows sliders, the less contrast that remains for the midtones. We find that using the Mid Contrast slider seems to undo some of the effect of the Highlights & Shadows adjustment, which is why we are adamant about minimizing the tonal width whenever possible.

Other ways to restore midtone contrast in the image are to use the Levels quarter tone controls or make a Curves adjustment, both of which we cover in this chapter.

Note

Using Levels

Levels enables you to have finer control of the exposure of your image and has some sophisticated features not found in the Levels controls in most other software programs.

To begin, set the Channel pop-up menu to RGB. That way you see a histogram of the Red, Green, and Blue channels superimposed on the Levels controls to help you adjust the settings, and when you set Levels you'll be adjusting the Levels for all three channels simultaneously.

Genius

You can set the pop-up menu to Luminosity to use Levels to adjust the overall luminosity of the image, but doing so means that you may accidentally introduce clipping in one or two channels in the highlights and/or shadows without being aware of it. That can cause you to lose some fine detail in the highlights or shadows. This is more of a risk with images containing highly saturated colors. Additionally, you can set the pop-up menu to affect a single channel at a time. Doing so you can use Levels to modify colorcasts because the color of the image is affected as you apply Levels to a channel individually, particularly as you adjust the brightness control.

To use Levels in it's most basic form, do the following:

1. **Hold down the ⌘ key, and click and drag the triangle on the right end of the histogram.** The image preview turns black. Continue dragging to the left until colored pixels begin to appear and then back off until the preview is pure black. The colored pixels show you where you're starting to introduce clipping in one or more channels. If the pixels appear white, then you're introducing clipping in all three channels.

2. **Release the ⌘ key and then visually tweak the position of the triangle.** This sets the white point of the image or, in other words, determines which pixels appear as pure white in the image, and then the rest of the pixels are adjusted accordingly.

3. **Repeat Steps 1 and 2 using the triangle on the left.** This time the image preview turns white as you set the black point or which pixels will appear as pure black.

4. **Adjust the middle triangle to adjust the overall brightness of the image.** Setting these three controls can greatly improve your image, as shown in Figure 6.25.

Note

Setting the black point in Levels affects a wider tonal range than by setting it using the Black Point slider in the Exposure brick.

Genius

The boxes beneath each triangle show the numeric setting of each Levels control, with the default position of the left triangle being 0 and the right being 1. Don't get too caught up in the precise numeric readouts. Primarily, Levels is a visual adjustment.

6.25 Setting the white and black points and midtone brightness can make a huge difference in an image.

Aperture offers additional controls for Levels called quarter tone controls. The quarter tone controls allow you finer control over the exposure, enabling you to lighten or darken parts of the tonal distribution. To access them, click the button shown in Figure 6.26 and two additional bars appear on the Levels display. In previous versions of Aperture, these controls were a substitute for a Curves adjustment. Once you get used to using them, they're an easy way to quickly add some midtone contrast.

Quarter tone control button

6.26 Use the levels quarter tone controls to modify midtone contrast in the image.

To use the quarter tone controls, do the following:

- Click the triangle beneath the 3/4 tone controls near the highlights and move it toward the center to darken the corresponding pixels and toward the highlight end to lighten them.

- Click the triangle beneath the 1/4 tone control near the shadows and move it toward the center to lighten the corresponding pixels and toward the shadow end to darken them.

- To increase midtone contrast, move both quarter tone controls slightly toward the middle.

- To have the quarter tone controls affect a wider or narrower range of tonalities, hold down the Option key, click and drag the associated bar to the right or left. Then adjust the triangle associated with the bar as usual.

Note

The Levels brick has two buttons to use to apply Levels automatically. The Auto button with the half–black, half-white circle uses the RGB mode to automatically set Levels in a way that will allow clipping in individual channels but will not introduce any luminosity clipping. The Auto button with the colored circle sets Levels for each channel individually. This can help correct some colorcasts. We rarely use the Auto buttons because we usually prefer not to introduce any clipping into our images.

Taking advantage of the Color controls

The Color brick allows you to fine-tune the colors in your image. Use it to modify the hue and/or saturation and luminance of specific colors within your image. That way if you want a different shade of red or blue and so forth, you can make it happen.

When you first open the brick you see six color blocks and an eyedropper. You can adjust up to six colors in the Color brick. (To adjust more colors, add an additional Color adjustment by going to the Action pop-up menu in the brick and choosing Add New Color adjustment.) Although you can click on any of the color blocks and adjust those colors, in most images you'll want to adjust specific colors that are in your image.

To use the Color controls to modify specific colors in your image, do the following:

1. **Click a color swatch.** If you're going to adjust multiple colors, you can choose the first one and go in order, or you can try to choose the closest color. It won't matter which way you begin. In Figure 6.27 we chose to adjust the color of his shirt and so the blue swatch is clicked to begin. In most images, you'll want to adjust the specific colors that are in your image rather than the more generic colors that appear by default in the color swatches.

2. **Click the eyedropper and drag it over your image to the problematic color.** As you do so, a loupe appears to help you see the area in detail.

3. **Click the problematic color to choose it.** The color swatch in the Color brick updates to reflect the color you chose.

4. **Adjust the hue, saturation, and luminance of the color as desired, as shown in Figure 6.28.** If necessary, also adjust the Range slider to limit how far the effect extends from the color you selected.

5. **Repeat as needed to adjust other colors, choosing a different color block in Step 1 each time until the image looks the way you want.**

6.27 Use the eyedropper to select the color you want to modify.

6.28 Modify specific colors as you choose by using the Color controls.

Sharpening the image

Aperture 3 has two sharpening adjustments that are available from the Adjustments pop-up menu: Sharpen and Edge Sharpen. Sharpen is available primarily for legacy reasons because it was the first sharpening adjustment that was available in Aperture 1. It exists in case you need to modify the settings you used on images that you adjusted using Aperture 1. However, you should use Edge Sharpen for all your newer images because it offers more control over the sharpening process. We use Edge Sharpen so often that we've opted to add it to the default set of adjustments that appears whenever you open the Adjustments Inspector. To add Edge Sharpen to the default set of adjustments, choose Add to Default Set from the Action pop-up menu in the Edge Sharpen brick.

To apply sharpening to an image do the following:

1. **Click the Edge Sharpen box in the Edge Sharpen adjustment brick to apply sharpening.**

2. **Zoom in to critical areas to be able to accurately judge the effects of the sharpening settings.** It's very difficult to accurately determine the amount of sharpening to apply if you don't zoom in.

3. **Adjust the Intensity slider to control the amount of sharpening to apply.**

4. **Adjust the Edges slider if necessary.** This slider determines which parts of the image are considered edges. The higher the setting, the more areas that are considered edges, and thus the more sharpening that's applied.

5. **Tweak the Falloff slider as desired.** Aperture applies the sharpening in three passes and by default it applies less sharpening on the second and third pass. Use this slider to increase or decrease the amount of sharpening applied on the second and third pass.

Taking advantage of Curves

The Curves adjustment is new to Aperture 3 and in our opinion was worth the wait. Using Curves, you can modify the lightness or darkness of various areas of the image and increase or decrease the contrast in different segments of the tonal range, as well as recover highlight data. To begin, select Normal in the Range pop-up menu and RGB in the mode pop-up menu.

Initially, you see a histogram superimposed over the curve. To use curves, do the following, bearing in mind that with any particular image you may need to omit a step:

- **Hold down the ⌘ key and begin to drag the White Point control (the triangle on the right edge.)** The preview goes black, and as you move the white point to the left, colored pixels appear indicating where data is being clipped in one or more channels. If the pixels appear white, then data is being lost in all three channels. Move the control back so that there is minimal, if any, clipping. With images that have specular highlights or that are quite contrasty, you may not be able to fully remove the clipping this way, but be certain you don't accidentally introduce any clipping.

- **Hold down the ⌘ key and begin to drag the Black Point control (the triangle on the left edge.)** The preview goes white, and as you move the black point to the right, colored pixels appear indicating where data is being clipped in one or more channels. If the pixels appear black, then data is being lost in all three channels. Move the control back so that there is minimal, if any clipping. With images that have blocked-up shadows or that are quite contrasty, you may not be able to fully remove the clipping this way, but be certain you don't accidentally introduce any clipping.

- **Click on the curve and drag it slightly up or down to lighten or darken pixels in that area.** With curves, points closer to the tonality that you adjusted will be affected more than those farther away.

- **To add some midtone contrast, consider adding a point about one-fourth of the way up the curve and pulling this point slightly down.** Add another point about three-fourths of the way along the curve and pull it up slightly. This increases the contrast in the middle half of the tonal range and decreases it slightly at the extreme ends. Of course, you can set these points anywhere along the curve to add contrast to as small or large a portion of the tonal range as you desire.

- **To remove a point that you've added, select it and then press Delete.** The point disappears.

- **To protect a range of tones so that they are not affected by changes you make at other places along the curve, lock the curve in that area by placing three points fairly close together.** That way when you adjust other points along the curve, that portion of the curve remains unaffected.

Figure 6.29 shows a Curves adjustment and Figure 6.30 compares an image before and after applying this Curves adjustment.

6.29 The Curves adjustment used in the "after" version in Figure 6.30.

6.30 Using Curves is an excellent way to bring out detail in your image and correct exposure issues.

Aperture 3's Curves adjustment enables you to work more specifically with the shadows and highlights in the image. To magnify the shadow portion of the curve so that you can make finer adjustments within it, choose Shadows from the Range pop-up menu. The curve display changes, as shown in Figure 6.31 to show just the lower quarter of the tonalties, meaning the shadow portion of the image. Make any adjustments that are needed and then change back to Normal range to make adjustments elsewhere on the curve.

The Highlights range option enables you to recover information that was recorded in the file but that is not currently visible. Although most of the time you'll want to use the Recovery slider for this purpose because it's easier, if the Recovery function isn't giving you the results that you hoped for, you can use Curves in the highlight range. One of the advantages of this is that you can apply highlight recovery per channel, which may yield better results with some images. In addition, you can opt to brush the effect in or out, thereby controlling where highlights are recovered and leaving specular highlights in other areas for more natural results. To use the Extended range to recover data, do the following:

6.31 Using the Shadow option enables you to make more precise adjustments to the shadows.

1. **Choose Extended from the Range pop-up menu in Curves.** The curve changes so that the curve occupies only one-fourth of the dialog and shows how much information is not currently visible. Most of the time we set the Channel pop-up menu to RGB and primarily affect the luminosity of the image; however, you can also opt to work in one channel at a time by choosing the individual channel and alter the color of the image.

2. **Move the White Point control over the right edge of the histogram data.** Initially, this decreases the contrast in the image.

3. **Move the point that's already on the curve up to the original line of the curve.** This restores contrast to the image.

4. **Lock down the curve to the left of that point by carefully adding three points close together to make sure that the changes you make in the extended range don't affect the rest of the image.**

5. **Grab the curve near the top corner and pull it down as far as necessary to recover the data, as shown in Figure 6.32.** This will vary by image and the amount of detail that needs to be recovered.

6.32 Using Extended Curves can help recover highlight detail such as the clouds in this image.

Converting an image to black and white

Many images take on new life when converted into monochromatic images. Although you may like a particular image in color, you may be surprised to see how effective it is in black and white. Rather than simply desaturating an image, use Aperture's Black & White adjustment or Black & White presets for more control over the final result. To convert an image into black and white using the Black & White adjustment, do the following:

1. **Choose Black & White from the Adjustments pop-up menu.** A new brick appears and the image immediately becomes monochromatic.

2. **Adjust the Red, Green, and Blue sliders as desired.** Moving a slider to the right lightens the pixels with those tones in the original, and moving it to the left darkens them, as shown in Figure 6.33. So if you want the areas that were blue in the original image to be lighter, move the Blue slider to the right. If you want them to be darker, move it toward the left.

179

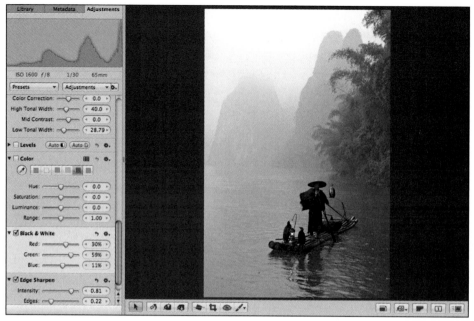

6.33 Adjust the Red, Green, and Blue sliders to tweak the appearance of the black-and-white conversion.

Converting an image to a color monochrome or sepia

The Color Monochrome brick can be used with or without the Black & White adjustment. To use it, do the following:

1. **Choose Color Monochrome from the Adjustments pop-up menu.** A Color Monochrome brick appears. By default, the monochrome choice is set to a sepia tone.

2. **Adjust the Intensity slider to control the strength of the sepia effect.**

3. **Click the arrow to the right of the sepia color swatch if you want to choose a different color for the color monochromatic effect.** A new color palate appears. As you hover the cursor over the colors in the color palate, the image preview updates to reflect the color monochrome using that particular color.

To specifically add a sepia effect, choose the Sepia adjustment from the Adjustments pop-up menu. A small brick appears containing an Intensity slider that you use to control the intensity of the sepia effect. We prefer the Color Monochrome option because it offers more control over the final effect, but the Sepia adjustment is faster if you like the tone of it.

Adding or removing a vignette

The Vignette and Devignette tools are separate controls available from the Adjustments pop-up menu. Although they seem to be opposite ends of the same spectrum, they're separate adjustments because Aperture applies them at different stages of the adjustment process. You can apply them whenever you want, but you can see from their location in the series of adjustment bricks that Aperture applies devignetting early on, whereas vignetting is added near the end when the final image is output.

Vignettes can be helpful to help guide your viewers' eyes toward your subject and away from any distractions near the edges of your image, as shown in Figure 6.34. Ansel Adams was a master of vignetting in the traditional darkroom.

6.34 Adding a vignette can improve an image by helping guide your viewers' eyes to the main subject.

To apply a vignette in Aperture, follow these steps:

1. **Choose the Vignette option from the Adjustments pop-up menu.** A new brick appears.

2. **Choose either Gamma or Exposure from the Type pop-up menu.** Gamma will yield a stronger overall result whereas Exposure will be more subtle.

3. **Set the desired intensity of the vignette.** We often begin by setting the Intensity to the maximum so we can easily see the effect and then back it off to a pleasing level. That helps us to set the Radius slider as well.

4. **Set the Radius slider to determine how far the effect should extend into the image.**

Devignetting is helpful to reduce any darkening around the corners or edges of an image that can occur with some lenses that were originally designed for film cameras rather than digital, or with some wide-angle lenses with lens shades or filters. Usually this type of accidental vignetting is not flattering to the image. To reduce vignetting, follow these steps:

1. **Choose Devignette from the Adjustments pop-up menu.** A new brick appears.

2. **Set the Intensity slider to determine how much lighter to make the corners.**

3. **Set the Radius slider to determine how far into the image the effect should extend.** Sometimes you'll need to readjust the Intensity slider as you adjust the Radius slider to achieve a good balance.

Removing chromatic aberration

Chromatic aberration appears when the Red, Green, and Blue channels do not focus on precisely the same spot. The result is a colored halo edge along high-contrast edges in the image, as shown in Figure 6.35, particularly near the edges of the image, although it can appear anywhere in the image.

6.35 Zoom in to 100 percent magnification or greater to check for chromatic aberration on high contrast edges.

To remove chromatic aberration, do the following:

1. **Choose Chromatic Aberration from the Adjustments pop-up menu.** A new brick appears.

2. **Increase the image magnification to see the chromatic aberration clearly.**

3. **Adjust the Red/Cyan and/or Blue/Yellow sliders to remove the colored edge, as shown in Figure 6.36.**

6.36 Adjust the sliders to remove the colored halos.

Removing noise

Aperture offers a Noise Reduction adjustment that primarily reduces chromatic noise (magenta, green, and blue blobs that appear in areas that should be smooth colors). The adjustment contains two controls: a Radius slider to control how far out the effect extends and an Edge Detail slider that controls how much edge detail to retain. The higher the Edge Detail setting the less noise reduction that's applied.

We find this adjustment can be helpful with some images, particularly when brushed in, but with images that have major noise issues, we tend to prefer third-party noise-reduction plug-ins that offer more controls.

Using Quick Brushes

Quick Brushes are very similar to the brushes you use when you brush an adjustment in or out. The main difference is that Aperture has additional adjustments that are only available as Quick Brush adjustments. These adjustments are designed to be brushed in or out but not necessarily applied to the entire image. In this section, we describe using the Quick Brushes, including the Retouch tool and the other Quick Brushes.

Using the Retouch Brushes

Without a doubt, the Quick Brush that we use the most frequently is Retouch in order to remove dust spots due to dirt on the sensor. We also use the Retouch Quick Brush to remove other distractions. To use Retouch, follow these steps:

1. **We recommend zooming in to 100 percent magnification when removing dust spots.** Otherwise it's quite possible that you'll miss some of the smaller spots and then be embarrassed when they suddenly are more visible when you output the image at a larger size. Begin in one corner and then move in a uniform way across the image and then down, making sure not to miss any areas.

2. **When you encounter a dust spot or streak, press X to access the Retouch tool or click the Brushes icon beneath the Viewer to the left, as shown in Figure 6.37 and choose Retouch.** A small dialog appears.

6.37 Access the Retouch tool from the Brushes icon and the Retouch dialog appears.

3. **Select Repair or Clone.** In Clone mode, Aperture makes an exact copy of the good pixels and places it over the area you want to hide. At times this is exactly what you need, but you have to be careful not to create obvious repetitions of areas because that will broadcast the fact that you cloned something out. In the Repair mode, Aperture copies the texture from good pixels but blends the color with the color in the problematic area. Often this leads to more subtle results, but which mode is better will depend on the area of the image that you're fixing, how detailed the area is, and whether the detail in the surrounding areas is similar or totally different. There are no hard and fast rules to follow

as to which mode to use, and the best advice we can offer is that if the surrounding area is fairly similar in detail, then begin by trying Repair mode. If you're removing a dust spot from a highly detailed area of an image where the nearby detail is of something else, then you may be better off with Clone mode and work at a very high magnification and with a tiny brush.

4. **Choose the Radius of the brush.** Normally, you want a brush that's fairly small because you can click and drag the brush to cover an area. You don't need to use a huge brush and cover large spots in a single click.

5. **Set the Softness of the brush.** The softer the brush, the more gradually the effect is feathered in, whereas the less soft, or harder the brush, the more discrete the edges of the clone or repair. In highly detailed areas, you may need a harder brush while when retouching areas of low detail such as sky or water or other backgrounds, a very soft brush may be better.

6. **Set the Opacity of the brush.** To cover an area completely, set the opacity to 100 percent, but if you need to blend a retouched area to help it look more natural and to hide any obvious cloning and repetition of patterns, you can retouch using a series of repairs and/or clones at partial opacities.

7. **When using Repair mode you have the option to have Aperture automatically choose the source.** We often begin by choosing this option, but if the results are unexpected and we discover that Aperture is using a source that doesn't work the way we have in mind, we leave that option unselected. In that case, as well as when using the Clone mode, hold down the Option key and click on the source pixels to load the brush with pixels.

8. **In Repair mode there is also the option to have Aperture automatically Detect Edges**. We find this option extremely helpful.

When you've set all the parameters for the Retouch tool, click and drag to cover the area. The direction that you drag the brush when using the Repair mode can make a difference in how well it works. If you aren't pleased with the initial results, try increasing or decreasing the radius slightly and/or dragging in a different direction. Often that will fix the problem.

After you use the Retouch tool, a new brick appears in the Adjustments Inspector. You can delete your retouches sequentially by clicking the Delete button in the brick, but you can't skip over several retouches and delete just one that was several steps back.

Using the remaining Quick Brushes

All the other Quick Brushes share a common control dialog and can be accessed either by choosing Quick Brushes from the Adjustments pop-up menu in the Adjustments Inspector and then choosing the specific Quick Brush, as shown in Figure 6.38, or by clicking the Quick Brush icon under the Viewer.

Once you choose a specific Quick Brush other than Retouch, the dialog shown in Figure 6.39 appears. Although compact, there are a lot of important options and controls packed into this dialog.

At the top are three choices: a brush to brush in the effect, a feather to use to help smooth the edges of the areas you brush, and an eraser to remove the effect. The feather and eraser are actually special types of brushes. All three brushes are controlled by the options in the rest of the dialog as follows:

- **Brush Size slider controls the size of the brush.** To increase or decrease the brush size, adjust the slider accordingly or drag two fingers up or down on a multigesture trackpad.

- **Softness slider determines how dis- crete or feathered the edges of the**

6.38 Access most of the Quick Brushes from the Adjustments pop-up menu in the Adjustments Inspector.

6.39 A lot of controls that make it even easier to brush on localized adjustments are packed into this small dialog.

brush are. The softer the brush, the more the effect will blend in gradually with areas that you haven't modified, whereas the less soft or harder the edges, the more abrupt the transition is. While often a soft brush is most helpful, there are times when you need the change to begin and end more abruptly, and in those cases you'll need to set this slider for a harder brush.

- **Strength slider determines how strongly the affect is applied.** Because you can reduce the strength of most of the Quick Brushes in the associated brick in the Adjustments Inspector after the fact, you could opt to apply the effect at full strength. However, if you start to brush in the effect and it's clearly too strong, it makes sense to reduce the strength of the brush initially. Keep in mind that you can set the strength at one setting for one stroke and at a different setting for the next stroke. That way you can work precisely and get exactly the results that best suit your image.

- **Detect Edges** causes Aperture to automatically constrain your brushstrokes to areas similar to where you initially begin the brushstroke. That way the effect doesn't accidentally seep into adjacent areas of the image. We use this option a lot and find it helps us to work more efficiently.

Use the Action pop-up menu in the upper right of the dialog to access additional controls including the options to see the brushstrokes. This is helpful when you make subtle adjustments that are difficult to see on the image. Taking the time to use the overlays, as shown in Figure 6.40, means you won't accidentally forget to include an area. Which overlay you use depends in part on personal preference and on the effect you're using.

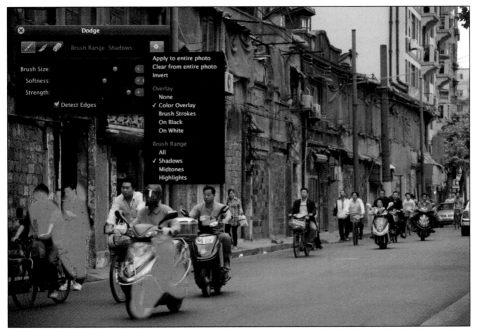

6.40 Take advantage of the overlays to see precisely where you've applied a Quick Brush.

187

Having the ability to limit the effect to the highlights, midtones, or shadows gives you a great deal more control over the effect. Although often you may opt to use the Quick Brushes set to All, keeping in mind the option to limit the effect to a specific tonal range enables you to have greater control over the various effects.

There is also the option to apply the effect to the entire image, whether you want it to apply to the whole image or use that as your starting place and then use the Eraser to remove it from a few areas. In cases where you want the effect to apply to the bulk of the image, it's a lot easier to begin that way rather than having to brush it in nearly everywhere.

There are a variety of Quick Brush effects. Use them as follows:

- **Use Skin Smoothing to reduce skin imperfections such as wrinkles and large pores.** The blur effect is somewhat subtle even when applied at full strength. Using skin smoothing on portraits can make you popular with your subjects as you make their skin look even better!

Note When using Skin Smoothing, remember to leave areas such as eyes, nostrils, mouth, teeth, hair, and earrings untouched. That way the image appears sharp, yet the skin appears smooth(er).

- **Use the Dodge Quick Brush to lighten areas and the Burn Quick Brush to darken areas, as shown in Figure 6.41.** We find it best to work at a reduced strength and then repeat the strokes using a higher strength setting as needed.

6.41 Using the Dodge and Burn Quick Brushes, you can brush in highlights and shadows to increase the sense of depth in your images.

- **Use the Polarize Quick Brush to deepen colors and shadows, as shown in Figure 6.42.** This uses a Multiply blend effect that is supposed to simulate using a polarizing filter; however, it does not remove glare from reflective areas. We find the results can be helpful but are not identical to what you'd expect if you were using a polarizing filter on the camera.

⦿ **Use the Intensify Contrast to increase the contrast by deepening the shadows while leaving the highlights mostly untouched.** This adjustment uses the Overlay blending mode to create the effect and differs from the Contrast Quick Brush in that the

6.42 The polarizing filter applied at full strength to part of the image.

Contrast brush causes the highlight tones to become noticeably lighter in addition to creating deeper shadows. The difference between the two brushes is shown in Figures 6.43 and 6.44, where both types of contrast have been applied to the entire image. If you don't want to risk blowing out any highlight values, choose the Intensify Contrast Quick Brush, whereas if you want darker areas to become darker and lighter areas to become lighter, choose the Contrast Quick Brush.

6.43 The Intensify Contrast adjustment has been applied to the entire image.

> **Note** To simulate a polarizing filter, we like to use the polarizing filter in Nik software's Color Efex Pro. We find that it gives a more realistic effect.

6.44 The Contrast adjustment has been applied to the entire image.

- **Use the Saturation or Vibrancy Quick Brushes to intensify the saturation or vibrancy in certain parts of your image.** Using the Saturation or Vibrancy brushes on your subject can help subtly guide the viewer's eye to your subject matter, as shown in Figure 6.45. By using the Quick Brush, you can brush in these effects separately from the other Enhance brick adjustments.

- **Use the Definition Quick Brush to brush in the Definition adjustment effects.** The Definition adjustment is the same as what's available in the Adjustments Inspector, but by using the Quick Brush you can brush the Definition in separately from the other Enhance brick adjustments. That way you can add midtone contrast, some saturation, and sharpness just where you want it in the image to help encourage the viewer's eyes to go there.

- **Use the Blur Quick Brush to blur any areas as desired.** You might try blurring the background to help draw attention to the foreground in your image.

190

6.45 Use the Saturation, Definition, and Vibrancy brushes to help draw attention to your subject.

- **Use the Sharpen Quick Brush to apply a basic sharpening effect to localized areas of the image.** We suggest you use this option sparingly because you have less control over the sharpening parameters this way than if you use the Edge Sharpen adjustment.

- **Use the Halo Reduction Quick Brush to remove any halos such as purple fringing that may occur with certain lenses.** The halo reduction is slightly different from the Chromatic Aberration adjustment and is not necessary with most lenses. However, if you check your image at an increased magnification of 100 percent or more and discover purple fringing, this Quick Brush can be invaluable.

- **Use the Noise Reduction Quick Brush to remove noise from specific areas of the image.**

Creating and Using Adjustment Presets

The new adjustment presets in Aperture 3 are major timesavers, as we've already mentioned with the white balance presets. There are a series of presets that Apple includes by default, and additionally you can create your own presets that contain a combination of various adjustments. In addition, you can add presets that you download from other sites. All presets can be applied to your images as they're being imported, or you can apply them to one or more images as you edit the images in Aperture. Using presets is a quick and efficient way to optimize images or at least get the adjustments close to where they need to be. After you apply a preset, you can always tweak the individual adjustment settings for any particular image.

To use the presets that come with Aperture 3, open the Adjustments Inspector and choose the Presets pop-up menu. As shown in Figure 6.46, you see a menu of the types of presets that are available. As you hover over the individual presets within each category, you see a preview of the image with the preset applied. Those previews are huge timesavers because you instantly see whether a preset is helpful.

6.46 Hover the cursor over any of the presets and a preview appears showing how the image will look if you apply that preset.

The presets are divided into groups. The first group is called Quick Fixes and primarily adjusts the exposure of the image. We've been pleasantly surprised that in many cases Auto Enhance does a good job of getting an image close to the way we want to see it. Unfortunately, it sometimes introduces clipping into one or more channels, so we often modify the white and black point Levels settings it creates after applying it. Nonetheless, as shown in Figure 6.46, Auto Enhance can provide a great starting place, particularly with low-contrast images, and helps when you initially view your images.

You can apply additional presets by selecting them. The image preview will update indicating when they've been applied. For example, we might use Auto Enhance and then opt to brighten the Shadows to see more shadow detail, and then perhaps use one of the White Balance presets to correct the colorcast of the image. With any of the presets, you can tweak the settings in the appropriate Adjustment brick.

Genius

To remove an earlier preset and apply a new one to an image, hold down the Option key while choosing the new preset. That way the new preset will be applied to the image *instead of* the earlier preset, rather than *in addition* to it.

The Color presets offer a variety of trendy effects you can apply. Seeing the previews is a huge help because it makes it very obvious when something is not a good choice.

As we discussed earlier, the White Balance presets offer access to the traditional white balance settings such as sunny, cloudy, shady, and so on, that are commonly used in cameras but that have been missing in earlier versions of Aperture.

The Black & White presets offer not only an additional method of converting the image to black and white, but a variety of presets that simulate the presence of various types of filters and infrared. If you want to convert your image to a monochrome, we highly recommend you check out the Black & White presets, at least as starting places.

If you have downloaded presets, such as the series of graduated neutral density filter effects for the Canon 5DMKII that we downloaded from www.maccreate.com, they also appear in the list of presets. The image preview updates to show the effect of each downloaded preset as well.

As helpful as all the default presets are, many people find the ability to create and apply custom presets even more useful. To create a custom preset, do the following:

1. **Open an image and make one or more adjustments to the image.**

2. **From the Presets pop-up menu, choose Save as preset.** A new dialog appears, as shown in Figure 6.47.

3. **In the new dialog, assign the preset a name that is easily recognizable.**

4. **In the right section of the dialog, remove any adjustments that you don't want to include in the preset.** For example, if you've modified the white balance in your image and applied a small S curve but only want to save the S curve as a preset, you'd select the White Balance adjustment in the right-hand column and click the minus icon (–) to remove it. Only the Curve adjustment remains.

5. **Click OK to save the new preset.** The new preset appears in the Preset pop-up menu and can be applied to images upon import or within Aperture.

Note   To apply a series of adjustments to multiple images, you can use the Lift and Stamp tool that we cover in Chapter 4.

6.47 Create custom presets using this dialog.

Using an External Editor

As full featured as Aperture is, there are still times when you want to open your images in an external editor such as Photoshop. We primarily do this when we want to create composite images. To
use an external editor you first need to specify the editor in Preferences. To set Preferences for
your external editor, do the following:

1. **Choose Aperture ⇨ Preferences.** A new dialog appears.

2. **Click the Export tab.**

3. **Click the Choose button to set the External Editor space to your external editor
such as Photoshop CS5, Elements, and so on.**

4. **Set the External Editor Color Space to use.** We use Adobe RGB 1998 because it's the
color space we tend to use within Photoshop.

5. **Close Preferences.**

After you establish the external editor, it's very easy to use it. To edit an image in an external editor such as Photoshop, after you've completed setting the Preferences, do the following:

1. **Select the image or images you want to open in the external editor.**

2. **Choose Photos ⇨ Edit With Photoshop CS5 (or whatever application you specified in Preferences) or press Shift+⌘+O.** Aperture creates a new version of the file as either a TIFF or PSD, depending on what you specified in Preferences, that contains all the pixel and adjustment information. The new file then opens in the external editor software. Make the desired changes.

3. **When you complete the adjustments in the external editor, choose File ⇨ Save or press ⌘+S.** Saving the image updates the file in Aperture. When you close the external editor, you can work on the image in Aperture again.

Caution

You must do a Save in the external editor, not a Save As. If you do a Save As, the file is stored outside the Aperture library and the image does not update in Aperture.

Using Third-Party Editing Plug-Ins

Over the past few years numerous third-party editing programs have been developed that enhance the optimizing options that are available within Aperture itself. There are plug-ins for sophisticated noise reduction, advanced sharpening, converting to black and white, creating HDR (high dynamic range) images from several exposures or HDR Toning from a single image, adding creative effects, adding creative borders, and so forth. Apple has a list of the various plug-ins at www.apple.com/aperture/resources/plugins.html#editing. We often use the plug-ins from Nik software, particularly Silver Efex Pro for converting to black and white and Color Efex Pro for creative effects; Dfine for Noise Reduction; Photomatix for HDR imagery; and some of the Topaz plug-ins. Many of these programs offer free trials so you can see the effects for yourself and decide which ones are the most helpful for you.

Note

We're able to offer our readers discounts on all Nik software programs. Use the promo code EANON, and on Photomatix, use the promo code EllenAnon.

Once you download the plug-ins and install them, they automatically go into the right place. You may need to relaunch Aperture to see them, and if the plug-ins have not been updated for use with a 64-bit program, you may see a message that says they only work with 32-bit programs. Follow the prompts that appear to reopen Aperture in 32-bit mode.

To use a third party plug-in that you've installed, do the following:

1. **Choose the image and then go to Photos ⇨ Edit With Plug-in.** A list of the plug-ins you've installed appears.

2. **Choose the plug-in you want to use.** Aperture creates a new version of the file complete with all the pixel information as well as any adjustments you've added in Aperture. That version of the file opens in a new dialog for the plug-in as shown in Figure 6.48 where we used Silver Efex Pro.

3. **Use the plug-in to make the desired changes and then click OK.** The file is saved into the Aperture library and visible with your other images. You can continue to modify it in Aperture if necessary.

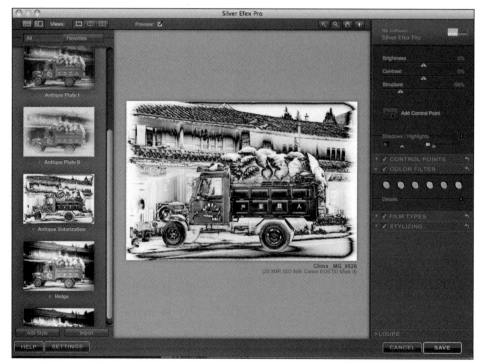

6.48 Plug-ins open their own interface. When you're happy with the settings, click OK or Save (depending on the plug-in).

Caution

Even if you make no additional changes to the file in Aperture, you can't reopen the file in an external plug-in and edit the settings you used. Once you click OK or Save, those changes are saved into the file.

What Options Do I Have to Create a Physical Copy of My Photos?

Ultimately, the reason we shoot is to share our best images with other people, whether digitally or as a printed image. However, getting a great print is a little more involved than just clicking the Print button. In this chapter, you learn everything from how to make sure your print on paper looks like the image on your screen to how to create different types of prints and even a custom book.

Color Management

One of the industry-defining features of the early Mac and LaserWriter was how the page on the screen in Aldus PageMaker looked just like the page that came out of the LaserWriter. This consistency spawned the desktop-publishing revolution. Over the years, we've all become used to What-You-See-Is-What-You-Get (WYSIWIG) printing, but setting your computer up so that you get prints at exactly the right size, layout, and color is still a little complex. The first step is making sure you have a color-calibrated workflow, and once set up, the next step is setting Aperture's Print panel to give you the size and layout of images you want. However, if you don't have a printer, Aperture has a built-in way for you to order high-quality prints. If you really want to go above and beyond to impress a client (or your grandparents), Aperture also has tools to enable you to build and order a beautiful, custom book.

Depending on a number of factors, including how old your monitor is, the quality of its internals, whether sunlight or tungsten bulbs illuminate it, and more, the exact same image file can look completely different on two different monitors. Furthermore, if you just click the Print button without doing anything, the resulting print will most likely look completely different than what you see on your monitor, and if you switch paper types, it will look different still. You might get lucky and get a print that matches your monitor fairly well, but this will be the exception and not the rule. Unless you're willing to do a little bit of work to create a color-calibrated workflow, you will always be playing Russian roulette when you click print.

There are a few reasons for this complexity. One is that your monitor is capable of displaying far more colors than your printer can print, and you need to help your computer determine the best way to go from the wider color space your monitor has to the more limited color space that your printer has. When we talk about a color space, we are talking about a subset of all possible colors created for some particular reason. For example, sRGB was designed to be a small color space (meaning it has fewer shades of each color than other color spaces) that looks roughly the same on all uncalibrated monitors. Adobe RGB 1998 is a color space that Adobe created to contain most colors that printers can output but that can also be displayed identically on a monitor. Figure 7.1 shows a CIE 1931 diagram (which represents all possible colors) with a triangle indicating the colors in the Adobe RGB 1998 and sRGB color spaces.

Genius The set of colors that a device can reproduce is referred to as the device's *gamut*.

Setting up a calibrated workflow so that your computer knows how your printer and monitor render each color is key to getting consistent prints of your photos. This process involves two key steps: calibrating your monitor and calibrating your printer. Although setting up a calibrated workflow might sound very complex, it's actually rather easy.

Calibrating your monitor

The first part of setting up a calibrated workflow is to figure out how your monitor renders colors. For example, a shade of red could look darker or bluer or more orange, and so forth, on your monitor than on another monitor. Calibrating your monitor lets your computer (and Aperture) know that it needs to correct this shade of red so that it matches the red standard.

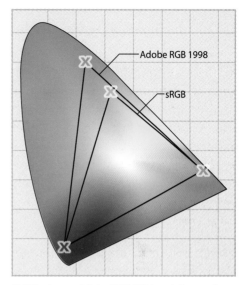

7.1 The larger Adobe RGB 1998 and the smaller sRGB color spaces on top of a CIE 1931 diagram with all colors.

To calibrate your monitor, you need a special device called a colorimeter. This device reads the light coming out of your monitor and uses it to build a color profile for your monitor. A color profile is a file that describes a device's color space. At the time of writing, there are three devices that we suggest checking out. The X-Rite Pantone Huey is a low-cost tool that can give reasonable results, although its results are not as accurate as other tools. The Datacolor Spyder 3 is a great midrange tool that generates very good profiles. The X-Rite ColorMunki (see Figure 7.2) is a very high-quality spectrophotometer that is capable of calibrating your monitor, projector, and printer. Although more expensive than the other two devices, the ColorMunki is our currently recommended calibration device.

Although these devices have very impressive names, they're fairly easy to use. Follow the directions for the device you purchase, but in general, you'll install a piece of software, launch it, hang the device from your monitor when prompted, and then save the resulting profile (and switch your system to use it).

Caution Pay attention to the lighting conditions in your room when calibrating your monitor. Even a calibrated monitor will look different in sunlight and under artificial lighting. We recommend making your room as dark as reasonable when calibrating your monitor and judging color, as it's easier to make a room dark than to match a specific lighting level.

Calibrating your printer

A monitor color profile tells your computer how to properly display the colors in an image file, and a printer color profile tells your computer how to convert the colors in the file into your printer's color space. Most printer manufacturers have profiles available on their Web sites for their printers and paper types. Make sure you pay close attention to the paper type specified in the profile name, because if you use a printer profile based on one type of paper such as glossy to print onto another paper type such as matte, your colors will be off. Many times, third-party print labs have their printer profiles available for download on their Web sites with instructions on how to use them.

Courtesy X-Rite

7.2 The X-Rite ColorMunki spectrophotometer.

While these generic profiles are usually pretty good for printers, you can create a custom printer profile to get the best results. Do so either by using a device like the X-Rite ColorMunki or by using a service such as Cathy's Profiles (www.cathysprofiles.com). Note that you will need a custom profile for each ink and paper combination you use with your printer.

Soft proofing

Even if you are very careful in creating your monitor and printer profiles, it's still possible that you will see a small difference between the image on the screen and the printed image. This difference can happen for a number of reasons, but the main difference is that we sometimes perceive a printed image differently than a displayed image. This difference can be more extreme with certain types of paper; for example, watercolor paper causes prints to appear less saturated.

Soft proofing is a way to preview how you perceive the print before actually printing it, as shown in Figure 7.3. As we explain next, you can then use Aperture's adjustment tools to modify the image so that the final output looks as good as possible.

7.3 The original image and how it appears soft proofed. Sometimes the difference is insignificant, but sometimes it is substantial.

Follow these steps to soft proof and adjust an image:

1. **Select the photo to print.**

2. **Choose Photos ⇨ Duplicate Version.**

3. **Choose View ⇨ Proofing Profile, and select the appropriate profile for your printer and paper type.** Note how the image changes. You are now soft proofing this image.

4. **Toggle soft proofing temporarily off by choosing View ⇨ Onscreen Proofing.** Pay close attention to how the image changes from the original as you turn soft proofing back on by again choosing View ⇨ Onscreen Proofing.

5. **Select the original version so that both versions are displayed, but change the primary selection back to the new version.**

6. **Open the Adjustments Inspector and adjust this new version so that it looks the same with soft proofing on as the original does with soft proofing off.** Unfortunately, when soft proofing is on, Aperture turns soft proofing on for every image in Viewer — you can't select both the original image and this new version and have Aperture only show a soft proof for this new version. Instead, you need to keep toggling Onscreen Proofing on and off as you adjust this new version. Your setup will look similar to Figure 7.4.

7.4 A soft proofing setup with the original image on the left and the soft-proof version you're adjusting on the right.

7. **Use this new version to print from rather than the original version as you follow the rest of the printing instructions in this chapter.**

Using Aperture's Print Dialog

After you finish soft proofing and adjusting your images, select them, and choose File⇨Print. You'll see a print dialog like the one in Figure 7.5. There are three key parts to the Print dialog. On the top left, you'll find all the different print style presets, including contact sheets and custom preset layouts (which we cover shortly). On the bottom left are all the print options (which we also cover shortly), but by default Aperture only shows a limited set. Click More Options to see the complete set of options as already done in Figure 7.5 (note that the button changes to read Fewer Options.). The right side of the dialog contains a preview of your print.

7.5 The Print dialog with the print style presets and options on the left and the print preview on the right.

Configuring a Standard Print

Typically, when photographers talk about wanting to make a print, they want to print one image per sheet of paper at a specific size. Aperture calls this type of print a *standard* print. Select Standard from the presets area to begin. Notice how the preview on the right displays your image as filling the page as much as possible. Next, you set a variety of options to control how Aperture places the image on the page and prints it.

Printer options

This is where you set which printer you're using and what size paper you're using. To add a new printer, choose Add Printer from the Printer pop-up menu, and Aperture opens the system-wide Add Printer dialog (which you can also access through the Print & Fax system preference). Choose your paper size from the pop-up list, but if you don't see the right size in the list, choose Custom and type the paper's dimensions.

Layout options

The next controls are the Layout options and the Margins options, as shown in Figure 7.6. These options control how your image is placed onto the page. Switch the orientation from Portrait to Landscape to change how the page is displayed in the preview area. Image Size lets you set your image to be a specific size, or choose Maximum to Fit to make the image take as much of the paper as possible (taking your margin settings into account).

If you select an image size that's smaller than the paper size, Aperture automatically increases the number of photos per page when possible. For now, set this number back to 1 (we cover the settings related to rows, columns, and number of photos per page when we discuss contact sheets). If you mouse over the preview, guidelines appear around your image. Move your mouse over one of

7.6 The Layout and Margins print options let you adjust where the image is on the page.

these guides, and when the cursor turns into a double-arrow, click and drag to adjust the margin sizes interactively, controlling where on the page Aperture prints your image. Alternatively, if you know the exact margin that you want to use, type its size into the Margins options area.

Although you won't typically use this next feature, it's good to have it in your bag of printing tricks just in case. If you selected an image size smaller than the page size, when you click on your image in the preview area, Aperture will display a heads-up display (HUD) that lets you scale up your image. Then you can click and drag your image to control which specific part Aperture prints. We recommend cropping your image beforehand when you have more control, and printing your full image rather than using the Print dialog to crop into an image.

Pay close attention to the Crop Image to Fill check box. Deselect this option. If this is selected, Aperture will crop your image to match the printable area's aspect ratio. For example, if you try to print a panorama onto a square sheet of paper, it will crop the panorama into a square image. While this is great for maximizing paper use, it's typically not what you want when printing an image.

Image and color options

Aperture has three groups of options to control your image and color. They are the Rendering, Image Adjustments, and Image Options groups, as shown in Figure 7.7.

Rendering options

The Rendering options control the color profiles and conversions that Aperture uses for your print, and these settings are crucial for having color-accurate prints. The first pop-up menu is to select whether you want Aperture or your printer to handle the color management. If you want your printer to manage color, choose Printer Managed. Aperture also displays a tip, reminding you to enable printer color management in the System Print dialog that appears when you click Print. If you choose to let Aperture manage color, which we recommend, select your printer and paper combination's profile from the list. In this case, Aperture displays a tip reminding you to disable color management in the next System Print dialog so that you don't accidentally double-convert your print's color.

7.7 The Rendering, Image Adjustments, and Image Options groups let you adjust your image's color.

When you choose to have Aperture handle color, you'll also see a Render Intent pop-up menu and a Black Point Compensation check box. As discussed earlier in the chapter, your printer, monitor, and image file all have different gamuts. To help your computer move between color spaces and to deal with these gamuts, it's helpful to give it a hint as to what part of the color space conversion is most important to you. Picking a rendering intent (see Figure 7.8) is how you provide this hint.

- **Perceptual Rendering.** This method takes all the colors in one device's space and scales them to fit within another device's space. This is useful for printing because it preserves the relationships between colors so that a color that appears more saturated on your monitor than a neighboring tone also appears more saturated on your print. However, perceptual rendering will cause all your colors to shift slightly — a specific shade of red on the printed page will not be the exact same color as what's displayed on your monitor.

Original Image

Out of Gamut

Perceptual

Relative Colorimetric

7.8 An exaggerated sample illustrating the original image and how it might be printed with perceptual or relative colorimetric rendering intents, assuming part of the original is outside the printer's gamut.

- **Relative Colorimetric.** This intent maps each color from the source (your displayed image) into the closest color that the destination (your printer) can reproduce. This means that a specific shade of red will match almost, if not perfectly, between a print and the display. However, if you have a lot of colors in the source that are outside of the destination's gamut, they might appear different on the screen yet the same in the print. For example, two different shades of very saturated orange could appear identical in a print because relative colorimetric rendering decided that the closest very saturated orange that the printer could create happened to be the same value.

In general, both methods will do a very good job, and you might not be able to tell the difference. However, if you have an image with a lot of very saturated colors or with very subtle color gradients, we recommend using perceptual rendering.

Caution

Regardless of which rendering intent you use, make sure to select Black Point Compensation. This option ensures that your shadows aren't clipped in your print by scaling the black values in your image to fit within your printer's gamut.

For Print Resolution, Auto automatically determines the best resolution for your print based on the print and image sizes, but you can also pick a standard size (Aperture uses 72, which is typically too low for high-quality prints) or type a custom resolution such as 360 for high-quality printing.

Image Adjustments

The Image Adjustments group provides two useful functions. The first is that sometimes, despite your best efforts at color management and soft proofing your prints, you'll find that your prints look a little better if you boost the brightness, contrast, or saturation before printing them. While you could make a new version, make those changes, and then print this new version, using these three sliders in the Print dialog is far easier.

The second part of the Image Adjustments group is the sharpening settings. As you've probably heard, you want to sharpen the image you're going to output after it's resized to the final print size. If you sharpen it before resizing, then your image won't appear to be sharpened properly because it's going to be scaled from the size you used to pick your settings. By selecting the Sharpen check box and setting the desired Amount and Radius settings (click the Loupe button to the left to open the Loupe tool so that you can zoom into your image and pick appropriate sharpening settings), Aperture sharpens your image appropriately now that it's scaled to its final print size. Similar to settings in Photoshop, Radius controls the size of the area around each object's edge that will be affected, and Amount controls how much the contrast in each edge will be exaggerated. Be careful not to set your Radius too high, as you might see halo artifacts around each object, especially with higher Amount settings.

Genius

While Aperture's sharpening is quite good, it doesn't provide as much control as you might want for the highest-quality prints. We recommend using an Aperture plug-in like Nik Software's Sharpener Pro before printing (and then not using Aperture's sharpen tool) to achieve the most precise, targeted sharpening.

Image Options

The last set of image and color options that directly affects how your image is printed is called, appropriately, Image Options. We recommend always leaving Rotate to Fit selected so that if you have a landscape image but your layout settings are set to portrait, Aperture will rotate your image to fit on the page. The border size and color controls will let you add a solid line border around your image. Lastly, to add a watermark to your image, select it from the pop-up menu, or if it doesn't appear, select Choose and browse for your watermark.

Metadata options

The final set of print options controls whether you see metadata with your print, and if so, what type of metadata, as shown in Figure 7.9. This can be useful if you're printing a selection of images to discuss with clients, and you'd like to have image information such as the filename available with the image.

From the Metadata View pop-up menu, select the metadata view that contains the metadata fields you want to see printed with your image (we cover creating custom views in Chapter 4). Use the Position and Font pop-up menus to determine where and with what font style Aperture will print your metadata. If

Metadata & Page Options

Metadata View:	None ⬍
Position:	Below Image ⬍
Font:	Helvetica Neue ⬍
	Regular ⬍ 6 ⬍
Logo:	None ⬍
Comment Lines:	◄ 0 ►

☐ Title
☐ Sub Title
☐ Page Numbers
☐ Crop Marks

7.9 The Metadata & Page options let you control the text that's printed with your image.

you have a company logo that you want to add to each printed page, select it from the Logo pop-up menu (if it's not there, select Choose to browse for the logo image).

Comment lines provide the specified number of blank lines below the metadata text for you to write comments onto. The Title and Sub Title check boxes control whether you see the project or album name as the title and a subtitle, which defaults to your name, in a larger font on the page. If you want a different title but don't want to rename your album or project, Aperture also lets you click on the title and subtitle text and to then type new text. Selecting the Page Numbers check box adds page numbers to each page, and selecting Crop Marks displays small crop marks where your page margins are.

Creating a contact sheet

To print a contact sheet, do the following:

1. **Select all the images that you want on the contact sheet.**

2. **Choose File ⇨ Print.**

3. **Choose Contact Sheets from the print presets area.** The Print dialog changes its preview and looks similar to Figure 7.10.

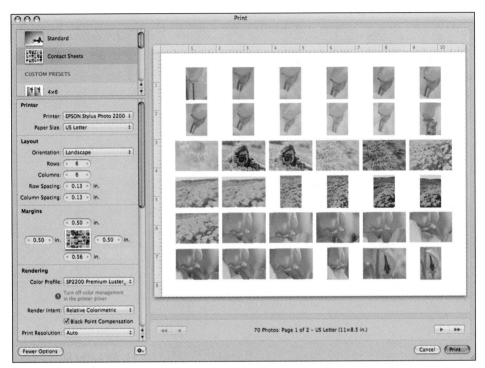

7.10 The Print dialog after selecting the Contact Sheets print preset.

The print options covered earlier about configuring a standard print still apply, with a few small differences.

The biggest difference in print options is that under the Layout options group, the Photos Per Page and Same Photo Per Page options (as well as a couple Layout group sizing options) have disappeared, and the row and column controls are now relevant. As you probably guessed, the Rows and Columns fields control how many rows and columns your contact sheet will have, and the Row Spacing and Column Spacing fields control the space between each row and column.

The next difference is that under Image Options, selecting the Rotate to Fit check box causes each thumbnail to rotate to match the page's orientation. For example, if you have portrait thumbnails on a page set to print in landscape mode, selecting Rotate to Fit causes the portrait thumbnails to rotate to have a landscape orientation. We recommend deselecting this check box.

Furthermore, the border and metadata options now apply to each individual image, although options like Title and Page Numbers still apply to the print page as a whole.

Caution

When printing a contact sheet, you'll want to use a light touch with any Image Adjustments, especially sharpening, as the settings are applied to each image. The settings that work for one image will most likely not work for all images.

Use the arrow buttons under the print preview to switch pages, assuming your contact sheet has more than one page, to make sure that everything looks as you expect before clicking Print.

Using built-in custom presets and creating your own

While the Standard and Contact Sheets print presets will meet most of your needs, sometimes you'll have custom print layout needs, such as printing two 4-x-6-inch images on one sheet of paper. Custom presets provide this flexibility.

Aperture provides a number of built-in custom presets. We recommend that you click these presets and look at what options Aperture changes to achieve each print style. For example, the 4×6 preset is based on the Standard print preset but has the image size fixed at 4×6 inches and automatically adjusts the number of photos per page to fill the selected paper size as completely as possible with 4-x-6-inch images. Same Photo Per Page is selected so that each page has two 4×6 prints of each image, and Crop Image to Fill is selected so that the print is guaranteed to be 4×6 inches and to have that exact aspect ratio, regardless of the original image's aspect ratio.

Sequence is similar, but rather than using a standard Image Size setting, it has a custom setting and Crop Image to Fill is selected, which creates a sequence of images that you might use to promote a show, for example. Again, remember that you can click on each image in the print preview and adjust how Aperture crops the image (and scale the image up or down as needed, too).

Review Sheet is based on the Contact Sheets preset. You can tell because under Layout, it doesn't have any individual image size options. Unlike the Contact Sheets preset, Review Sheet has no space between the rows, fewer rows and columns overall, and a few settings changed under Metadata & Page Options.

While these different custom presets provide some diverse printing options, chances are they're not exactly the settings you want, and you'll still want to create your own presets for your specific needs.

The Action pop-up menu at the bottom of the Print dialog provides three commands to help you manage your custom presets: Save Preset, Duplicate Preset, and Delete Preset.

To create a custom preset, follow these steps:

1. **Select an existing preset that's closest to the preset you want to create, even if it's just the straightforward Standard or Contact Sheets preset.**

2. **Choose Duplicate Preset from the Action pop-up menu and give the new preset a name.** Note how Aperture displays a dot, as shown in Figure 7.11, to the left of the preset's thumbnail. This dot means that the pre-set has unsaved changes.

7.11 The small, embossed dot means that the preset has unsaved changes.

3. **Change whatever print options you need to change for your preset.** While you might save certain Image Adjustments, such as brightness, to account for how your printer prints, we recommend not saving sharpening settings as part of a preset to avoid accidentally oversharpening an image.

4. **Choose Save Preset from the Action pop-up menu.**

5. **Click Print to print your image using this preset.** In the future, you'll be able to select this new preset from the Custom Presets list to quickly print another image (or group of images) with the same settings.

As you might expect, at some point if you want to remove a preset, select it and choose Delete Preset from the Action pop-up menu.

> **Note**
> Often, you'll change a setting in a custom preset just for a particular image or group of images, such as adjusting a sharpening setting. You don't need to save the preset each time you change it, unless you explicitly want to save the adjusted settings as part of the preset.

Clicking the Print button and its settings

After you set up your print (or prints) the way you want them, click Print on the bottom right. Aperture opens the standard system Print dialog, as shown in Figure 7.12. Make sure to click the disclosure triangle, select Color Management from the pop-up menu, and choose the appropriate setting. Remember, if you told Aperture to manage your color (which we recommend), you select

No Color Adjustment. If you told Aperture that your printer would manage your colors, choose the appropriate color management settings here.

7.12 The system Print dialog and Color Management settings.

Once you finish adjusting your Color Management settings, click Print, and Aperture spools your print job.

Ordering Prints

If you don't own a printer, Aperture provides a tool to order prints via a third-party print service. Unfortunately, you have no control over the paper type or other print settings. To order a print, follow these steps.

1. **Select the images you want to have printed.**

2. **Choose File ⇨ Order Prints.**

3. **Use your Apple ID to sign in.** This is the same ID you use to log in to the iTunes Store. If you don't have an Apple ID, click the Create Account button and follow the steps. The screen changes to display the order form.

4. **As shown in Figure 7.13, use the text fields, to select the number of each size of prints that you want to order, and click Continue when done.** The screen changes to display just your order.

Select Prints

Select Prints   Review   Verify   Send

(Sign Out)

Quick Order: [4 x 6]

Prints

4 x 6	$0.12 each	0
5 x 7	$0.49 each	0
Wallet	$0.99 for 4	0
8 x 10	$1.99 each	0
16 x 20	$9.99 each	0
20 x 30	$14.99 each	0
4 x 6	$0.12 each	0
5 x 7	$0.49 each	0
Wallet	$0.99 for 4	0
8 x 10	$1.99 each	0
16 x 20	$9.99 each	0
20 x 30	$14.99 each	0
4 x 6	$0.12 each	0
5 x 7	$0.49 each	0
Wallet	$0.99 for 4	0
8 x 10	$1.99 each	0
16 x 20	$9.99 each	0

Availability is based on your
United States billing address. (Manage Account)   **Order Subtotal:**   **$0.00**

Secure connection   (Cancel)   (Continue)

7.13 Use the Select Prints screen to control how many of each type of print for each print you want to order.

5. **Review your order and click either the Back button to make changes or the Continue button to go forward.** The screen changes again to display shipping and billing information.

6. **Type your shipping and billing addresses as well as your e-mail address for a receipt.** This last Verify screen also includes the estimated tax and shipping charges.

7. **Click Place Order to confirm your order.**

While Aperture's Order Prints tool is quite convenient and priced nicely, for full control over your prints, we recommend using the techniques described in Chapter 8 to create a ready-to-print digital version of your image and send it to a print service that provides more control, such as mpix.com.

Genius

For other types of prints, such as a card or calendar, export your images to iPhoto by generating previews for your images (which we cover in Chapter 10), choosing File ➪ Show Aperture Browser from iPhoto, and dragging and dropping your Aperture images into an iPhoto album. Then order the desired print product from within iPhoto.

215

Creating a Book

One of Aperture's unique features is the ability to lay out and order a completely custom book of your photos. Creating a book comes down to three main steps: picking the type of book you want to make, laying out the pages in your book, and ordering your book. This section covers how to do each of these tasks and describes in depth how to lay out a page to customize your book.

Creating a new book album and picking themes

To create a new book, follow these steps.

1. **Select the images you want to put into your book.**

2. **Choose File ⇨ New ⇨ Book.** Aperture displays the New Book dialog shown in Figure 7.14.

3. **Type your book's title into the Book Name field.**

4. **Select the type of book from the Book Type pop-up menu.** In addition to the standard Apple books, you can also download Photo Book Plug-Ins from the Apple Web site for third-party book printers, such as Graphistudio and Couture Book. Choose Learn More from the Book Type pop-up, and Aperture opens the Photo Book Plug-Ins page in your Browser. Lastly, choose Custom if you want to create a completely custom book that you will print yourself.

7.14 The New Book dialog lets you pick a book type and style.

5. **Select your book's theme from the list on the left.** As you click on each theme, a theme preview appears on the right side of the dialog. If you're creating a Custom book type, click New Theme to enter your book's page size and margin information.

6. **Click Options & Prices to see a list of prices and finishing options for your book.**

7. **Click Choose Theme to confirm these options, create your book album in the Library Inspector, and to open the Book Layout Editor.**

8. **Choose whether you want a Hardcover or Softcover book, if your book type provides the option, by clicking the appropriate button at the top of the Book Layout Editor.** Because this choice affects page layout, changing it later might adversely affect your book's pages.

Note It's possible to add images from multiple projects and albums to the book by dragging the images onto the book's icon in the Library Inspector.

Genius Any custom themes you create are saved in /Users/yourUserName/Library/ Application Support/Aperture3/Book Themes. To share your theme with another person, copy your custom theme from that folder to the same location on the other person's computer.

Navigating the Book Layout Editor

Whenever you have a book album selected in the Library Inspector, Aperture displays the Book Layout Editor that you see in Figure 7.15 instead of the standard Viewer. This editor lets you control the pages in your book and the layout of those pages including the images, text, and maps placed on the page. There are two main parts to the Book Layout Editor: the Pages pane and the Book Editor Viewer.

- **Pages pane controls.** The Pages pane is on the left side of the Book Layout Editor. It lets you quickly see and navigate between pages in your book, add and remove pages, change page templates, and more. At the top of the Pages pane, there are buttons to switch your book's theme and to switch cover type (if available).

Pages pane

Book Editor Viewer

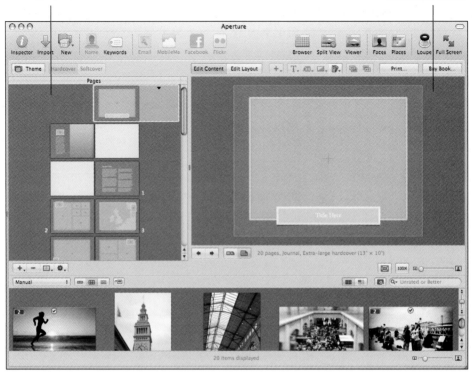

7.15 The Book Layout Editor replaces the standard Viewer when working on a book and allows you to see, navigate between, and edit the pages in your book.

● **Book Editor Viewer.** The Book Editor Viewer is similar to a regular Viewer, but it displays a book page instead of just a photo. Because normal Viewer functions such as View ⇨ Zoom to Actual Size are disabled with the Book Editor Viewer, Aperture provides three controls in the bottom right of the Book Editor to fit the Book Editor Viewer to the available space, zoom it to actual size, and to manually select the zoom scale for the Viewer. There are also buttons at the bottom of this viewer to switch between viewing a single page or a full spread and to go to the previous or next page. At the top of this viewer are buttons to control the contents of the page, and we cover these buttons more in detail in the rest of this chapter.

Aperture prepopulates the Pages pane with a variety of page types. These prepopulated pages help show what options are available with this theme and provide a nice starting point to start creating your book.

Note

At the bottom right corner of the Pages pane is the Book Actions pop-up menu. This menu contains many commands we refer to throughout the rest of the chapter.

Placing images and text

As you click on different pages in the Pages pane, Aperture changes the page currently displayed in its Viewer. Notice how many pages have gray areas with a crosshatch in the middle and blocks of *lorem ipsum* text. These are placeholders for images and text, respectively.

Changing the text is fairly straightforward. Double-click on the *lorem ipsum* text or *Section Title* text and type in the text you'd like to appear. We'll cover how to customize your text's appearance shortly.

Placing images is almost as easy. Start by dragging and dropping an image from Browser onto the gray placeholder area (if Browser isn't visible, choose View ➪ Split View or press V). Double-click on a placed image to open the Image Scale HUD, which lets you zoom your placed image in or out, and click and drag your placed image to move it around within the image box. For example, if you've placed a landscape image onto a portrait placeholder box, you can drag the image around to control how it's being cropped into a portrait image.

Caution

If you're unable to place an image or edit text, make sure the Edit Content button at the top of the Book Editor Viewer is selected and not the Edit Layout button.

Note

When you place an image into a book, Browser displays a small maroon badge with a number indicating how many times this image has been placed into this book.

Genius

The Rebuild Book commands in the Book Actions menu will remove any changes you've made to the book's design, revert to the default series of pages, and automatically fill the image placeholders with either all your images or the selected images, depending on which command, Rebuild Book With All Images or Rebuild Book With Selected Images, you choose.

Rather than placing images manually into each image placeholder, Aperture can automatically place either your selected images or all images that haven't been used yet in the book. To automatically place a specific group of images, select the images in Browser and choose Autoflow Selected Images from the Book Actions pop-up menu. Aperture places the selected images into your book, shown in Figure 7.16, starting with the first empty image placeholder. To have Aperture automatically place any unused images into your book, simply choose Book Actions ⇨ Autoflow Unplaced images.

Some layouts will also let you place a photo as the page background. To do so, drag an image from Browser onto the background area of the page, and let go when Aperture highlights the background.

To unplace an image, select the photo box and press the Delete key. To remove a background image, click the Set Background pop-up menu, highlighted in Figure 7.17, and choose either No Background or a background color. Figure 7.17 also highlights the other customization menus that we refer to throughout the rest of the chapter.

7.16 A before and after view of an empty page and a page with text and images filled out.

Set Photo Filter pop-up menu

Set Metadata Field pop-up menu

Set Page Background pop-up menu

Set Text Style pop-up menu

7.17 The text, metadata, photo filter, and page background customization menus provide formatting options for each type of item on the page.

Adjusting metadata boxes

Some themes have special text fields that are linked to a particular image placeholder and display that image's metadata. You cannot directly type in new metadata values for the image here (use the Metadata Inspector if you wish to adjust an image's metadata), but you can change what metadata is displayed in the box and link the metadata box to a different image.

To change the metadata box's metadata view, select the metadata box, click the Set Metadata Field pop-up menu, and select the new metadata you want displayed. Note that this menu doesn't provide access to the standard metadata views and isn't customizable. There is only a limited subset of metadata that you can have automatically displayed in a metadata box.

To link a metadata box to a different image, follow these steps:

1. **Select the metadata box.**

2. **Choose Book Actions ⇨ Unlink Metadata Box.**

3. **Select both the image you want to connect to the metadata box and the metadata box by ⌘+clicking on each.**

4. **Choose Book Actions ⇨ Link Metadata Box.** The metadata box should now be displaying metadata values for the new image.

Configuring item options

Each photo and text box (including metadata boxes) has a number of configuration options related to both style and how the box contents are placed into the box.

To start with, the Set Photo Filter menu provides a number of filters that you can quickly apply to an image, including the page background image. To use them, select a photo and then select a filter from this menu.

There are two ways to apply a different style to a text or metadata box. The first is to select the text box and then click the Set Text Style menu. This menu, with an example shown in Figure 7.18, lists all the preset styles from this book template. You can choose a different text style by picking one from the menu.

Alternatively, if you highlight the text you want to style and choose Edit ⇨ Show Fonts, Aperture opens the standard System Font dialog. Use this dialog to pick custom fonts, sizes, and colors for your text.

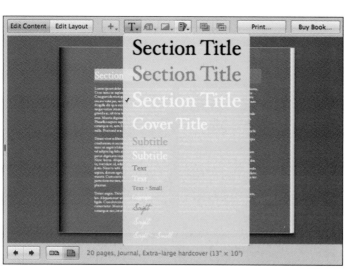

7.18 An example Text Style menu, showing the preset options from the built-in Journal theme.

The next set of configuration settings deals with how each box's contents are placed into its box. If you select a photo box and choose Book Actions ⇨ Photo Box, you see four options:

- **Scale to Fill.** This option is the default and scales the image up to fill the photo box completely, regardless of aspect ratio.

- **Scale to Fill Centered.** This option scales the photo so that it fits completely into the photo box at the proper aspect ratio. The photo will be centered in the photo box.

- **Scale to Fill Left.** This option scales the photo so that it fits completely into the photo box at the proper aspect ratio. The photo will be placed along the left side of the photo box.

- **Scale to Fill Right.** This option scales the photo so that it fits completely into the photo box at the proper aspect ratio. The photo will be placed along the right side of the photo box.

The Photo Box Alignment options are available both when in Edit Content and Edit Layout mode. However, to make the text box options active, click the Edit Layout button.

Now, if you select a text box, you'll notice that the Book Actions ⇨ Text Box Alignment menu is active. Use this menu to select whether a text box is left aligned, centered, and so on. We cover the other options available when in Edit Layout mode later in the section on customizing page layout.

Working with Browser's extra book features

In addition to showing you how many times an image is used in a book, as mentioned previously in this chapter, Browser has three extra buttons when attached to the Book Editor, as indicated in Figure 7.19.

Show Viewer for this Browser button   Show All Images button

Show Unplaced Images button

7.19 Browser gains buttons for Show Viewer for this Browser, Show Unplaced Images, and Show All Images when attached to the Book Editor.

On the right, Browser now has buttons to toggle between showing all images in the book album and only showing images that haven't been placed into the book. It's useful to have Browser set to Show All Images while you collect images to put into your book and to switch to Show Unplaced Images mode while placing images.

The other button Browser gains is the Show Viewer for this Browser button. When the Book Editor is open, there's no obvious way to make an adjustment to an image beyond the Book Editor's photo filters, aside from leaving the Book Editor and finding the image in its project. Instead, if you select an image (or images) in Browser and click this button, Aperture temporarily switches the Book Editor out for a normal Viewer so that you can inspect your images and make any adjustments. Click this button again to close Viewer and return to the Book Editor.

Note   The Loupe still works even when the Book Editor is open, allowing you to zoom in on your images to check for sharpness and such. However, it doesn't magnify the entire page contents. It only lets you loupe the images on the page or in Browser.

Using maps

Some themes, such as Photo Essay and Journal, also have map elements on certain pages. These maps integrate with Places, allowing you to flag a specific place or to draw a journey between places. If you haven't yet set a specific place, it's possible to add a new place on the map while creating the book.

To set a map's initial location, either drag a photo with a location set onto the map or follow the following instructions on how to manually add a new place to the map. Double-click on the map to open the Map Options HUD, as shown in Figure 7.20.

There are four main controls in the Map Options HUD:

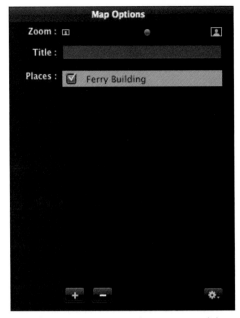

7.20 The Map Options HUD lets you control the locations marked on the map, the lines between locations, and other options.

- ⦿ **Zoom slider.** This lets you change the map's scale.

- ⦿ **Title.** This lets you adds stylized title text to the map.

- ⦿ **Places.** This lists the locations flagged on the map. If you're going to set the map to display lines and arrows between locations, drag and drop each location name in the list to rearrange them into the order that you want Aperture to draw the lines.

- ⦿ **Action pop-up menu.** This contains controls to display how the map's displayed.

To add additional locations to the map, you can either drag additional photos tagged with a location to the map or follow these steps:

1. **Double-click the map to open the Map Options HUD.**

2. **Click the Add (+) button in the bottom left.**

3. **Start typing the location in Places and Aperture displays a pop-up menu with matching locations.**

4. **Pick the correct location from the list.**

5. **The new location will now appear in the list in the Map Options HUD and on the map.**

To delete a location, select it in the Map Options HUD and click the Remove (–) button in the bottom left.

The Action pop-up menu in the Map Options HUD has a number of commands to help you configure your map to create a finished map, as shown in Figure 7.21, and they are as follows:

- **Return to Starting Place.** If you have your map set to draw lines between locations, this option will close the loop and draw a line from the last place to the first place.

- **Move Label.** This option causes the label, if visible, for the selected place to move to a different side of the place pin, making it easier to read the label.

- **Show Lines with Arrowheads / Show Straight Lines / Hide Lines.** These options toggle between showing a line between places with arrowheads, without arrowheads, and not drawing any lines.

- **Show Place Marker Text.** Show or hide the place labels.

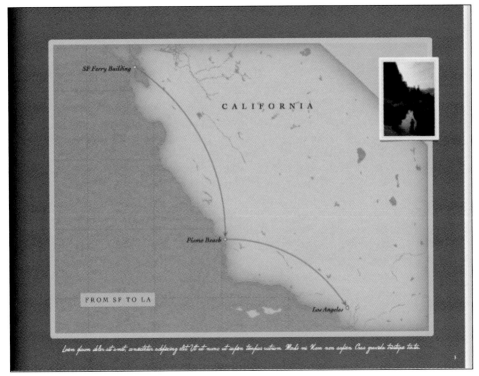

7.21 A finished map, showing different locations, lines with arrows between locations, location names, and a map title.

● **Show Region Text.** Show or hide the larger labels, such as the country name, on the map.

● **Center Map on Places.** Zoom the map automatically to show all places marked on the map.

● **Reset Map.** Reset the map display back to the book's default.

Genius

Instead of manually typing a location into the Map Options HUD, double-click on the map and then click and drag the map around to move it. Control+click on a location and choose Add Place to interactively add places to the map.

Switching page styles

To switch page styles between different preset master pages, select the page in the Pages pane and either click the Set Master Page button at the bottom of the Pages pane or click the disclosure triangle that appears next to the selected page. Aperture opens a menu, such as the one in Figure 7.22, with the available page styles. Note that the right and left pages might have different options; for example, the left page has options for styles that span both pages.

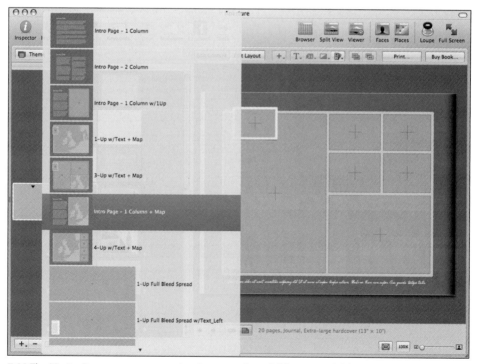

7.22 The Master Page pop-up menu, showing a number of different available page styles.

Adding and removing pages

To add a new page, select the previous page in the Pages pane, click the Add Pages button, and choose Add New Page. Aperture creates a blank page with what it determines to be the appropriate master layout. Choosing Duplicate Page makes a duplicate of the previous page's layout and images, with the layout adjusted to reflect whether the new page is on the left or right side of the book. Note that the default Apple books are limited to 99 pages.

To remove a page, select the page and click the Delete Pages button. Books require an even number of pages and at least 20 pages. If needed, Aperture inserts a blank page later in your book to accommodate these restrictions.

Customizing page layout

While there are plenty of preset page masters to choose from, sometimes you will still want to adjust the page layout. To begin, click the Edit Layout button at the top of the Book Editor.

The easiest place to begin customizing a page layout is to drag the different boxes around on the page to rearrange them. As you do so, Aperture displays Smart Guides along the page, and snaps the box to them to help you line up your different boxes. Use the Bring Forward and Send Backward buttons at the top of the Book Editor, shown in Figure 7.23, to move items behind and in front of one another. These commands are also in the Book Actions menu under the Arrange submenu.

Add pop-up menu   Bring Forward button

Send Backward button

7.23 The Bring Forward, Send Backward, and Add buttons provide additional commands to modify the page's layout.

Resize a box by selecting it, clicking on one of the handles that appears, and dragging that handle. Hold the Option key while dragging to cause Aperture to scale the box around the middle rather than only the side you're dragging.

You can type specific sizes and locations for your boxes by using the Layout Options pane, as shown in Figure 7.24. To open it, choose Book Actions ⇨ Show Layout Options. When you select a box on the page, Aperture fills the Layout Options pane with the box's information. Type new numbers in these fields for precise control over each item's layout.

The Book Actions menu contains a number of other useful layout commands:

7.24 The Layout Options pane lets you type exact values for each box's size, position, and rotation.

- **Photo Box Aspect Ratio submenu.** To quickly apply a specific aspect ratio to a photo box, instead of manually resizing it, select the photo box and choose an aspect ratio from this submenu.

- **Text Box Columns.** To change the number of columns in a text box, select the text box and choose the number of columns from this submenu.

- **Page Numbers.** To force page numbers to be always on or off or to let Aperture automatically determine when to show them, choose the appropriate option from this submenu.

- **Enable/Disable Plate Numbers.** By default, Aperture does not display image numbers in its metadata boxes. Enable Plate Numbers if you want to automatically have plate numbers.

To add a completely new element to the page, whether you want an image, text box, metadata box, or map, either click the Add button at the top of the Book Editor or choose Book Actions ⇨ Add and select the appropriate item. Position, size, and format it using the commands covered in this chapter.

Remove an element by selecting it and pressing the Delete key.

At any point, if you want to return to the original page master, choose Book Actions ⇨ Reapply Master, and Aperture resets the page to its default.

Editing master pages

Master pages are the default starting layouts for the different pages in your book. Aperture lets you customize these masters, either by editing an existing one or creating a new one.

To see the masters, choose Book Actions ⇨ Show Master Pages. Aperture opens the pane you see in Figure 7.25. As you scroll through this list, you can click on any master page to open it into the Book Editor Viewer. Edit the master's layout as you would any other page to make changes directly to the master. Note that you cannot make changes to the cover page.

7.25 The Master Pages pane lets you quickly modify and add new master pages to your book.

To add a new master page, follow these simple steps:

1. **Select an existing master page.**

2. **Click the Add (+) button and select Add New Page.** This adds a new master to the Master Pages pane.

3. **Double-click its name to give it a new, descriptive name.** You can edit its layout as previously described.

If, after customizing a normal book page, you decide that you want to add these changes to the master, rather than redoing all the changes on the master, simply select the page and choose Book Actions ⇨ Save Page ⇨ To Document Master. If you want to turn your changes into a new master page, rather than modifying the existing master, choose Save Page ⇨ As New Document Master instead. Then show the Master Pages pane, find this new master, and double-click its name to give it a more descriptive name.

By default, when you create a new master, whether by explicitly adding a new master or by saving a page in your book as a new master, Aperture creates versions of this page for both the right- and left-hand sides of your book. You will most likely want to tweak each version of this master. For example, you might have a text field on the left for a page on the left but want the text field to be on the right for a page on the right. To do so, click the left and right sides of your master to make changes to each version.

If you instead want this master to have one layout for both the left and right sides of your book, choose Book Actions ⇨ Unify Master Page. Rather than displaying two thumbnails for each side of the page, your master will now only have one thumbnail representing both sides, as shown in Figure 7.26. To split a master so that the left and right sides have different versions, select the master and choose Book Actions ⇨ Split Master Page.

Split master pages

Unified master pages

7.26 Unified and split master pages in the Master Pages pane.

Printing or ordering your book

When you finish creating your book, you can either print it yourself, save it as a PDF to send to a third-party print service, or buy it directly through Aperture. To print it or save it as a PDF, click Print in the Book Editor. Aperture opens the standard system Print dialog. Either set your print settings and click Print or choose PDF ⇨ Save as PDF to create a PDF version of your book.

To order a copy of your book directly from within Aperture, do the following:

1. **Click Buy Book in the Book Editor.** Aperture displays a sheet like the one in Figure 7.27.

2. **Log in using your Apple ID or create one if you don't yet have one.**

3. **Adjust the quantity of books you want to order.**

4. **Click Preview Book to see a PDF preview of what your book will look like.**

5. **Click Continue, type your billing and shipping information, and click Place Order to confirm your order.** Aperture uploads your book in the background to the appropriate print service, and your new book arrives in the mail in a few days!

Choose Quantity

(Sign Out)

Quantity Verify Send

Product		Item Price		Item Total
	San Francisco Tour	$49.99	1	$49.99
	Extra-large Hardcover Book 13 x 10 inches; 33 x 25.4 cm 20 pages		Save 10% when you order 25 books or more.	
			Preview Book	

Availability is based on your United States billing address. (Manage Account)

Order Subtotal: $49.99

🔒 Secure connection (Cancel) (Continue)

7.27 The very handy book order sheet.

How Can I Share My Images Digitally?

ne of the great things about digital photography is that you no longer need worry about sending original slides through the mail. However, there are any file formats and sizes that you need to decipher in order to send a digital version of your image. Aperture simplifies your digital sharing workflow, tting you e-mail or post an image to the Web with a single click. Furthermore, ou can use Aperture to create advanced presentations, such as slide shows d Web pages, with just a few clicks. This chapter explores the powerful ols Aperture provides to share your images digitally.

The most basic form of image exporting in Aperture is exporting a copy of the master version your photo (typically the RAW file) or exporting a specific size and resolution of the selected ve sion of your photo, complete with all the adjustments you've made. You might export the mast for backup reasons, to provide someone else with your RAW file, or to export the RAW file so th you can open it in a different converter. Typically, though, you export a version of your photo fo specific purpose, whether it's to e-mail to a client or to enter into a contest.

Fortunately, Aperture is very consistent, and wherever you can export a master or a version of yo photos you will see a nearly identical set of options. In this section, we cover the different optio available when exporting masters and versions of your photos.

Exporting masters

The basic steps to export a master are quite simple.

1. **Select the images whose masters you want to export.**
2. **Choose File ⇨ Export ⇨ Master.** Aperture opens the dialog in Figure 8.1.
3. **Select the folder to save the masters into.**
4. **Click Export Masters.**

After you click Export Masters, you can check the status of your export by opening the Activi window (Window ⇨ Show Activity). When finished, Aperture will have created copies of th selected master files in the selected folder for you to do with as you please.

At the bottom of the dialog there are two options that you can select. Selecting Include Aud Attachments causes Aperture to export a copy of any audio attachments for the selected imag alongside the exported masters. Selecting Show alert when finished causes Aperture to open ɑ alert dialog when it's finished exporting your images.

Aperture also provides options to rename your master files and to control how it exports the ma ter's metadata.

8.1 The Export Master dialog lets you export copies of your original master files out of Aperture.

Folder and filename options

By default, Aperture puts your exported masters into the folder you select. However, you can also set it to create subfolders for your master images automatically and perhaps create an image year/month/day hierarchy for your exported masters.

To pick a different subfolder format, click the Subfolder Format pop-up menu and choose one of the presets. If the preset allows you to set a custom name, make sure to type the custom name into the Custom Subfolder Name text field. To return to the default, no subfolder option, select None.

To create your own subfolder format, follow these steps.

1. **Choose Edit from the Subfolder Format pop-up menu.** Aperture opens the Folder Naming dialog in Figure 8.2.

8.2 The Folder Naming dialog lets you create or modify folder naming presets.

2. **Select an existing preset to modify it, or click the Add (+) button to create a new folder naming preset.** Make sure to give your new preset a name.

3. **Drag and drop the tokens on the left from the Include area into the Format text field to create your preset.** Table 8.1 describes a select group of tokens that aren't obvious. If you add a Custom Name token, type a default Custom Name in the appropriate field. If you add a Counter token, set its starting number and the number of digits to use (for example, when the counter's value is *5*, one digit displays *5* whereas four digits would display *0005*). Note that as you adjust your tokens, the Example field updates to show you a sample filename.

4. **Type any text you want to be part of the preset into the Format text field, such as your initials.**

5. **Select a token in the Format text field and press Delete on your keyboard to remove it.**

6. **Click OK to finish creating your preset.**

Caution

If you use a counter, Aperture will continue increasing the counter number for each export unless you manually reset it by typing a zero into the Increment counter starting at field.

Table 8.1 A Few Unintuitive Tokens for Naming Presets Such as Folder Naming Presets

Token Name	Effect
Counter	Adds a counter to the preset that keeps increasing by increments until you reset it.
Index #	Adds an index number that starts at 1 and resets for each export.
Sequence #	Adds text such as "1 of 5" to the preset where the first number is the current item and the second number is the total number of items being exported.
/	Creates a new subfolder. For example, Image Year/Image Month will create a folder for each year (based on your export selection) and sub-folders for each month within each year.

In addition to being able to set custom subfolder names, the Export Master panel also lets you control how your exported masters are named. Use the Name Format pop-up menu to control filenames. Choose Master File Name to return to the default (which gives you the original file-name) or choose Edit to open the File Naming dialog. This dialog is nearly identical to the Folder Naming dialog covered earlier, and you create and edit file naming presets in the same manner.

Genius

Rather than opening an export dialog and choosing Edit from the Subfolder and Name Format pop-up menus, access the File and Folder Naming dialogs directly by choosing Aperture ➪ Presets ➪ Folder Naming and File Naming.

Metadata options

When exporting a master file, there are three metadata options to pick from, with the default being not to export any metadata.

- **Don't Include IPTC.** This option will not export any metadata with the master.

- **Include IPTC.** This causes Aperture to embed the image's IPTC metadata into the master file.

- **Create IPTC4XMP Sidecar File.** This creates an XMP file alongside the master file with the image's IPTC information, without changing the contents of the master file.

Note

The Aperture-created XMP file only contains the image's IPTC information and not the full set of metadata on the image. The Lightbox XMP plug-in (www.lightbox software.com) allows you to export an XMP file with more information.

237

Exporting versions

Whereas exporting a copy of your master file will give you a duplicate of your original, unadjusted file in the original format at the original resolution, exporting a version will export an image with the size, format, and quality that you choose containing all your adjustments. You will most likely find yourself exporting versions of your images far more often than the master, whether it's a low-resolution JPEG version to send to a client or a high-quality TIFF version to send to a commercial print house.

The basic steps to export a version are quite similar to exporting a master:

1. **Select the image(s) to export.**

2. **Choose File ⇨ Export ⇨ Version.** Aperture opens the dialog in Figure 8.3.

8.3 The Export Version dialog allows you to pick from preset, common formats and sizes or to create your own.

3. **Set the subfolder and name format, or create a custom format as described in the previous section.**

4. **Choose a preset image format and resolution, or follow the instructions in the next section to create your own Image Export preset.**

5. **Select whether or not you want Aperture to display an alert when you finish exporting.**

6. **Click Export Versions.**

Managing image export presets

The Image Export dialog lets you manage your saved image export presets, making it easy to create commonly used image settings to export with. For example, we have an agent who prefers to receive an initial batch of lower-resolution images and then a second set of his selected images at a higher resolution. We have two presets set up, one for the initial submission and one for the final submission. By picking the appropriate preset from the Export Versions sheet, it's easy to guarantee our images are at the right size and format.

To open the Image Export dialog, either choose Edit from the Export Preset pop-up menu or choose Aperture ➪ Presets ➪ Image Exports. There are two main parts in the Image Export dialog, as seen in Figure 8.4. On the left is the list of presets, and on the right are all the available settings for each preset.

8.4 The Image Export dialog allows you to manage your export presets, whether you want to change an existing preset or to create a new one.

To create a new preset, click the Add button (+) in the bottom left. Select a preset to change its options, and if you change a built-in preset, you can click Reset Preset to restore it to its default state.

We cover adding watermarks to a preset in the next section, but here are the different options available for each preset.

- **Image Format.** Use this pop-up menu to select the image's file type, whether it's JPEG, PNG, TIF, or PSD. TIF and PSD also have higher-resolution 16-bit options available.

- **Include Metadata.** If you select this check box, Aperture embeds your image's metadata into this exported version. Sometimes, such as when posting an image to the Web, you might not want to have your metadata embedded into an image, especially GPS meta-data. Note that this option is not available for PNG images.

- **Image Quality.** When you select JPEG for the preset's image format, use this slider to adjust how much compression the image will have. Lower numbers mean a more com-pressed/smaller but lower-quality file.

- **Size To.** Choose whether this preset exports the image at its original size, scaled to fit within a specific dimension that you type in (specified either in pixels, inches, or centi-meters), or scaled to a percentage of the original image size.

- **DPI.** Specify the dots per inch resolution at which to export your images.

- **Gamma Adjust.** This option lets you apply a gamma curve to your image to adjust the midrange brightness. In general, we recommend using a color-calibrated workflow and making adjustments to your image rather than relying on this setting. However, if you're creating an export preset for a specific purpose and find that the midrange brightness of your images is consistently off for that purpose, the Gamma Adjust slider lets you add a correction to the preset.

- **Color Profile.** This pop-up menu allows you to select the color profile that Aperture embeds into this version. We typically recommend ProPhoto or Adobe RGB (1998) for most display or print purposes, and sRGB for Web or e-mail.

- **Black Point Compensation.** Selecting this check box causes Aperture to scale the black and white values in your image to fit within the export color space. This prevents shadow areas from becoming solid black and highlight areas from becoming solid white, but it might also cause subtle tonal changes throughout your image.

Note You can also control whether Aperture exports Faces and Places metadata with your images. Unfortunately, these settings are global and apply to all exported files. These options are available by choosing Aperture ➪ Preferences ➪ Export.

Note It's always smart to set your on-screen proofing profile to match the color profile your export preset uses to double-check your image's color when exporting, making any needed adjustments. We describe how to soft proof your images in Chapter 7.

Adding watermarks

Aperture makes it easy to automatically add a watermark to your exported images. The first step is to prepare an image of your watermark. (You'll need to do this using another program such as Photoshop or Elements.) We recommend creating a PSD, TIF, or PNG file with a transparent background. We also recommend creating several different-sized watermarks, one for each preset to which you want to add a watermark. That way you're not trying to use the same watermark for a 2048-x-2048-pixel image that you're using for a 640×640 image. Note that Aperture scales watermarks down if you choose, but it won't scale them up.

After you create an image file with your mark, follow these steps to add a watermark to an export preset:

1. **Choose the Export Preset you want to use.**

2. **Select the Show Watermark check box.**

3. **Use the Position pop-up menu to choose where you want the mark to appear.**

4. **Use the Opacity slider to adjust the mark's opaqueness.**

5. **Click Choose Image and select your watermark image, or drag and drop your watermark image onto the image view.**

6. **Select the Scale watermark check box if you want Aperture to scale the mark proportionately to how it's scaling down your image.**

7. **Click OK to finish editing your preset.**

E-mailing Images

E-mailing an image is one of the most common reasons to export an image, and Aperture has simplified this to a one-button click. Simply select your images and click the Email button in the toolbar, as shown in Figure 8.5, or select your images and choose File ⇨ Share ⇨ Email.

Chances are, though, that you want to select how Aperture exports your images to an e-mail and what mail program it creates a new e-mail within. To access those options, open the Export preferences by choosing Aperture ⇨ Preferences and clicking the Export button. Figure 8.6 highlights the options related to e-mailing an image.

8.5 Select your images and click the Email button to quickly export them and attach them to a new e-mail message.

8.6 The Export tab in Aperture preferences has options to control how Aperture e-mails images.

The first pop-up menu lets you pick what mail program Aperture uses to create a new e-mail for you, be it AOL, Eudora, Mail, or Microsoft Entourage. The second pop-up menu lets you choose what image export preset Aperture uses for your e-mail. Choose the Edit item to open the Image Export dialog to create or modify a preset as discussed previously in this chapter.

Slide Shows

While slide shows might initially make you think of the carousels of slides that your Great Aunt Matilda used to show for hours on end (here's Matilda waving to the north, here's Matilda waving to the south, and for variety, here's Matilda waving to the east), digital slide shows are far more engaging than traditional slide shows. Aperture 3 lets you create advanced slide shows with transition effects, custom timing, video, music, and more. Plus, it's easy to export your show to the Web or to an iPad.

Creating a new slide show

There are two ways to make a slide show in Aperture. The first is more of an impromptu show, where you just pick images, pick a preset, and give the show. The second involves creating a slide show album, possibly adjusting specific settings on your show, and being able to quickly give this same show again in the future or export a movie of the show.

To create an impromptu slide show, select a group of images and choose File⇨Play Slideshow. Aperture opens the Play Slideshow dialog, as shown in Figure 8.7.

Choose your preset, described in the following list, from the pop-up menu, and click Start to start playing your show.

8.7 The Play Slideshow dialog lets you quickly create and play a slide show with little customization.

- **Dissolve.** Fade between static images.

- **Fade through Black.** Transition between static images by fading out to black and then in to the new image.

- **Manual.** Click to advance slides with a dissolve transition.

- **Slow Dissolve.** Like dissolve, but shows each slide for 5 seconds with a 5-second dissolve instead of 3 seconds with a 2-second dissolve.

- **Classic.** Fade between static images with a title slide.

- **Ken Burns.** Pan and zoom across your images while they're on-screen.

- **Photo Edges.** Display your images against a textured background with a virtual two-colored matte around each image.

- **Scrapbook.** Present your images on pages that look like they're out of a real photo album.

- **Shatter.** Each image is broken apart into 3-D planes and spun around, transitioning into the new image.

- **Sliding Panels.** Have your images slide in and out of preset panels that fill your screen.

- **Snapshots.** Create a sliding stack of your images, where each photo initially appears white and then your photo appears with a flash transition.

- **Watercolor Panels.** Display your images against a colored and textured background, with subtle zoom effects on each image.

Creating a custom slide show preset

It's also possible to edit or create your own slide show preset by choosing Edit from the pop-up menu or by choosing Aperture ➪ Presets ➪ Slideshow. Figure 8.8 shows Aperture's Slideshow Presets dialog. As usual, there's a table listing your existing presets as well as Add, Remove, and Reset buttons on the left. Select a preset to see its properties on the right.

8.8 The Slideshow dialog allows you to customize or add slide show presets.

Your preset options are as follows:

- **Theme.** This sets the general style for the preset, possibly determining what other options are user configurable. For example, choosing a Shatter theme disables the Transition and Transition Duration options.

- **Timing.** Choose from among manually advancing each slide, showing each slide for a fixed period of time, or adjusting the slide durations so that they all fit within the selected background music's duration.

- **Background.** Select the color that appears in any empty background area.

- **Transition.** Select the visual effect Aperture uses to move from slide to slide.

- **Show title slide.** Show a slide with text, defaulting to the show's name.

- **Slide Duration.** This determines how long the slide appears on-screen.

- **Inset.** Control the spacing between the edge of the screen and the images.

- **Transition Duration.** Decide how long the transition should last.

- **Play music during slideshow.** Select this option and then use the audio browser to pick a DRM-free song from your iTunes library or Aperture's built-in music to add background music to your preset. Click the Play button to preview a song.

Caution Any music you use in an Aperture slide show must be free of any type of digital rights management (DRM).

Using the Slideshow Editor

When you want more control over your slide show and to save it for later, instead of using the Play Slideshow command, you can create a new slide show album and use the Slideshow Editor to configure your show.

To create a new slide show, select some images and choose File ➪ New ➪ Slideshow. In the dialog that appears (see Figure 8.9), give your show a name and select what type of transitions you want. Clicking each transition name shows a preview on the right, and most of these are similar to the previously mentioned slide show presets. The Classic and Ken Burns themes provide the most customization options, but the other presets have potentially more appealing visual effects and styles.

After you select a theme, Aperture opens the Slideshow Editor, as shown in Figure 8.10. Note how when you move your mouse over the browser you get a playhead, and Aperture adjusts the Viewer to show what the contents of the slide show are at that point in time. As you move your mouse left or right, you see any animating effects or transitions that happen while this photo is on-screen. This is called *skimming*. There are also a number of buttons in the Slideshow Editor to help you create and play back your show.

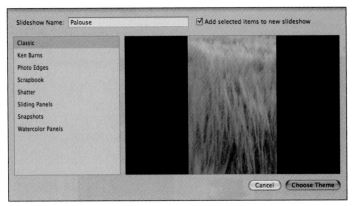

8.9 The New Slideshow sheet lets you pick what type of slide show you're creating.

- **Theme.** Click this button to switch your slide show's theme.

- **Play Slideshow.** Click to play your slide show in full-screen mode.

- **Preview Slideshow.** Click to play your slide show in your viewer.

- **Slideshow Action pop-up menu.** This menu has useful commands to help set up your show. For example, to turn off the time indicator above the playhead that appears while skimming, click the Action pop-up menu button and toggle View Playhead Info. We refer to this button more throughout this section.

- **Slide Duration.** With Classic or Ken Burns themes, this button lets you record custom per-slide timing.

- **Slideshow Settings.** Click this button to access default settings for the entire show or individual settings for the selected slides.

- **Audio Browser.** Toggle the Aperture Audio Browser to pick background music for your slide show.

● **Export.** Export a movie of your slide show.

● **Show Viewer for this Browser.** Temporarily switch out the Slideshow Editor Viewer with a normal Viewer so that you can zoom in and adjust the selected images. Double-clicking an image in the Slideshow Editor's Browser automatically triggers this button.

Theme button   Export button

Show Viewer for this browser button   Slideshow settings button

Slide duration button   Audio browser button

Slideshow action pop-up menu

Preview slideshow button

Play slideshow button

8.10 The Slideshow Editor lets you create your slide show just the way you want it, and the highlighted buttons provide the tools to do this customization.

Arranging a slide show

The order that your images appear in the Slideshow Editor's Browser is the order in which they will play back. Use the normal Browser sorting techniques to either sort them into some default (such as by date) or drag and drop the images into a manual sort order.

Periodically, you'll want to insert a blank slide, perhaps to separate sections of your slide show. To do so, select the image that you want to insert a blank slide after. Then, from the Slideshow Action pop-up menu, choose Insert Blank Slide or Insert Blank Slide With Text. The only difference between the two is that the With Text version adds a text field with the words "Text Slide" to the blank slide. Select the slide and then click on that text to edit it. Choosing Edit ➪ Show Fonts allows you to customize the text font and color.

Adjusting the show's settings

The default settings for your slide show affect all slides. To access them, click the Slideshow Settings button and choose Default Settings. You'll see the options in Figure 8.11. Many of these are self-explanatory, such as the Play slide for field that controls the slide's duration. The Aspect Ratio allows you to control the slide show's overall aspect ratio. Devices can have a wide range of aspect ratios, such as 16:10 for an Apple 23-inch cinema display and 3:2 for an iPhone. If you're creating your show for a specific device, start by setting the Aspect Ratio pop-up menu to match that device. Otherwise, when you need to export to a specific device, we recommend temporarily changing your show's aspect ratio to match that device and then adjusting the border, inset, and text options so that your shows look great when you export them.

If the Crop pop-up menu is set to Fit In Frame and if the show's aspect ratio is different than an individual slide, Aperture adds black bars around the slide to fill out the empty space (instead of cropping or scaling your image). If

8.11 The Default Settings group allows you to adjust show-wide preferences.

the Crop pop-up menu is set to Fill Frame, then your image will be scaled up and cropped to avoid black bars. Choosing Ken Burns Effect from the Crop pop-up menu causes Aperture to pan and zoom your image so that you eventually see the whole image, but there's never any black area showing in Viewer.

One slightly unintuitive control is the set of arrows next to the Transition pop-up menu. This control lets you set the direction from which a transition happens (for example, left to right or right to left) by clicking the appropriate arrow if the transition has a direction. Some transitions, such as dissolve, do not have an associated direction.

Adjusting individual slide settings

To adjust an individual slide or group of slides, select the appropriate images, click the Slideshow Settings button, and click Selected Slides. This set of options, shown in Figure 8.12, is very similar to the default settings, but it lets you override each setting for a specific slide. There are three main differences: Photo effect, Crop settings, and Text.

- **Photo effect.** Selecting this check box automatically applies an effect that you pick from the pop-up menu (black and white, sepia, or antique) to this slide.

- **Crop settings.** Clicking Edit next to the Crop pop-up menu causes Viewer to change to look like Figure 8.13. In this mode, if you choose Fill Frame, Aperture overlays a green crop rectangle, fixed to the show's aspect ratio, to let you control how your image is cropped. Click and drag this rectangle to move it

8.12 The Selected Slides settings let you customize settings for a particular slide or group of slides.

around or drag the edges to adjust the crop region. Finally, if you choose Ken Burns Effect, you see two crop regions: a green one indicating the starting crop and a red one indicating the ending crop. Adjust these as previously described, and click the Swap button on the starting crop if you want to swap the starting and ending crops.

● **Text.** Select the Text check box to add text to a slide. Use the pop-up menu to pick between displaying a specific metadata field or custom text. Use the Font and Color buttons below the Text pop-up menu to set the font style and color. Click and drag the text box that appears on the slide to position the text, and use the handles around the text box to resize it.

8.13 When you click Edit next to the Crop pop-up menu, Aperture displays the crop options on top of Viewer as well as crop rectangles when you select the Fill Frame or Ken Burns Effect crop.

Periodically, you'll find yourself wanting to give each slide a custom duration. Rather than clicking on each slide and setting its duration, it's much easier to use the Slide Duration button to record custom timing. Note that this option is only available with the Classic and Ken Burns themes. To use the Slide Duration button, follow these steps.

1. **Select the slide where you want to start recording custom timing.**

2. **Click the Slide Duration button.** Aperture adds the overlay to Viewer, as shown in Figure 8.14.

When the slideshow is playing, press the return key to set the slide's duration. Press the spacebar to play/pause. **3.0** seconds | Done

8.14 The Slide Duration overlay provides instructions for how to record custom slide durations as well as displaying the elapsed time for each slide.

3. **Press the spacebar to start playing the show.** The overlay in Figure 8.14 shows the elapsed time in its timer.

4. **Press the Return key to set the slide's time and to move on to the next slide.**

5. **Press the spacebar when you finish setting slide durations.**

At any point, you can repeat these steps to record new custom timing, and you can use the Slideshow Settings/Selected Slides settings to change a slide's duration without rerecording the timing.

Adding video clips

Adding video to a slide show is quite straightforward because Aperture essentially treats your video clip just like it does your images. Simply drag your video clip onto the Slideshow Album in the Library Inspector to make sure it's in the slide show, use the Slideshow Editor's Browser to position the clip where you want it to be in the show, and you're done.

Just like with an image slide, there are a number of options available for a video slide including photo effects, cropping, transitions, text, and more. There is an extra option for video slides, however, related to the clip's audio track. The Slideshow Settings/Selected Slides settings have four new sliders. The first three, Volume, Fade In, and Fade Out, control the clip audio's volume and how long (if at all) Aperture takes to fade the clip's audio in or out. Set the Volume slider to 0% to not use any of the clip's audio.

There's also a slider and a Reduce volume of main track check box to control any background music in your slide show. Selecting this check box causes Aperture to reduce the background music's volume by the amount specified with the slider so that you can hear the clip's audio instead.

Adding music

To add music to your slide show, start by clicking the Audio Browser button. Aperture opens the audio browser, as shown in Figure 8.15. Use the pop-up menu at the top to switch between Aperture-provided music, audio files from your camera and movie clips, and your iTunes library and playlists. Drag a song from the audio browser onto the empty area in Browser to add it to your slide show. Aperture displays a green bar behind your images representing the main audio file. If your slide show is longer than the main audio file, the green background ends before the last slide. Either drag an additional audio file onto your show or set the main audio file to loop by going into the show's default settings and selecting Loop main audio track. To delete an audio file, select the green area representing the audio file so that it has a white border around it and press Delete on your keyboard.

8.15 When you add a DRM-free sound file to your slide show from the audio browser, Aperture displays a green area in Browser representing the sound file.

To open the Audio Adjustments heads-up display (HUD), either double-click the main audio clip or select the clip and choose Adjust Audio from the Slideshow Action pop-up menu. The Audio Adjustments HUD (see Figure 8.16) lets you modify the audio file's volume and fade in and out duration.

To have Aperture automatically time your slides so that your show lasts exactly as long as your audio, choose Fit Slides to Main Audio Track from the Slideshow Action pop-up menu. Aperture can also automatically analyze your audio file to determine where the beats happen so that your transitions are guaranteed to happen on beats in the music. Simply choose Align Slides to Beats from the Slideshow Action pop-up menu, and Aperture adjusts your timing. To revert your timing, select the slide to revert and choose Reset Selected Slide from the Slideshow Action pop-up menu.

It's also possible to add a second audio track to your show. For example, you might have recorded some narration using Garage Band, and you'd like it to start with a particular slide. To add an audio file as a secondary audio track, select it in the audio browser and drag it onto an image in Browser. It will appear as a thin, green bar, as shown in Figure 8.17. To

8.16 The Audio Adjustments HUD allows you to adjust your audio file's volume.

8.17 A second audio track lets you add prerecorded narration to your slide show in addition to background music.

adjust the in/out points on the second audio track, move your mouse over its endpoints and your cursor changes to double-arrows. Click and drag to adjust the in/out points. Click and drag the bar to adjust that point in your slide show that the track starts playing; select it and press Delete to remove the track.

Just like with the main audio track, you can double-click to open the Audio Adjustments HUD. When adjusting a secondary audio track, you can set how much the main audio track's volume fades out while the secondary track is playing by selecting Reduce volume of the main track to and adjusting the slider.

Playing and exporting your shows

Once you have your show set up the way you want, click the Preview Slideshow button to watch it play back in Viewer. To play it back full screen, click the Play Slideshow button. If you have multiple monitors, you can choose on which monitor your slide show plays back by choosing Aperture ➪ Preferences ➪ Appearance and changing the View slideshows on pop-up menu. To pause your slide show, press the spacebar; to end it early, press Esc.

To export your slide show as a QuickTime movie, click Export. Aperture opens the Export dialog shown in Figure 8.18. Choose where you want to save your movie and what format you want to export it for. If you don't see the right preset, choose Custom and type your desired export settings. To have Aperture add your movie to iTunes so that you can sync it right away to your iPhone, select the Automatically send slideshow to iTunes check box.

8.18 The Export Slideshow dialog allows you to save your slide show as a QuickTime movie.

Note If you want to play your slide show on an iPad, use the Apple TV preset.

Genius Aperture uses JPEG previews of your photos in its slide shows. If the images in your slide show aren't as sharp or as high of quality as you expect, you need to adjust your preview settings. Choose Aperture ➪ Preferences ➪ Previews, increase your Photo Preview size to the needed resolution, and increase the Photo Preview quality. Make sure to regenerate your old previews after changing this setting by selecting your old images, Control+clicking them, and choosing Update Previews. Keep in mind that higher-quality previews require more hard drive space.

Web Pages

While slide shows are a great, multimedia-oriented way to present your work, many times it's more effective to create a Web Page of your images. In addition to letting you easily post images to Facebook, Flickr, and MobileMe (which we cover later in this chapter), Aperture makes it easy to create custom Web Pages of your images that you can upload to your own Web site.

Comparing Web Journals, Web Pages, and Smart Web Pages

A Web Journal is a Web site where the main pages have groups of images intermixed with text that you type yourself, as shown in Figure 8.19. A Web Page (called a Web gallery in previous versions of Aperture) displays a contact sheet of thumbnails for images you pick by hand on the main pages (also shown in Figure 8.19), and a Smart Web Page is just like a Web Page except Aperture automatically populates the Web Page contents based on the Smart Album's setting. All three types of pages can display image metadata on the main page, and all three types have detail pages with larger versions of each image and optionally more or different metadata.

The main way to figure out which type of page you want is to think about what you want to do with the Web site. If you want to create a Web site about a trip you took, and putting images and stories together, you would create a Web Journal. If you just want to show images that you explicitly pick, then use a normal Web Page. However, if you need to make a Web site around a specific criteria (for example, all photos of this person or from this place), then you should create a Smart Web Page.

8.19 Web Journals let you mix text and images whereas Web Pages are focused on just images.

Creating and configuring a new Web Page

To create a normal Web Page, select a group of images and choose File⇨New⇨Web Page. Aperture displays a dialog to pick a theme and to give your Web Page a name. Aperture then adds the Web Page album to your project, and at any point you can drag more images to this album.

After creating your Web Page, you see the Webpage Editor in Figure 8.20. You can change themes at any point by clicking the Choose Theme button. There are three key parts to this editor: the Pages pane, the Detail Images pane, and the Preview pane. Use the Pages pane to select the main gallery page that you want to work on or use the Detail Images pane to select an individual image's page. Then use the various options to control how the page looks in the Preview pane. The Preview pane provides a live preview of how your finished site will look.

Pages pane

Detail Images pane   Preview pane

8.20 The Webpage Editor allows you to create custom Web pages, and the Pages and Detail Images panes let you select which page to load into the Preview pane to edit.

Aperture automatically places the images in the Web Page album onto your site. The images' order in Browser mirrors their order on the site, and the Browser sort-order pop-up menu, which defaults to sorting by date, lets you quickly sort your images by a certain criteria, such as rating. Of course, you can simply drag and drop images into the order you want to create a custom order. At any point, you can choose a different sort order to re-sort your images.

To edit text, such as a copyright notice or site header, double-click the text field on the page, and if it's user-editable, Aperture lets you begin editing the text. Although you can open the System Fonts panel by choosing Edit ⇨ Show Fonts, you cannot change the typography for a Web Page.

There are also buttons above and below the Preview pane that control your Web Page's layout. The Theme button lets you switch your site's template. The Metadata Set button changes what metadata set is displayed with your image. Choose Enable Plate Metadata from this pop-up menu to display image numbers. Note that the main thumbnail pages can and typically should have a different metadata set than the individual detail pages.

Below the Preview pane are buttons to go to the previous/next page in the selected group (that is either within the main pages or within the detail pages). Use these instead of scrolling through the Pages and Detail Images panes. The Columns and Rows fields let you control the layout of your thumbnail grid, and the Fit images within pop-up and size fields let you control how much space each thumbnail receives. The options for the Fit images within pop-up are:

- **Rectangle.** Use the size fields to define a rectangle, and Aperture makes the thumbnails fit within the specified size.

- **Square.** This is similar to Rectangle except the width and height fields are locked together to create a square.

- **Width.** Only the width size is changeable, and Aperture makes all thumbnails have the same width.

Go to a detail page by either selecting it in the Detail Images pane or by selecting the image's thumbnail in the Preview pane and clicking the arrow button that appears. The configuration options for the detail pages are very similar to the main pages. It's important to note that any options you set on a detail page for the metadata set or image size apply to all detail pages. Figure 8.21 shows a sample detail page.

Creating and configuring a Smart Web Page is very similar, except you can't manually pick what images are included in the Web site, as the smart settings criteria you set do this filtering for you. To create a Smart Web Page, choose File ⇨ New ⇨ Smart Web Page. Rather than displaying the theme dialog as with a regular Web Page, Aperture instead creates a Web Page with a default theme and displays the standard Smart Settings dialog, where you set your criteria for what images Aperture automatically adds and places onto the smart Web Page. Configure a Smart Web Page just as you do a normal Web Page.

8.21 Detail pages show individual images.

Export your Web Page by clicking Export Web Pages in the top right of the Webpage Editor. This opens a standard Save dialog, except there are two extra pop-up menus below it. The pop-up menus allow you to choose what Web export presets to use for your thumbnails and for the detail images. To create your own Web export presets, choose Edit from either pop-up menu. The options are nearly identical to the image export presets covered earlier in the chapter. When you click Export, Aperture creates a folder in the specified location on your hard drive with your Web site, which you can then upload to your Web server.

If you have a MobileMe account and want to upload your Web site to HomePage (note that this is not a fancy MobileMe gallery, which we cover later in this chapter, but rather the Web site you just created hosted on MobileMe), click Publish to MobileMe. This opens the Publish to MobileMe sheet displayed in Figure 8.22. Give your Web site a name, note the URL and how it includes the name, pick your thumbnail and detail image presets, and click Publish to export and upload your site to MobileMe.

Publish Album As: MonkeyPark

http://homepage.mac.com/joshanon/MonkeyPark/

Thumbnail Image Preset: Web Thumbnails – JPEG – Medium Quality

Detail Image Preset: Web Detail – JPEG – High Quality

Cancel   Publish

8.22 The Publish to MobileMe sheet allows you to export a Web site and upload it to MobileMe with just a couple of clicks.

Creating and configuring a new Web Journal

Creating a Web Journal is very similar to creating a Web Page, with the only difference being that you choose File ➪ New ➪ Web Journal instead of Web Page. Even the Webpage Editor for a Web Journal (see Figure 8.23) looks very similar to the editor for a Web Page, although there are a few key new buttons.

- **Add Text Block.** Click this button to add a custom text field to your Web Journal so that you can type text about the surrounding images.

- **Add Page.** Unlike a Web page, where the number of main pages depends on how many images are in the album and the number of rows and columns per page, the layout of each main Web Journal page is up to you. Click this button to add a new main page.

- **Remove Page.** This button deletes the selected main page and unplaces any images on the page.

- **Page Template.** This button reveals a pop-up menu that lets you adjust the main page template, if your selected theme allows, choosing between a header with text only or a header with text and an image.

- **Webpage Editor pop-up Action menu.** This button's pop-up menu has commands to reorder the main pages and to automatically create new main pages from the selected images based on criteria such as one page per day.

- **Show All Images/Show Unplaced Images.** Because you manually place the images in Browser onto your Web Journal, this button lets you quickly toggle between seeing all images in the album and seeing unplaced images only.

Add text block button

Webpage Editor action pop-up menu   Show All Images button

Page template pop-up menu   Show Unplaced Images button

Remove page button

Add page button

8.23 The Webpage Editor for a Web Journal is quite similar to a Web Page's editor, although there are a few extra buttons.

Placing images onto a Web Journal is fairly straightforward. Drag them from Browser onto the empty area or next to an existing thumbnail in the Preview pane. Aperture places the image and shows you a badge on the thumbnail indicating how many times (if any) you've placed the image into a Web Journal. Some themes have an empty, gray rectangle in the header to represent an image placeholder. Drag and drop an image onto this placeholder, and click this placed image in the Preview pane to adjust its scale and crop window.

Add a text block after a group of images by clicking the Add Text Block button. Add new pages as needed or select a group of images and choose a command, such as New Page for Each Day, from the Webpage Editor pop-up Action menu to have Aperture create main pages for you.

When you move your mouse over the Preview pane, group boxes appear, as shown in Figure 8.24. These boxes indicate an image or text block in your Web Journal. Click and drag the block's header to move the block around the page. Click the Remove button that appears on the block to delete it. Text blocks have an extra button to switch between header and paragraph text.

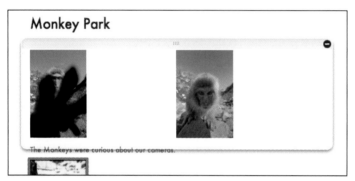

8.24 As you move your mouse over your Web Journal, group boxes for each image or text group appear with extra controls.

When you're ready to publish your Web Journal, follow the same steps described in the section on creating and configuring a new Web Page.

MobileMe

MobileMe is a set of online services offered by Apple for $99 per year (as of this writing). One of its nice features is that it provides a sophisticated gallery system, where you can view slide shows and upload new images, which are synced back to Aperture, right from your Browser. Aperture 3 makes it easy to create a MobileMe Gallery album.

Setting up a MobileMe Gallery album

To set up a new MobileMe Gallery album, follow these steps:

1. **Select the images to initially include in your gallery.**

2. **Choose File ⇨ Share ⇨ MobileMe Gallery.** Aperture opens the New MobileMe Gallery Album sheet, as shown in Figure 8.25.

Would you like to publish this album to your Gallery?

This will create an album in Josh Anon's MobileMe Gallery. The album can be viewed with Safari or any modern web browser. The title of this album will be visible to everyone viewing your Gallery.

Album Name: Japan 2010 Gallery

Album Description: Here are some of my favorite images from my trip to Japan in early 2010.

Album URL:

Album viewable by: Everyone

Allow: ☐ Downloading of Optimized Images
☐ Uploading of photos via web browser
☐ Adding of photos via email or iPhone
☐ Show email address to visitors
username@gallery.me.com

Options: ☐ Hide album on my Gallery home page
☑ Show: Version Name as photo title

Cancel   Publish

8.25 The New MobileMe Gallery Album sheet provides options to set up your gallery.

3. **Configure how you want your album to work.** We recommend deselecting the Downloading of option, which is selected by default.

4. **Use the Album viewable by pop-up menu to set your privacy settings for this gallery.** To create a new login for this gallery, choose Edit Names and Passwords from this pop-up, and Aperture swaps the New MobileMe Gallery Album sheet for the Edit Names and Passwords sheet, as shown in Figure 8.26. Use the Add (+) and Remove (–) buttons to add or remove users, double-click in the Name and Password columns to set those values, and click OK when finished to return to the New MobileMe Gallery Album sheet.

5. **Click Publish to export your new album to your MobileMe Gallery.**

Name	Password	Albums
dslru	abc123	

+ − Name may consist of a–z, 0–9, underscores and a single dot (.)
Password should be four characters or more; capitalization matters.   Cancel   OK

8.26 The Edit Names and Passwords sheet lets you add or remove users for your Web galleries. Note that the users in this list are for all your Web galleries, and not just the one you're currently creating.

To view your MobileMe Gallery, go to http://gallery.me.com/*UserName* where UserName is your MobileMe login (for example, *sjobs*). In your Web browser, click the album you just exported to view it. If you set your album to not be visible on the Gallery home page, use the Edit MobileMe Gallery Album sheet we describe in the next section to see your album's URL.

Adjusting the settings on your MobileMe Gallery album

After you set up a MobileMe Gallery album, Aperture lists that album in the Library Inspector at the bottom under MobileMe Gallery, as seen in Figure 8.27. When you click the album, Aperture loads and displays it like any other project or album, except there's a new pop-up menu that says MobileMe in the tool strip.

This pop-up menu has three commands:

- **Settings.** Open the MobileMe Gallery Album Settings sheet. We cover these settings shortly.
- **Visit MobileMe Gallery.** This command opens your gallery album in your Web browser.
- **Tell a friend.** This creates a new mail message with an invitation to your album. Aperture uses your e-mail program, which you set in Preferences when you configured e-mailing images from Aperture.

Add or remove images to your MobileMe Gallery album within Aperture like you would a normal album to add or remove them from your Web site. Click the Publish button next to your album's name in the Library Inspector to force Aperture to sync your changes immediately (this also down-loads any new images you've uploaded elsewhere to your album).

8.27 A MobileMe Gallery album looks just like a normal album except there's an extra MobileMe pop-up menu.

To set Aperture to automatically check for new photos that people have uploaded to your album, outside of Aperture, choose Aperture ➪ Preferences ➪ Web, and the Web dialog appears, as shown in Figure 8.28. Use the pop-up menu to set when, if ever, Aperture should automatically check for new photos across all MobileMe Gallery albums. This preference pane also allows you to set whether your images will include location information and to see how much free space you have remaining on the MobileMe server.

For all other options, you can use the Settings command in the MobileMe pop-up menu. This opens the MobileMe Gallery Album Settings sheet, as shown in Figure 8.29, which is nearly identi-cal to the sheet you used to create your album. The main difference is that this sheet displays your album's URL, and clicking it opens your gallery in your Web browser.

8.28 The Web dialog allows you to set how often Aperture checks for updates to a MobileMe Gallery album, among other things.

8.29 The MobileMe Gallery Album Settings sheet lets you adjust your album's settings after you create your album.

To remove a MobileMe Gallery Album, select it in the Library Inspector and choose File➪ Delete MobileMe Album.

Facebook

In the past few years, Facebook has exploded from a private social-networking site with its membership limited to select colleges into one of the most trafficked sites on the Web. Everyone and his or her Uncle Bob seem to have a profile. Aperture 3 provides direct Facebook integration, which lets you directly publish your images to Facebook rather than using Facebook's clunky image uploader.

Setting up Facebook access within Aperture

The first time you go to export your images to Facebook, you need to set up access to your Facebook account from within Aperture. Start by selecting a group of images to share.

1. **Choose File ⇨ Share ⇨ Facebook.** Aperture asks if you want to set up access to your Facebook account. Click the Set Up button.

2. **Type your login e-mail and password in the Facebook Login sheet that appears, as shown in Figure 8.30.** To have Aperture store your Facebook information, select the Keep me logged in to Aperture Uploader check box. If you don't have a Facebook account, click the Sign up for Facebook link at the bottom left of this sheet to create an account.

8.30 The Facebook Login sheet is where you log in and set up Aperture's access to your Facebook account.

3. **Click Login.**

4. **Click Close, assuming you entered your login correctly.** Otherwise, address any errors that Aperture displays in the sheet.

After clicking Close, Aperture displays a new sheet that lets you actually publish your images to Facebook.

Publishing images from Aperture to Facebook

The first steps to publishing your images are the same as setting up Facebook access within Aperture — select your images (or an item in the Library Inspector) and choose File ⇨ Share ⇨ Facebook. As long as you set Aperture to store your Facebook login information, you'll go directly to the New Facebook Album sheet. Otherwise, you need to log in as described in the previous section.

In the New Facebook Album sheet that appears, as shown in Figure 8.31, type a name for your album and select whom it should be visible to. We recommend choosing Friends of Friends or Only Friends rather than Everyone to help protect your privacy. Click Publish to send your images to Facebook. Aperture displays a progress wheel next to your album's name under the Facebook group in the Library Inspector.

Do you want to publish "BBC" to Facebook?

This creates an album in Josh Anon's Facebook account. To use a different Facebook account, click Change Accounts.

Album Name: `Recent Images`

Photos Viewable By: `Only Friends`

I certify that I have the right to distribute these photos and that they do not violate the Terms of Use.

(Change Accounts...)   (Cancel) (Publish)

8.31 In the New Facebook Album sheet, you can type a name for your album name and determine your privacy settings.

Just like with MobileMe albums, add or remove images from your Facebook album within Aperture and then click the Publish button next to your album's name, as shown in Figure 8.32, in the

Library Inspector to send your changes to Facebook. To delete an album, select it in the Library Inspector and choose File ⇨ Delete Facebook Album.

When you select your Facebook album in the Library Inspector, its contents look a lot like a

8.32 Select your Facebook album in the Library Inspector to see its contents, and click the Publish button to send your changes to Facebook.

normal album except there's a Facebook pop-up menu in the tool strip. This pop-up has commands to adjust your album's settings or to open the album in your Web browser. This Settings dialog is nearly identical to the one in Figure 8.31 that you used to set up your album, but there's also a Remove Account from Aperture button. Clicking this logs you out of Facebook (from within Aperture) and removes all information about your Facebook account from Aperture.

Flickr

Flickr is another very popular way to share photos, and unlike Facebook where photos are a feature and not the primary purpose, Flickr is all about sharing photos. Some art directors even use Flickr to find images that they want to use in their campaigns. From within Aperture, sharing images via Flickr is very similar to sharing via Facebook. In fact, it's possible to set up Flickr's photo stream to display in your Facebook photo stream (you'll need to do this via Facebook's Web site, not within Aperture) so that any image you upload to Flickr from Aperture also appears on Facebook.

Setting up Flickr access within Aperture

As you might expect, you need to log in to your Flickr account from Aperture to upload images. To do so, follow these steps.

1. **Select the images in Browser or item in the Library Inspector that you want to upload to Flickr.**

2. **Choose File ⇨ Share ⇨ Flickr.**

3. **Click the Set Up button when Aperture asks you if you want to set up Aperture to publish to Flickr.** Aperture opens your Web browser and directs it to the Flickr login page.

4. **Log in to Flickr.** We recommend selecting the Keep me signed in check box, which keeps you signed in for two weeks.

5. **Click OK, I'll Authorize It when Flickr asks about linking Aperture Uploader to your Flickr account.**

6. **In Aperture, if the New Flickr Set sheet doesn't automatically appear, click the Set Up button again.**

7. **Follow the steps in the next section to publish and modify images on Flickr.**

Caution If you have problems getting Aperture to recognize that you're logged into Safari, make sure that Private Browsing is not selected in Safari (Safari ⇨ Private Browsing). Private Browsing prevents sites like Flickr from storing cookies, which can make Aperture think you're not logged in to Flickr.

Publishing images to Flickr

Start by selecting images in Browser or the item in the Library Inspector that you want to share, and choose File ⇨ Share ⇨ Flickr. Aperture opens the New Flickr Set sheet, as shown in Figure 8.33. Type a name for your photo set, adjust your privacy settings using the Photos Viewable by pop-up menu, and use the Photo Size pop-up menu to pick how Aperture should optimize your images. If you don't have a Flickr Pro account, some of the photo size options will be disabled. Click Publish to upload your images and to create your set.

Do you want to publish "BBC" to Flickr?

This creates a "set" of photos in joshanon's Flickr Photostream. To use a different Flickr account, click Change Accounts.

Set Name: BBC

Photos Viewable by: Only You

Photo Size: Web Images

Change Accounts...   Cancel   Publish

8.33 The New Flickr Set sheet allows you to create a set of photos on Flickr from within Aperture.

As with Facebook and MobileMe, Aperture creates an album in the Library Inspector within the Flickr group for each Flickr set you create. Add and remove images as you would a normal album, and when you want to publish your changes, click the Publish button next to the album name in the Library Inspector.

Within the album, use the Flickr pop-up menu to adjust your set's settings by choosing the Settings command. The Settings command opens a sheet that's identical to the New Flickr Set sheet. The Flickr pop-up menu also has a Visit Flickr Gallery command that opens your Browser to this set.

To delete this set, select it in the Library Inspector and choose File ⇨ Delete Flickr Album.

Genius

Rather than uploading full-sized images to Flickr directly, if you want to post larger versions, first export optimized versions of your images to your computer and then use Flickr's Web site to upload these optimized versions.

Using Other Export Plug-ins

As you work with a digital workflow, you'll notice (if you haven't already) that there always seem to be two steps involved with getting an image to someone or some service. First, you prepare a specifically sized and optimized version, and then you send it to that person or service.

Aperture's image export presets make it incredibly easy to prepare images at whatever size, resolution, and format you need, but you still have to upload those exported images somewhere. Fortunately, third-party export plug-ins help Aperture make your workflow even simpler by reducing exporting and uploading (and other tasks) into one step.

For example, if you want more control over how Aperture posts your images to Flickr, including the image title, you can either export optimized versions by hand and then use Flickr's Web site to upload them or you can purchase Connected Flow's FlickrExport plug-in and use it to upload, optimize, and control your images from within Aperture.

As another example, Lightbox XMP, as shown in Figure 8.34, lets you write XMP metadata either as sidecars with any referenced master images you select, or it lets you export versions of your images with the metadata stored in XMP either in a sidecar or embedded in the exported version.

As a last example, PhotoShelter, which provides a great online content management system for photographers, has a plug-in for uploading from Aperture to PhotoShelter (see Figure 8.35), so that you can upload either your master images or versions of your files. Josh, for instance, creates two folders on PhotoShelter for each project. The first is a JPEG folder that contains the optimized versions of his images that are suitable for posting to the Web, and the second is a Masters folder where he uploads backup copies of his master image files.

Lightbox XMP

○ Referenced Master sidecar only
○ Export sidecar files only
◉ Export image and sidecar
○ Embed XMP into exported image version
○ Sidecar and embed XMP into exported image version

Export: ◉ Version
○ Master

Version Preset: [TIFF – 50% of Original Size ⬍]

Export Name Format: [Current Version Name ⬍]

Custom Name: [Enter Name Text Here]

File Name Example: Heart Island.tiff

(?)   (Cancel) (Export)

8.34 The Lightbox XMP export plug-in allows you more options for exporting XMP metadata with your images than what Aperture provides.

Because each plug-in is different and there are so many, we can't go into full detail about how to use all of them. Here are a few general tips, however:

- **Plug-in location.** If you have multiple accounts on your computer and want each person to have access to this export plug-in, copy the plug-in to the folder at /Library/ Application Support/Aperture/Plug-Ins/Export/. If you're the only person who will use the plug-in, you could also put it at /Users/*YourUsername*/Library/Application Support/ Aperture/Plug-Ins/Export/.

- **Opening the plug-in.** Select the images to export and choose File ➪ Export. A list of all your installed export plug-ins appears. If you don't see your plug-in, make sure it's installed in one of the previously mentioned locations.

- **Using the plug-in.** While each plug-in varies a bit, you will often see radio buttons you can click to switch between exporting a version or master file and then pop-up menus to select the appropriate presets for your export (such as in Figure 8.34), just like you do when exporting either a version or master file.

PhotoShelter Personal Archive

Upload | Account | Preferences

PHOTOSHELTER

You are logged in as joshanon@mac.com.

New Folder

Africa
Alaska
Antelope Valley
Berkeley
Bosque
Breckenridge
Chanukkah
Chicago
Cincinnati
Cook Islands
Default

Export: ● Version
○ Master

Version Preset: TIFF – 50% of Original Size

Export Name Format: Current Version Name

Custom Name: Enter Name Text Here

File Name Example: Heart Island.tiff

Cancel | Export

8.35 PhotoShelter's Aperture plug-in makes it easy to export images to PhotoShelter at whatever size and format you want.

To see a full list of the various export plug-ins available for Aperture, go to www.apple.com/aperture/resources/ and click the Export Plug-ins link.

How Can I Use Aperture with My HDSLR's Video Files?

One of the biggest new features in dSLRs is the ability to shoot high-definition video. Yet most of the tools designed to work with these video files are geared toward cutting them together into a sequence and not actually managing and organizing the files. Fortunately, Aperture 3 makes it so that you can manage your video files just as easily as you do your images, and it even lets you pull still images out of your video files.

How Does Aperture Handle Video Files?

Put simply, video files in Aperture appear just like any other file, except when you have your metadata display set to display badges you see a small movie icon on each video file like in Figure 9.1. It's easy to organize your video files into projects and albums, set ratings, labels, and other metadata on them, and to even include them in slide shows. While you can't make adjustments to a video file, aside from basic trims, just being able to manage your video files alongside your images is a huge step forward for anyone shooting video with a dSLR.

9.1 Videos appear just like any other file in Aperture, although they will show a movie badge to distinguish them from your still images.

Importing Video Files

As you might expect, video files appear in Aperture's Import panel just like any other file. If for some reason you don't see your movie clips, look in the File Types brick (choose File Types from the Import Settings pop-up menu) and make sure that Exclude videos is not selected. In grid view, your movie files will again have a small badge indicating that they're movie files (see Figure 9.2), and in List view, their type will be QuickTime movie.

9.2 Movie files in the Import panel appear just like your images.

If you switch to Viewer mode in the Import panel, Aperture displays transport controls over your movie, when you move your mouse over it, that allow you to play your movie and to step through or scrub through it. Follow the instructions in the next section to learn how to use these controls.

To finish importing your movie files, make sure they're selected and click Import Checked.

Viewing Video Files

Select a video file in Browser just like you would an image, and open Viewer. You will see a still frame (by default the first frame in your video file). When you move your mouse over Viewer, a set of transport controls appears in the HUD, as indicated in Figure 9.3.

There are four key playback controls in this HUD that you can use to view your video files.

9.3 The playback controls for a video file appear in an HUD over Viewer.

- **Play/Pause.** Click this button to play or pause your movie. The spacebar is the keyboard shortcut for this button.

- **Next Frame/Previous Frame.** These buttons let you step to a particular frame in your movie. This is useful if you intend to extract a JPEG still from your movie.

- **Time slider.** This slider indicates where the playhead is in your movie, and you can also click and drag this slider to scrub through your movie.

- **Volume slider.** Use this slider to adjust the playback volume.

Note

When you have a video file selected, the Metadata Inspector replaces the Camera LCD display with information about your clip's length, size, and frame rate.

Editing a Clip

While Aperture lets you manage your clips quite effectively, its video-editing capabilities are quite limited. They're even more limited than in QuickTime Player Pro, as you can't perform any adjustments on the image itself, not even a brightness change. However, it is possible to perform two types of adjustments: changing the clip's poster frame and adjusting the clip's in and out points.

Genius

Aperture has settings for separate video and audio external editors so that you can do more sophisticated editing in an external program. Set those editors under Aperture ➪ Preferences ➪ Export, and edit your file by choosing Photos ➪ Edit with External Editor.

Setting the clip's poster frame

A poster frame is simply the frame that Aperture uses as your movie's thumbnail. If you think about a shot, you typically try to record extra frames before and after the main action (the extra frames are referred to as head and tail) to make it easier to edit the clip into a sequence. However, to make it easier to tell at a quick glance which clip you're looking at, you will probably want to set the clip's thumbnail to be more representative of the clip's action than the first frame.

Follow these simple steps to set the poster frame:

1. **Select the clip in Browser.**

2. **Use the transport controls in Viewer, and play or scrub to the frame you want to use as the clip's poster frame.**

3. **From the Transport Controls HUD Action pop-up menu, choose Set as poster frame.** Notice that your clip's thumbnail in the Browser updates to display the new frame.

Trimming the clip

Chances are the clip you recorded is longer than you want to actually show people. For example, when you pressed the Stop Recording button on your camera, you probably shook the camera slightly, and it would be nice to edit that bump out of your clip. Aperture 3's main video-editing capability is trimming a clip, where you adjust the in and out points to remove any unwanted head and tail on your video clip. To trim a clip, follow these steps:

1. **Select the clip in Browser.**

2. **From the Transport Controls HUD Action pop-up menu in Viewer, choose Trim.** Aperture changes the HUD to the Trim HUD, as shown in Figure 9.4.

9.4 The Trim HUD allows you to adjust your clip's in and out points.

3. **Click the yellow handles representing the in and out points in your video and drag them to the desired in and out points.** Note that there is no Snap to Playhead feature or way to zoom in for a frame-accurate trim. It can take a couple tries to set the right in and out frames on long clips.

4. **Click Trim to finish trimming your clip.**

To reset your clip's in and out points, choose Reset Trim from the Transport Controls HUD Action pop-up menu.

Exporting a Video Clip

It's possible to export either your original clip or the trimmed version of your clip. Select it and choose either File ⇨ Export ⇨ Master or Version, respectively. Unfortunately these commands don't provide any transcoding options.

If you want to reencode your video or to cut together a sequence of video clips that you export as one movie, you have to repurpose another Aperture feature. Specifically, create a new slide show with your clip (or clips) and use the Classic theme. Assemble it as we describe in Chapter 8, and pay close attention to the aspect ratio setting. You will probably also want to turn off the show title. Then follow the steps in Chapter 8 to export your clip or sequence in one of a number of preset formats or to enter your own export settings.

Genius

If you're going to display your video on an iPad, use the Apple TV export preset.

To create a still JPEG image from your movie, scrub to the appropriate frame and choose New JPEG from frame from the Transport Controls HUD Action pop-up menu. Aperture creates a JPEG of the frame at the same resolution of your video, stacked with your video.

Working with Audio Files

In addition to managing video files, Aperture also handles audio files, such as voice memos that some cameras can record and attach to an image.

Importing audio files

By default, Aperture shows any audio files or audio attachments in the Import window. Audio files will have a gray background with a speaker icon, and images with an audio attachment have a speaker badge, as shown in Figure 9.5. If you do not see your audio files or this badge, make sure that Exclude audio files and Exclude audio attachments are not selected in the File Types brick.

Playing audio

If your audio file is attached to an image, the playback controls are in the Metadata Inspector (see Figure 9.6). Click the Play button to hear your audio file, and click and drag the Time slider to scrub through your audio file. When you mouse over the Time slider, Aperture displays handles around the in and out points for your audio attachment. Click and drag these handles to adjust the audio file's in and out points.

9.5 The speaker badge indicates that the image has an audio attachment.

If you're working with an audio file that isn't attached to an image, its playback controls will appear in an HUD over the image in Viewer. To change your audio file's in and out points, click Trim, and Aperture displays in and out handles around your audio file that you can click and drag to trim your file. Click Trim again to confirm your changes.

Library	Metadata	Adjustments

Canon EOS-1D Mark IV   AWB **RAW**
EF24-105mm f/4L IS USM   ⊙ ▦

| ISO 400 | 24mm | 0 ev | f/8 | 1/25 |

▶ ◇ ━━━━━━━━━━━━━━━   00:04 🔊

| General | ⬍ | ⚙▾ |

9.6 An audio attachment's playback controls are in the Metadata Inspector.

Attaching and detaching audio files

If you use your camera's built-in microphone to record a voice memo, it will most likely be automatically attached to an image. But if you use it to record an audio file or use a separate audio recording device, you will just have an audio file, such as an MP3 or AAC file. It's possible to associate this audio file with a specific image or to detach an audio file from an image so that you can leave them as separate files or attach them to a different image.

Attaching audio files

There are two ways to attach an audio file to an image. The first way involves attaching an audio file that you've already imported into Aperture with an image in the same project. Do the following:

1. **Select the image to which you want to attach the audio file.**

2. **Click the Metadata menu and choose Attach Audio File.** Aperture opens the Attach Audio File sheet, as shown in Figure 9.7.

3. **Select the audio file to attach.**

4. **Click Attach.** Your audio file disappears from Browser because it's now attached to the selected image from Step 1.

Caution

If you're attaching an existing audio file to an image, the two items must be in the same project or the audio file won't appear in the Attach Audio File sheet.

The second way to attach an audio file involves bringing a new audio file from the Finder into Aperture and attaching it to an image. To do so, simply select an image and display it in Viewer.

Then drag and drop your audio file from the Finder onto Viewer. Aperture displays a green outline around your image, and when you drop the audio file it attaches it to the selected image.

Attach Audio File

Choose an audio file to attach to the selected image. The trim setting from the selected audio version will be preserved. The remaining versions and all metadata for the selected audio file will be removed.

Version Name ▲	Date
03 Duck And Run	11/23/08 2:46:53 PM PST

03:30, 191.72 kbps, MP3   Cancel   Attach

9.7 The Attach Audio File sheet lets you pick an audio file to link to the selected image.

Detaching audio files

To split an audio attachment out into its own file, select an image with an audio attachment and choose Detach Audio File from the Metadata menu. Aperture creates a new audio file item in your project.

How Can Aperture Make My Workflow Smoother?

©Josh Anon

Throughout each chapter, we cover the major features that make Aperture the cornerstone of our digital workflows. Yet what really sets Aperture apart is its attention to the small details that help make your workflow more efficient, whether that's working with multiple computers and multiple libraries or running a tethered shooting session. This chapter covers many of the smaller but important workflow-improving features in Aperture 3.

ays to indicate an image's status, ranging from whether the image has an adjustment to whether has an audio attachment. Chapter 3 explains how to configure your metadata overlays to see adges if you currently don't see them in Browser or Viewer. However, there are some uncommon adges in Aperture that we haven't covered yet. Table 10.1 provides a quick reference list to those adges so that you don't have to dig through each chapter to figure out what each badge means, d Figure 10.1 helps you identify them.

Table 10.1 Aperture Image Badge Descriptions

Badge	Description
Referenced	This image has a referenced master.
Offline master	This image's master is on a drive that's not currently connected, and the master is offline.
Master not found	This image's master can't be found.
RAW/JPEG	This image has both a RAW and JPEG master (simultaneously shot), and Aperture displays the first badge when the RAW file is the master and the second when the JPEG is the master.
Video	This image is a movie file.
Stack	This is a stack of images, and the badge displays how many images are in the stack.
Set metadata	This image has user-set metadata.
Adjusted	This image has one or more adjustments applied.
Externally edited	This image has been externally edited and has its own master file.
Audio attachment	This image has an audio attachment.
Placed	How many times this image has been placed into a book, Web gallery/journal, or light table.
Album pick	Out of the stack of images, this image is the album pick and the top of the stack. Note that an album pick is not necessarily the stack pick displayed at the project's root, and different albums can have different album picks.
Low quality	This image is a low enough resolution that it might not look good when printed in a book or used in a Web gallery.
MobileMe	This image was downloaded from a MobileMe gallery.

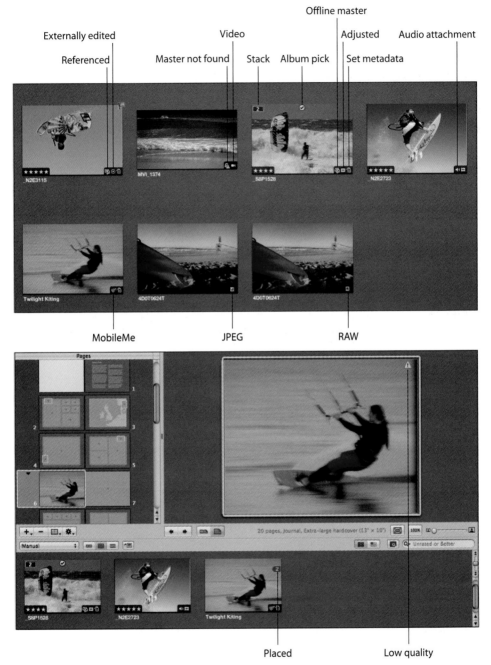

10.1 There are a variety of different badge images that you might see in Aperture.

Managing Photo Previews

One of Aperture's great features is the ability to make multiple adjustments and versions of your images without actually modifying your files on disk. Unfortunately, sometimes you want to quickly access your modified images, such as to sync to your iPhone, to set as your desktop background, or to include in an iDVD project, without having to export versions of your images. Aperture can automatically create JPEG previews of your images, with all your adjustments, that you can use whenever you see the media browser, such as in iWork, or even drag right from Aperture and drop onto another application.

However, it's important to pay close attention to how you set your preview preferences so that you don't slow down Aperture or waste tons of disk space on unneeded previews. If you're automatically generating previews, Aperture updates your preview every time you make a change to an image, which can slow Aperture down.

Genius

We keep our Aperture libraries on external drives but sync our photos to our iPhones. To avoid photos suddenly disappearing if we sync when our drives aren't plugged in, we use iPhoto's Aperture importer (which uses Aperture previews) to create albums in iPhoto with our Aperture-managed images that we then sync to our iPhones. Because our iPhoto libraries are empty (aside from these Aperture images) and live on our main hard drives, they're always available when we sync our devices.

Controlling preview preferences

We recommend setting your preview preferences as soon as possible so that you get Aperture creating previews the way you want right away. Start by opening the Previews preferences pane (Aperture ⇨ Preferences and click Previews), as shown in Figure 10.2. There are a number of options to set here.

- **New projects automatically generate previews.** If selected, Aperture starts creating preview JPEGs for your images as soon as you start importing images into a project. We recommend deselecting this so that Aperture doesn't waste time creating previews for images that you throw away. After all, how often do you keep and use every image you import? However you'll need to remember to have Aperture create previews for some of your images as part of your workflow.

10.2 The Previews preferences pane lets you adjust how Aperture creates its photo previews.

- **Use embedded JPEG from camera when possible.** We recommend selecting this option so that rather than having to open your RAW file and generate a preview (which takes processing time), Aperture uses the camera-created JPEG that some cameras automatically create when you take the photo.

- **Share previews with iLife and iWork.** Use this pop-up menu to choose when Aperture updates its data file that contains information about your previews. Because we leave Aperture running most of the time, we leave this set to Always. Leaving it set to Always (rather than When quitting Aperture or Never) also makes it so we never wonder why other iApps aren't seeing our latest previews.

- **Photo Preview.** This pop-up menu controls the dimensions for your previews. We leave these set to monitor resolution so that full-screen slide shows look good using previews rather than the original files. Preview JPEGs are easier for computers to open and process instead of the full RAW files.

- **Photo Preview quality.** Use this slider to adjust the JPEG compression setting in your previews. A higher quality means less compression. We find a value around 8 to be a good balance between quality and disk size.

Genius

To turn off automatic preview generation for an existing project, select the project in the Library Inspector and deselect Maintain Previews for Project from the Library Inspector Action pop-up menu.

Generating previews

You're probably asking yourself how and when we create previews for our images, since we turn off automatic preview generation. Our workflow is to only create previews for images once we've done an initial ratings and adjustment pass. Typically we filter a project to show the images we rated as 3-star and higher and then create previews for those files.

To create previews, select the images in Browser, Control+click them, and choose Update Preview. Aperture will show its progress in the Activity window.

If an image already has a preview, Update Preview won't regenerate the preview. If Aperture thinks your preview is up to date but you're not seeing your latest adjustments, select the image, Option+Control+click it, and select Generate Preview.

To delete an image's preview, select the image, Control+click it, and choose Delete Preview.

Previews and stacks

When you use the media browser in the iApps to browse your Aperture library, you might have noticed that you don't see the full contents of your stacks. Aperture only displays the stack pick. Aperture does respect the album pick (if it's different than the main stack pick) and displays the album pick in that album in the media browser. If you want to see the full contents of the stack, then make a new Smart Album with the image and select the Ignore stack groupings option.

 Genius Once you create a preview for an image, you can drag it from Aperture and drop it onto another program. If you drag an image that isn't a stack pick, Aperture correctly drags that image's preview rather than the stack pick.

Working with Multiple Libraries

At some point, you will end up with a second library. You might create one to separate your work and personal images, or perhaps you'll create one library for each year's worth of wedding shoots that you archive and remove from your main drive at the end of the year. Or perhaps you have more than one computer, such as a laptop and desktop, and you have a library on each computer. Whatever the reason, it's good to know how to use multiple libraries with Aperture.

In previous versions of Aperture, it was a little clunky to work with multiple libraries and to move images among them. Fortunately, Aperture 3 has simplified this whole process.

Switching libraries

The most basic task when using multiple libraries is to switch to a different or even completely new library. Start by choosing File ⇨ Switch to Library. At the top of this menu is a list of the various libraries that Aperture recognizes on your computer. If you see the library you want to use, select it. To reset this menu, choose Clear Menu. To pick a different library or to create a new library, select Other/New, and Aperture opens the dialog shown in Figure 10.3.

Which library do you want Aperture to use?

You can select a library from the list, find another library, or create a new library. The same library will be used the next time you open Aperture.

Aperture Library (current default)

Aperture Library

Drobo Media ▸ 🖼 Aperture Library

Version 3.0.3, 22324 versions, 23669 masters

(Other Library...) ⚙ Scanning for libraries... (Create New...) (Choose)

10.3 The Switch to Library dialog lets you pick an existing or new library to load into Aperture.

- **If you see the desired library in the list, select it and click Choose.** Note that when you select the library, Aperture displays information about the library's location, version, and contents.

- **If you don't see your desired library, click Other Library and browse for your library.** Select it and click the Select button to switch to that library.

- **To create a new, empty library, click Create New, select where you want the library to live, give your library a name, and click Create.** Aperture automatically opens this new library.

Genius

To set which library Aperture uses while opening Aperture, hold down the Option key and then open Aperture. Aperture shows you a dialog nearly identical to Figure 10.3. Select the library you want to use and click Choose to continue opening Aperture.

Moving images between libraries

At some point, you will need to move images from one library to another. The simplest way to do so is to export your masters from the first library and to import them into the second. While this works well if you haven't made any adjustments or set any custom metadata (if you export an XMP file with your master, Aperture exports some of your metadata with the image), it's not adequate for most users' needs.

Exporting a library

Fortunately, Aperture provides a better way to export images from one library to another. Specifically, it lets you export an album, project, or folder as a library, which contains all your adjustments and metadata that you can then import into the second library. Follow these steps to export your new library:

1. **Select the album, project, or folder in the Library Inspector.**

2. **Choose File ⇨ Export ⇨ Album/Project/Folder as New Library.** Aperture opens the sheet in Figure 10.4.

10.4 The Export Library sheet contains controls for exporting your project or album as a library.

3. **Select where you want this new library to live.** If you have referenced masters that you want to keep referenced, make sure the Consolidate masters into exported library option isn't selected. However, if you want to make sure your new library has its own copy of all your master images, select this option. We recommend always selecting this option if you're transferring your library to another computer. If you don't want Aperture to have to rebuild previews for your images in the new library, select Include Previews in exported library. Note that this will make your exported library larger, sometimes significantly so.

4. **Click Export Library to start exporting.** Use the Activity (Window ⇨ Show Activity) to track your export status.

Genius

A faster way to export albums, projects, and folders is to select them in the Library Inspector and then drag and drop them into the Finder. While Aperture exports them, the new library will have _exporting appended to its name. Aperture removes that extension once it's finished exporting.

Importing a library

After you export your library, the next step is importing it into another Aperture library. To import a library, choose File ⇨ Import ⇨ Library/Project and browse to select the library you exported. (The command includes the word Project in case you want to import a project from an earlier version of Aperture.) You will see the dialog in Figure 10.5. If you want to add the contents of this library without modifying your current library, click Add. If you want to merge the two together (this is useful if you're working with one project on multiple computers), click Merge.

Do you want to merge "Test Project"?

If you merge, all matching items will be updated and other items will be copied to the current library. If you add, all items will be copied to the current library.

[Add]   [Cancel] [Merge]

10.5 Aperture prompts to see if you want to add copies of or merge the images in the library you're importing.

When merging libraries, sometimes there will be a conflict. For example, if you exported a project from your desktop to your laptop, made similar changes in both places, and then tried to merge the library from your laptop with the one on your desktop, you will create a conflict because a file has been changed in both libraries. If Aperture finds a conflict, it prompts you with the dialog shown in Figure 10.6 about how you want to resolve the conflict.

Which library should be used when a conflict is detected?

Some items have been edited in both the current library and the imported library. Aperture will resolve all conflicts with the library you choose.

⊙ Current Library (Aperture Library)

○ Imported Library (Test Project)

Cancel   OK

10.6 Aperture lets you pick which library's data it should use to resolve any merge conflicts.

You resolve a conflict by picking which library is accurate. Unfortunately it doesn't provide any information about what the conflict is, and it will apply your pick to all conflicts it finds. If you have merge conflicts, to be safe, we recommend clicking Cancel, reimporting this library, and clicking Add instead of Merge so that Aperture imports its contents as a copy into your library, rather than possibly replacing existing, good data.

Note If you drag and drop a library onto Aperture from the Finder, Aperture prompts you if you want to add or merge this library into the open library.

Genius The Projects View also lets you merge libraries into specific projects. To do so, select the project in the Projects View, Control+click and choose Import ⇨ Library/Project, and select the library to merge.

Working with multiple computers

A very common reason to work with multiple libraries is that you have multiple computers. While you will need to establish a workflow that best fits your setup, here are our recommendations based on our setup. Specifically, we have laptops with limited storage that we take into the field and use on site and desktops with large hard drives in our offices.

- **Create a new library for each shoot on your laptop.** If you have just one Aperture library on your laptop containing multiple shoots, then you need to export a subsection of it to import into the master library on your desktop. If instead you create a new library for each shoot, when you're done you can import it as is to your desktop. Furthermore, if you like to keep a library with shots from multiple recent shoots on your laptop, you can add the single-shoot library into your existing laptop library and then delete the separate one-shoot library.

- **Use managed files on the laptop.** When you're tired or working quickly, as often happens in the field, it's easy to lose track of what folders you're putting your images into, how you're renaming your files, and all the other settings. We try to keep Aperture's settings on our laptops as idiot-proof as possible, and managed files give us one less thing to worry about.

- **Connect your laptop to your desktop**. Use either FireWire target disk mode or networking, or connect your laptop directly to your desktop's external hard drive with your master Aperture library. We prefer using Target disk mode because it's significantly faster than copying large files over a network (especially our wireless ones) and because we don't have to change our external hard drive's connections to hook them up to our laptops.

Note To enter Target disk mode, connect two Macs with a FireWire cable, then reboot one of them while holding down T on that computer until you see the screen fill with the FireWire icon. That computer appears listed as an external hard drive for your other computer. You can then move or copy files between them.

- **If needed, open your laptop's library from your desktop and export the library to a temporary location.**

- **Switch to your main Aperture library and import the library.** At this point, do any bulk file management, such as switching managed files to referenced files, and if you exported a temporary library, it's now safe to delete it.

- **Alternatively, use a portable external hard drive in the field as a backup and copy the library onto it daily.** Then connect the external drive to your desktop computer at your home/office and import the library from there.

Genius If you use a Vault with your laptop, keep your Aperture libraries in the /Users/Shared folder, which isn't encrypted. That will improve Aperture's performance on your laptop, as it won't have to decrypt files while you use it.

Controlling Tethered Shooting

A useful feature for studio photographers is the ability to shoot tethered. This means that your camera is hooked up to your computer, and as you press the Shutter Release button, Aperture automatically downloads each image and adds it to a project. Then, you can quickly check the image's overall exposure or zoom in to check your focus. Clients also like tethered shooting, as they can quickly see what you're shooting on a large display and provide feedback as to what, if any, changes they want.

Configuring a tethering session

To start a tethering session, choose File⇨ Tether⇨Start Session. This command opens the dialog in Figure 10.7. Notice how these options are very similar to the import options we cover in Chapter 2.

This dialog lets you pick whether your images will be managed or referenced, how they'll be named, what metadata preset is applied, whether they're backed up, and what

10.7 The Tether Settings dialog lets you control the import options for your tethering session.

adjustment preset Aperture applies as it imports your images. We recommend selecting the Show HUD check box in the bottom left, as the tethering HUD has useful status information. Click Start Session once you enter your settings.

Running a tethering session

Running a tethering session is quite straightforward. Press the Shutter Release button on your camera, and Aperture downloads your image and adds it to the selected project. When you're ready to stop the session, choose File ➪ Tether ➪ Stop Session. Note that while the session is running, you see a small camera icon in the Library Inspector next to the project you're importing into.

We recommend using the Tether HUD (see Figure 10.8, which is also accessible by choosing File ➪ Tether ➪ Show Tether HUD) because in addition to having a Stop Session button, it shows you what camera it's using, which helps you make sure Aperture recognizes your camera. The Auto Select option controls whether Aperture will select each image as it downloads it. Leaving the Tether HUD up while in a tethering session also provides a helpful hint that you're running a session so that you can stop it when finished.

10.8 The Tether HUD provides useful status information about your camera and the last image shot during a tethering session.

Genius
Make sure to check Apple's Web site to see whether your camera is compatible with Aperture's tethering system. Currently, because of their proprietary nature, some Canon cameras do not work with it. If your camera is listed as compatible but you have a busy message on your camera when connected, make sure your camera's communication method is set correctly (typically to PC Connect and not Print/PTP).

Customizing Keyboard Shortcuts

One of Aperture's most underrated features is its ability to customize the keyboard shortcuts for nearly every command, including commands that don't have keyboard shortcuts. Furthermore, Aperture lets you save those command sets and to export them from one machine to another.

Open the Command Editor (see Figure 10.9) by choosing Aperture ⇨ Commands ⇨ Customize. The Command Editor has three main areas: The keyboard display lets you dynamically inspect what different keys are bound to commands, the Command List allows you to manage every command and their respective shortcuts, and the Key Detail area displays a list of every command associated with a given key and the various modifier keys (such as Shift, Control, and Option).

10.9 The Command Editor provides a quick way to customize Aperture's keyboard shortcuts.

The simplest way to set a keyboard shortcut is as follows:

1. **Sort through the Command List until you find the command whose shortcut you want to change.**

2. **Select the command.**

3. **Press the shortcut, including the ⌘ key and any modifier keys.** If the shortcut is already bound to another command, Aperture prompts you whether you want to change what the shortcut does. The first time you change a shortcut, Aperture prompts you to make a copy of the default command set, as you can't modify the default set. Click Make Copy and give your command set a new name.

4. **Click Save to save your changes and to close the Command Editor.**

There are other ways to use this editor, though. If you click a key in the keyboard display, Aperture updates the Key Detail area to show all the different commands associated with this key and different modifiers. For example, the N key is bound to the Light Table Zoom Navigator, New Project, Add Noise Reduction, and New Folder, depending on the modifier key. To change which modifiers a given key uses (for example, perhaps you want ⌘+Shift+N to be New Project and ⌘+N to be New Folder), drag the command names in the Key Detail's Command column around until they're set up how you'd like. You can also drag a command from the Command List to the Key Detail table to set a new hotkey.

Clicking the Keyboard button at the top right shows you what keys have shortcuts attached to them for the selected command group (in the Command List area), and Aperture updates the display as you select the different modifiers at the top. You can also drag commands onto the keyboard display or drag them from the keyboard to add and remove commands interactively. Note that as you drag commands over the keyboard display, Aperture updates the contents of the Key Detail area to reflect the selected key.

To create a new command set, follow these steps:

1. **Open the Command Editor.**

2. **Select the set you want to copy or the Default set from the pop-up menu in the top left.**

3. **Choose Duplicate.**

4. **Give your command set a name and click OK.**

To switch command sets without opening the Command Editor, choose your desired set from the Aperture ➪ Commands menu. To export a command set, select it from the Aperture ➪ Commands menu and then choose Aperture ➪ Commands ➪ Export. Import that file on another machine by choosing Aperture ➪ Commands ➪ Import.

Using Aperture with Automator

Automator is a workflow tool that ships with Mac OS X. It lets you easily assemble workflow actions by dragging and dropping different pieces. For example, you could create a workflow to get the images you have selected in Aperture, export versions of them at a certain size, and load them into Keynote, one image per slide.

We're going to walk through a simple example, exporting images, applying a quartz composition filter, and reimporting them into Aperture. If you've ever used Photo Booth and played with the funky filters, those are all quartz composition filters, and the filters range from simple ones like black and white or sepia tone to funky ones like color pencil and thermal camera. These filters aren't available directly in Aperture, but this workflow makes it easy to apply them anyway. Follow these steps:

1. **Open Automator.** It's in your Applications folder and looks like Figure 10.10 when running.

2. **Go into the Photos group, select Get Selected Items, and drag it onto the area at the right.** Automator now looks like Figure 10.11.

10.10 Automator is a useful tool for creating complex workflows quickly and easily.

3. **Drag the Export Versions action onto the right, after the Get Selected Images task.** Set your export options as desired.

10.11 Drag and drop workflow actions from the library on the left to the workflow area on the right.

4. **Drag Apply Quartz Composer Filter onto the right.** Select what filter you want to apply, such as Color Pencil, and set any additional task options for that filter. Automator prompts you to add a copy files step because this action modifies your images. Choose Don't Add, as a fresh copy of your images was already exported in the previous action to modify.

5. **Drag Import Photos after Apply Quartz Composer.** Click Options and select the Show this action when the workflow runs check box so that Automator prompts you each time you run this action for where and how Aperture should import your images.
   Alternatively, if you always want to import your images the same way to the same project, type your settings and leave Show this action when the workflow runs deselected. Your completed workflow will look like Figure 10.12.

6. **Select a few images in Aperture.**

7. **Click the Run button in the top-right corner of Automator.** When it finishes running, look at your newly imported images with the quartz composition filter applied.

10.12 A completed Automator workflow to apply a quartz composition filter to a group of images.

Caution Sometimes Automator actions have similar names. Make sure the icon for the action matches the icon for the program you want to use (for example, Aperture and not iPhoto) or read the action description in the bottom left that appears once you select the action.

When your workflow is working, save your Automator action. Automator provides a number of different formats, including workflow, application, and plug-in. Use workflow when you want to open the Automator workflow into Automator and make changes. Use application to create a stand-alone file that you can double-click to run without opening Automator. Use plug-in to create a plug-in for a specific application, such as Finder. For example, if you made a workflow with an Import Photos action, you could save it as a Finder plug-in named *Import to Aperture* so that you could Control+click any Finder item and choose Automator ⇨ Import to Aperture.

Genius

If your camera doesn't work with Aperture's tethered shooting, you can set up an Automator folder action so that any file placed in the folder is imported into Aperture. Then use your camera's software, such as Canon's EOS Utility, to control the tethering session, setting it to save each image into that special folder.

Vaults and Backup

Your digital files are your film negatives, and to a working photographer, they're also your income. Protecting these files is crucial! The first step to protecting your files is to figure out a backup strategy, starting with where you store your photo library.

One of the most common causes of lost data is hard drive failure. Unfortunately, drives don't last forever, and if your library's only on one drive, it's quite possible that you'll lose all your images at some point. Rather than storing our libraries on a single drive, we use redundant arrays of independent disk (RAID) storage devices for our primary photo library. RAID systems let you automatically store your data to multiple hard drives at once, but the combined drives appear as one drive to your computer.

Note

When setting up a RAID system, we recommend buying drives from different manufacturers if possible, so that if a manufacturer has a bad run of drives, your drives don't all fail together.

Currently, we use Drobos from Data Robotics (see Figure 10.13), which are special cases with fast interfaces (including FireWire 800 and eSATA) that automatically reconfigure their RAID settings as you add or remove drives. Literally, you just add new drives or swap out old drives as you need more storage, and the Drobo automatically reconfigures itself to provide efficient, protected data storage. With the original Drobo, one drive can fail but your data will still be safe, and with newer systems like the Drobo S, more drives can fail but your data will still be safe (assuming you're using all the drive bays).

While keeping your images on a RAID array helps prevent image loss due to hard drive failure, it won't protect you if there's a fire or some other natural disaster. The simplest way to protect yourself in this case is to keep a second copy of your data at an off-site location. For example, perhaps you buy a second Drobo that you keep in your house rather than your studio. Every so often, take your spare drive to your computer and sync your data either using vaults as we describe shortly or by using a program like RSyncX that updates your backup drive with any changes that you make on your main drive.

RAID arrays aren't a viable option while shooting in the field because they're too large to be easily portable. When we shoot in the field, we use a two-tiered backup system. The first is that we use field storage devices (specifically Sanho HyperDrive COLORSPACE UDMAs) to back up our memory cards when we download them to our computers. Then we have small, portable hard drives on which we keep an Aperture vault or export the albums and projects as libraries, so that as we organize our

Image courtesy Data Robotics Inc.

10.13 Drobo products, from Data Robotics, provide an easy and low-cost way to set up a RAID system for your photo library.

images on our computers, all our changes are synced to our backup drive. Furthermore, should our computer die, Sanho sells an accessory for the HyperDrive so that you can back up to the HyperDrive and an external hard drive at the same time. We feel that this setup gives us the best balance between portability, flexibility, and reliability.

Using vaults to back up your images

A vault is a special backup of your photo library that Aperture incrementally updates when you update the vault. Specifically, each time you update your vault, Aperture's smart enough to only copy over any changes you've made, rather than making a full copy of your library each time. You can create multiple vaults, such as one that you update daily, and another on a hard drive that you keep off-site that you update weekly.

Caution Aperture does not back up referenced files within a vault, only managed files. If you use referenced files in your workflow, see the section on Alternate backup strategies for how to back up your images.

Choose Window ➪ Show Vaults or switch to the Library Inspector and click the Vault Pane button to display the Vault pane, as shown in Figure 10.14.

Creating a vault

Creating a new vault is simple. Follow these steps:

1. **Connect your external drive for the vault.**

2. **Open the Vault pane.**

3. **Choose Add Vault from the Vault Action pop-up menu or choose File ➪ Vault ➪ Add Vault.** Aperture opens a dialog indicating how many files will be backed up. Click Continue to proceed.

Vault status

Full Vault   149.7GB of 627.9GB available

Vault

Update all vaults

10.14 Use the Vault pane in the Library Inspector to manage your vaults.

4. **Choose where you want your vault to live and give it a name.**

5. **Click Add, and Aperture creates an empty vault.** Update it right away to create the initial backup.

Updating a vault

The Vault Status button, located to the right of each vault's entry in the Vault pane, indicates how up to date the vault is. A black icon means the vault is up to date, a yellow icon means that the vault contains all the master files from your library but not all your adjustments, and a red icon means that there are masters in your library that haven't been backed up.

To update a specific vault, either click the Vault Status button or select the vault and choose Update Vault from the Vault Action pop-up menu.

To update all your vaults, click the Update All Vaults button or choose File ➪ Vault ➪ Update All Vaults.

Genius If you have to manually copy your vault to a new drive or rename your backup drive, reconnect your vault to Aperture by selecting the vault in the Vault Pane, choosing Update Vault Path from the Vault Action pop-up menu, and selecting the vault on your drive in the dialog.

Restoring from a vault

Restoring your library from a vault is straightforward. While hopefully you'll never have to restore a library due to a drive failure, if you purchase a new computer, you can use these easy steps to restore a vault into a fresh Aperture installation rather than manually copying your library over.

1. **Connect the hard drive with your vault to your computer.** Wait for it to appear in Finder.

2. **Open Aperture.**

3. **Choose File ⇨ Vault ⇨ Restore Library.** Aperture opens the sheet in Figure 10.15.

Restore Library

Restoring your library will recover the most recent data that has been archived in a vault. The library you are currently viewing will be saved and Aperture will open the newly-restored library.

Source Vault: Full Vault

Cancel   Restore

10.15 The Restore Library sheet lets you choose which vault to use to restore your library.

4. **Choose your vault from the Source Vault pop-up menu.** If it's not listed, choose Select Source Vault and navigate to your vault.

5. **Click Restore.** When prompted to confirm, click Restore again.

Note If you use a vault to back up your library, we highly recommend storing it on an external hard drive so that if your primary drive fails, you don't lose your vault, too.

Deleting a vault

To delete a vault, select it in the Vault Pane and choose Remove Vault from the Vault Action pop-up menu or choose File⇨Vault⇨Remove Vault. Aperture prompts you to either remove and delete the vault, or to just remove it. If you only remove it, it will still be on your hard drive, and you can still restore from it at a later date. If you choose Remove and Delete, Aperture deletes the vault from your drive.

Alternate backup strategies

While vaults are quite convenient, they don't back up referenced images and therefore aren't the ideal backup solution for every photographer. Fortunately, there are plenty of other backup tools out there.

Time Machine

The simplest backup tool, Time Machine, comes standard with every Mac that has OS X 10.5 or later installed. Time Machine is sort of like a vault, but it operates on your entire hard drive and not just your Aperture library. It's like a vault in that it's an incremental backup — it only backs up files that have changed since the last backup. But it goes far beyond an Aperture vault, too. It keeps hourly backups for the past day, daily backups for the past month, and weekly backups until its area of the hard drive is full. Should you need to restore a file, Time Machine's interface lets you go back in time to find and restore the files you want.

To use Time Machine, choose System Preferences⇨Time Machine, and you'll see the pane in Figure 10.16. Make sure the big switch is set to On. Click Options to select any folders you don't want to back up. Then connect an external hard drive, and when prompted, if you want to use that drive for Time Machine, click Yes. Note that the initial backup takes a while, but subsequent back-ups will be significantly faster.

Note Because hard drives can always fail, we recommend either using a RAID system like a Drobo for your Time Machine backups or having two different external hard drives that you use for backup. Should you use a Drobo, the Drobo FS supports Time Machine natively. Otherwise, you'll need to set up a sparse disk image on your Drobo for your backup. Look online for help on how to do this.

10.16 The Time Machine System Preferences pane lets you control what Time Machine backs up and to turn it off and on.

Other physical storage

An alternative to using hard drives to back up your data is to use another type of physical storage such as a DVD. or a tape drive. Tape drives, while once popular backup solutions, aren't common on the desktop now, and we don't recommend them for the typical user.

Using DVDs is sort of a middle ground. While it seems like a great idea (hey, my data's being laser-etched into a disc — isn't that better than a hard drive?), DVDs can also go bad, and sometimes they don't even last a year. At the very least, make sure to use archival gold DVDs, which last longer, and look for DVD-R and not DVD-RW discs. The DVD-RWs, or rewritable variety, don't last as long as the write-once type. DVDs are also convenient for keeping a copy of your data off-site, as they take far less space than a hard drive.

Unfortunately, because DVDs typically only hold about 4GB (a bit more if you use a dual-layer disc), you'll probably need a lot of discs to back up your images. If you choose to use DVDs to back up your work, we recommend that you use referenced files. That way, you can point third-party programs that automatically distribute large chunks of data among a number of DVDs at your image folders. Plus, you can periodically also burn your Aperture library to a disc to back up your project structure and metadata.

Online backup

A different alternative is to use an online backup service. There are a number of services that photographers would be interested in, but they primarily fall into two camps. The first camp is a photography-oriented backup service, designed to both archive your photos and to provide gallery and sales features, and the second camp is a general-purpose backup solution, designed to back up your entire hard drive.

Some of the photography services include PhotoShelter (www.photoshelter.com), SmugMug (www.smugmug.com), and Swiss Picture Bank (www.swisspicturebank.com). PhotoShelter and SmugMug (as of this writing) charge either a monthly or yearly fee, and they have different rates depending on what features you need, ranging from basic gallery services to terabytes of storage with online sales and custom Web site templates. Josh currently uses PhotoShelter to drive his Web site. He uses its Aperture export plug-in to upload his master files to a RAW folder within his PhotoShelter archive, and he uploads JPEG versions of his images, with all his adjustments burned in, to another folder that he then posts publicly.

Swiss Picture Bank is a newer service, but what's special about it is that your data has a lifetime guarantee through the Foundation for Data Permanence so that if Swiss Picture Bank goes out of business, your data is always safe and accessible. Furthermore, rather than paying an annual fee, you pay once for however much storage you need and have that for life.

Unfortunately with these services, you have to manually select what images you want to upload to the sites and upload them yourself. But that's a small price to pay to be able to access your images anywhere and for some of the other features these sites provide.

The more general services, like Mozy (www.mozy.com) and Carbonite (www.carbonite.com) provide programs that monitor the data on your computer and upload any new or changed files whenever you make a change. These services cost less (each is roughly $60 per year for unlimited backup, compared to the $60 per month you might pay PhotoShelter for storage), but they don't provide any gallery or photo sales features.

Should you choose to use an online backup service, remember that the initial backup can take a significant amount of time depending on how much data you have to back up and your network connection, possibly even weeks. Furthermore, we recommend not relying on an online service as your only backup solution, as restoring your data can also take a significant amount of time.

Caution When choosing an online backup service, read its privacy policies carefully to make sure your data is only accessible by you, even if the company goes out of business.

Using Aperture's Database Repair Tools

At its core, Aperture uses a database to contain and organize information about your images, ranging from where the files are on disk to where each thumbnail is stored to what faces are tagged in each image. Unfortunately, once in a while, it's possible for something bad to happen, such as the power going out while Aperture is using its database, which causes the database to become corrupt.

Aperture 3 includes a first aid tool that you should use as the first problem-solving step when you encounter problems with Aperture. It can fix everything from images showing the wrong thumbnails to Aperture not being able to open the library file and can be faster than restoring your library from a backup.

To access the Library First Aid tools, follow these steps:

1. **Quit Aperture if it's running.**
2. **Find the problematic Aperture library in the Finder.**
3. **Hold down the ⌘ and Option keys and then double-click the library file.** Aperture displays the Library First Aid dialog, as shown in Figure 10.17.

10.17 Use the Library First Aid tool to try to repair your library in case you have problems.

4. **Select the appropriate option (described in the following list) and click Repair/Rebuild.**

Within the Library First Aid dialog, there are three repair options:

- **Repair Permissions.** Select this option if Aperture can't open or display either the library or some of the images within the library. Note that this option requires an administrator password for your computer. Also note that if Aperture can't open your images because they're referenced and have missing masters, this option will not reconnect your images for you.

- **Repair Database.** If Aperture is displaying the wrong metadata for various images (or not displaying any metadata) or having trouble with something other than accessing your image files, select this option.

- **Rebuild Database.** This option uses the different data files within your Aperture library to rebuild the library's database. Use this option as a last resort if Repair Database fails, as it can be quite slow.

If you still have problems with your library after using the Library First Aid tool, we recommend simply restoring your library from your most recent backup.

Genius

Because of how Aperture stores some of its internal files, your library can become fragmented across your hard drive. If you notice Aperture's performance slowly degrading over time, try using a defragmentation program on the drive that you use to store your Aperture library.

Index